HIPAA Regulatory Desk Reference

J.D. Robinson

HIPAADeskReference.com

Visit **HIPAADeskReference.com** for

- ✓ Discounts on HIPAA Courses
  - ○ HIPAA for Executive Leaders
  - ○ HIPAA for Frontline Professionals
  - ○ HIPAA for Compliance Officers
  - ○ HIPAA for IT Professionals
- ✓ Live HIPAA Training
- ✓ Live Remote Cybersecurity Awareness Training
- ✓ HIPAA News & Updates
- ✓ Free HIPAA Compliance Resources
- ✓ The HIPAA Quick Guide
- ✓ …and more!

Intentionally Blank

HIPAA Regulatory Desk Reference

J.D. Robinson

HIPAADeskReference.com

Published By: Laramie Compliance, Nashville, TN

First Edition

ISBN: 979-8-88940-429-3

Library of Congress Control Number: 2024900328

Printed in United States of America, January 2024

Important Disclaimer

Intentionally Blank

Table of Contents

Preface

The Health Insurance Portability and Accountability Act (HIPAA) stands as a cornerstone, dictating how the healthcare industry should be safeguarding the privacy and security of patient information. This book, dedicated to making the HIPAA law and regulations readily accessible, aims to serve as a the go-to guide for healthcare professionals, managers, compliance officers, students, and anyone interested in understanding HIPAA.

In my work consulting with healthcare practices on cybersecurity and compliance measures, I have been continually surprised to find so many healthcare practices with little or no HIPAA compliance program. This is a risk and a disservice to both the practice and the patient. My hope is that by having available the text of the regulations, small and medium practice managers and compliance officers will find it easier to attain and maintain compliance and keep you off the HHS "Wall of Shame."

The primary objective of this book is to present HIPAA's regulations in a clear, accessible manner. While the main content delves into the regulatory specifics, this non-legal section is designed to provide readers with a foundational understanding of HIPAA's history, purpose, and overall significance in the healthcare industry. By setting this groundwork, I hope to enhance your comprehension and appreciation of the subsequent legal discussions.

As you navigate through the pages of this book, I encourage you to reflect on the importance of HIPAA not just as a legal requirement, but as a vital component of ethical healthcare practice. Whether you are a seasoned professional or new to the field, my hope is that this book will enrich your understanding of HIPAA and empower you to uphold the highest standards of patient privacy and care.

J.D. Robinson

Intentionally Blank

Introduction

Welcome to this comprehensive exploration of the Health Insurance Portability and Accountability Act (HIPAA), a pivotal piece of legislation that has profoundly impacted the landscape of healthcare information management in the United States. This book is designed to serve as a detailed guide for healthcare professionals, experts, students, and anyone interested in understanding HIPAA's complexities and its practical applications.

The "Wall of Shame"

Yes, it's real. While it's not called the "Wall of Shame," HHS/OCR does maintain a website that has listed all healthcare breaches over 500 records. Once you make it on this website, you're there forever. Even if the breach originated from your business associate (such as an IT company), if your patients are affected, then YOUR practice will show up on the *Wall of Shame*. This is why it's important to not only take seriously the security and compliance of your own practice but also to ask your business associates to *prove* that they are compliant, too. That's why HIPAA requires that you "gain satisfactory assurance" that your business associates are compliant (45 CFR §164.308(b)(1)).

> **See the *Wall of Shame*: visit HIPAADeskReference.com**
> for an up-to-date link to the official HHS/OCR breach listing.

A note about "Required" versus "Addressable"

In the HIPAA regulations, you'll find certain controls listed as being either "Required" or "Addressable." There are some ostensible professionals who erroneously claim that "Addressable" controls are "optional." I'm here to tell you that they absolutely are NOT optional. Pay special attention to how the regulation differentiates between required and addressable (see X). If you determine that an addressable control isn't necessary as written for your practice, be sure to follow the guidance in the regulation to document how you came to that conclusion and what compensating control(s) you implemented instead. Always maintain all documents, paperwork, notes, screenshots, assessments, etc. for the requisite six years. During an audit, OCR is going to want detailed *evidence* that you properly followed the law and regulations.

Historical Background and Importance

HIPAA was enacted by the U.S. Congress in 1996, primarily to modernize the flow of healthcare information, stipulate how personally identifiable information maintained by the healthcare and healthcare insurance industries should be protected from fraud and theft, and address limitations on healthcare insurance coverage. The Act has since evolved, encompassing a broad range of rules and standards designed to secure electronic protected health information (ePHI) and ensure patient's rights and privacy.

Scope of This Book

This book delves into various aspects of HIPAA, including its rules, regulations, and their implications in the healthcare sector. While the main content focuses on the legal intricacies of HIPAA, this introduction aims to set the stage by providing a fundamental understanding of the Act's history, purpose, and significance. Additionally, we explore how HIPAA has evolved over time to meet the changing landscape of healthcare information technology and patient privacy concerns.

How to Use This Book

This book is structured to guide readers from the basics to more complex aspects of HIPAA. The initial sections, including this introduction, offer a foundational understanding, ideal for those new to the subject. Subsequent chapters delve into detailed legal text and case studies, beneficial for professionals seeking in-depth knowledge. Legal text is presented, formatted for readability, and up-to-date as of this writing.

As you embark on this journey through the intricacies of HIPAA, remember that this act is not just a set of regulations, but the reflection of a commitment to protecting patient privacy and securing health information. Whether you are a healthcare provider, a policy maker, a compliance professional, or a student, this book aims to enhance your understanding of HIPAA and equip you with the knowledge to navigate its regulations with confidence and competence.

Abbreviations & Acronyms

BA – Business Associate
BAA – Business Associate Agreement
CFR – Code of Federal Regulations
CE – Covered Entity
CIRCIA - Cyber Incident Reporting for Critical Infrastructure Act
CISA – U.S. Cybersecurity and Infrastructure Security Agency
CMS – Centers for Medicare and Medicaid Services (within the Department of Health and
     Human Services)
EHR/EMR – Electronic Health Records / Electronic Medical Records
ePHI – Electronic Protected Health Information
FIPS – Federal Information Processing Standards
FTC – Federal Trade Commission
HHS – Department of Health and Human Services
HIPAA – Health Insurance Portability and Accountability Act
HITECH – Health Information Technology for Economic and Clinical Health Act
IT – Information Technology
NIST – National Institute of Standards and Technology
NPP – Notice of Privacy Practices
OCR – Office for Civil Rights (within the Department of Health and Human Services)
PHI – Protected Health Information
PSQIA – Patient Safety and Quality Improvement Act
SAMHSA – Substance Abuse and Mental Health Services Administration
TPO – Treatment, Payment, and Operations

Intentionally Blank

45 CFR PART 160—GENERAL ADMINISTRATIVE REQUIREMENTS

Authority:42 U.S.C. 1302(a); 42 U.S.C. 1320d–1320d–9; sec. 264, Pub. L. 104–191, 110 Stat. 2033–2034 (42 U.S.C. 1320d–2 (note)); 5 U.S.C. 552; secs. 13400–13424, Pub. L. 111–5, 123 Stat. 258–279; and sec. 1104 of Pub. L. 111–148, 124 Stat. 146–154.
Source:65 FR 82798, Dec. 28, 2000, unless otherwise noted.

Subpart A—General Provisions

§ 160.101 Statutory basis and purpose.

The requirements of this subchapter implement sections 1171–1180 of the Social Security Act (the Act), sections 262 and 264 of Public Law 104–191, section 105 of Public Law 110–233, sections 13400–13424 of Public Law 111–5, and section 1104 of Public Law 111–148.

[78 FR 5687, Jan. 25, 2013]

§ 160.102 Applicability.

(a) Except as otherwise provided, the standards, requirements, and implementation specifications adopted under this subchapter apply to the following entities:

(1) A health plan.

(2) A health care clearinghouse.

(3) A health care provider who transmits any health information in electronic form in connection with a transaction covered by this subchapter.

(b) Where provided, the standards, requirements, and implementation specifications adopted under this subchapter apply to a business associate.

(c) To the extent required under the Social Security Act, 42 U.S.C. 1320a–7c(a)(5), nothing in this subchapter shall be construed to diminish the authority of any Inspector General, including such authority as provided in the Inspector General Act of 1978, as amended (5 U.S.C. App.).

[65 FR 82798, Dec. 28, 2000, as amended at 67 FR 53266, Aug. 14, 2002; 78 FR 5687, Jan. 25, 2013]

§ 160.103 Definitions.

Except as otherwise provided, the following definitions apply to this subchapter:

Act means the Social Security Act.

Administrative simplification provision means any requirement or prohibition established by:

(1) 42 U.S.C. 1320d–1320d–4, 1320d–7, 1320d–8, and 1320d–9;

(2) Section 264 of Pub. L. 104–191;

(3) Sections 13400–13424 of Public Law 111–5; or

(4) This subchapter.

ALJ means Administrative Law Judge.

ANSI stands for the American National Standards Institute.

Business associate:

(1) Except as provided in paragraph (4) of this definition, business associate means, with respect to a covered entity, a person who:

(i) On behalf of such covered entity or of an organized health care arrangement (as defined in this section) in which the covered entity participates, but other than in the capacity of a member of the workforce of such covered entity or arrangement, creates, receives, maintains, or transmits protected health information for a function or activity regulated by this subchapter, including claims processing or administration, data analysis, processing or administration, utilization review, quality assurance, patient safety activities listed at 42 CFR 3.20, billing, benefit management, practice management, and repricing; or

(ii) Provides, other than in the capacity of a member of the workforce of such covered entity, legal, actuarial, accounting, consulting, data aggregation (as defined in § 164.501 of this subchapter), management, administrative, accreditation, or financial services to or for such covered entity, or to or for an organized health care arrangement in which the covered entity participates, where the provision of the service involves the disclosure of protected health information from such covered entity or arrangement, or from another business associate of such covered entity or arrangement, to the person.

(2) A covered entity may be a business associate of another covered entity.

(3) **Business associate** includes:

(i) A Health Information Organization, E-prescribing Gateway, or other person that provides data transmission services with respect to protected health information to a covered entity and that requires access on a routine basis to such protected health information.

(ii) A person that offers a personal health record to one or more individuals on behalf of a covered entity.

(iii) A subcontractor that creates, receives, maintains, or transmits protected health information on behalf of the business associate.

(4) **Business associate** does not include:

(i) A health care provider, with respect to disclosures by a covered entity to the health care provider concerning the treatment of the individual.

(ii) A plan sponsor, with respect to disclosures by a group health plan (or by a health insurance issuer or HMO with respect to a group health plan) to the plan sponsor, to the extent that the requirements of § 164.504(f) of this subchapter apply and are met.

(iii) A government agency, with respect to determining eligibility for, or enrollment in, a government health plan that provides public benefits and is administered by another government agency, or collecting protected health information for such purposes, to the extent such activities are authorized by law.

(iv) A covered entity participating in an organized health care arrangement that performs a function or activity as described by paragraph (1)(i) of this definition for or on behalf of such organized health care arrangement, or that provides a service as described in paragraph (1)(ii) of this definition to or for such organized health care arrangement by virtue of such activities or services.

Civil money penalty or *penalty* means the amount determined under § 160.404 of this part and includes the plural of these terms.

CMS stands for Centers for Medicare & Medicaid Services within the Department of Health and Human Services.

Compliance date means the date by which a covered entity or business associate must comply with a standard, implementation specification, requirement, or modification adopted under this subchapter.

Covered entity means:

(1) A health plan.

(2) A health care clearinghouse.

(3) A health care provider who transmits any health information in electronic form in connection with a transaction covered by this subchapter.

Disclosure means the release, transfer, provision of access to, or divulging in any manner of information outside the entity holding the information.

EIN stands for the employer identification number assigned by the Internal Revenue Service, U.S. Department of the Treasury. The EIN is the taxpayer identifying number of an individual or other entity (whether or not an employer) assigned under one of the following:

(1) 26 U.S.C. 6011(b), which is the portion of the Internal Revenue Code dealing with identifying the taxpayer in tax returns and statements, or corresponding provisions of prior law.

(2) 26 U.S.C. 6109, which is the portion of the Internal Revenue Code dealing with identifying numbers in tax returns, statements, and other required documents.

Electronic media means:

(1) Electronic storage material on which data is or may be recorded electronically, including, for example, devices in computers (hard drives) and any removable/transportable digital memory medium, such as magnetic tape or disk, optical disk, or digital memory card;

(2) Transmission media used to exchange information already in electronic storage media. Transmission media include, for example, the Internet, extranet or intranet, leased lines, dial-up lines, private networks, and the physical movement of removable/transportable electronic storage media. Certain transmissions, including of paper, via facsimile, and of voice, via telephone, are not considered to be transmissions via electronic media if the information being exchanged did not exist in electronic form immediately before the transmission.

Electronic protected health information means information that comes within paragraphs (1)(i) or (1)(ii) of the definition of *protected health information* as specified in this section.

Employer is defined as it is in 26 U.S.C. 3401(d).

Family member means, with respect to an individual:

(1) A dependent (as such term is defined in 45 CFR 144.103), of the individual; or

(2) Any other person who is a first-degree, second-degree, third-degree, or fourth-degree relative of the individual or of a dependent of the individual. Relatives by affinity (such as by marriage or adoption) are treated the same as relatives by consanguinity (that is, relatives who share a common biological ancestor). In determining the degree of the relationship, relatives by less than full consanguinity (such as half-siblings, who share only one parent) are treated the same as relatives by full consanguinity (such as siblings who share both parents).

(i) First-degree relatives include parents, spouses, siblings, and children.

(ii) Second-degree relatives include grandparents, grandchildren, aunts, uncles, nephews, and nieces.

(iii) Third-degree relatives include great-grandparents, great-grandchildren, great aunts, great uncles, and first cousins.

(iv) Fourth-degree relatives include great-great grandparents, great-great grandchildren, and children of first cousins.

Genetic information means:

(1) Subject to paragraphs (2) and (3) of this definition, with respect to an individual, information about:

(i) The individual's genetic tests;

(ii) The genetic tests of family members of the individual;

(iii) The manifestation of a disease or disorder in family members of such individual; or

(iv) Any request for, or receipt of, genetic services, or participation in clinical research which includes genetic services, by the individual or any family member of the individual.

(2) Any reference in this subchapter to genetic information concerning an individual or family member of an individual shall include the genetic information of:

(i) A fetus carried by the individual or family member who is a pregnant woman; and

(ii) Any embryo legally held by an individual or family member utilizing an assisted reproductive technology.

(3) Genetic information excludes information about the sex or age of any individual.

Genetic services means:

(1) A genetic test;

(2) Genetic counseling (including obtaining, interpreting, or assessing genetic information); or

(3) Genetic education.

Genetic test means an analysis of human DNA, RNA, chromosomes, proteins, or metabolites, if the analysis detects genotypes, mutations, or chromosomal changes. Genetic test does not include an analysis of proteins or metabolites that is directly related to a manifested disease, disorder, or pathological condition.

Group health plan (also see definition of *health plan* in this section) means an employee welfare benefit plan (as defined in section 3(1) of the Employee Retirement Income and Security Act of 1974 (ERISA), 29 U.S.C. 1002(1)), including insured and self-insured plans, to the extent that the plan provides medical care (as defined in section 2791(a)(2) of the Public Health Service Act (PHS Act), 42 U.S.C. 300gg–91(a)(2)), including items and services paid for as medical care, to employees or their dependents directly or through insurance, reimbursement, or otherwise, that:

(1) Has 50 or more participants (as defined in section 3(7) of ERISA, 29 U.S.C. 1002(7)); or

(2) Is administered by an entity other than the employer that established and maintains the plan.

HHS stands for the Department of Health and Human Services.

Health care means care, services, or supplies related to the health of an individual. *Health care* includes, but is not limited to, the following:

(1) Preventive, diagnostic, therapeutic, rehabilitative, maintenance, or palliative care, and counseling, service, assessment, or procedure with respect to the physical or mental condition, or functional status, of an individual or that affects the structure or function of the body; and

(2) Sale or dispensing of a drug, device, equipment, or other item in accordance with a prescription.

Health care clearinghouse means a public or private entity, including a billing service, repricing company, community health management information system or community health information system, and "value-added" networks and switches, that does either of the following functions:

(1) Processes or facilitates the processing of health information received from another entity in a nonstandard format or containing nonstandard data content into standard data elements or a standard transaction.

(2) Receives a standard transaction from another entity and processes or facilitates the processing of health information into nonstandard format or nonstandard data content for the receiving entity.

Health care provider means a provider of services (as defined in section 1861(u) of the Act, 42 U.S.C. 1395x(u)), a provider of medical or health services (as defined in section 1861(s) of the Act, 42 U.S.C. 1395x(s)), and any other person or organization who furnishes, bills, or is paid for health care in the normal course of business.

Health information means any information, including genetic information, whether oral or recorded in any form or medium, that:

(1) Is created or received by a health care provider, health plan, public health authority, employer, life insurer, school or university, or health care clearinghouse; and

(2) Relates to the past, present, or future physical or mental health or condition of an individual; the provision of health care to an individual; or the past, present, or future payment for the provision of health care to an individual.

Health insurance issuer (as defined in section 2791(b)(2) of the PHS Act, 42 U.S.C. 300gg–91(b)(2) and used in the definition of *health plan* in this section) means an insurance company, insurance service, or insurance organization (including an HMO) that is licensed to engage in the business of insurance in a State and is subject to State law that regulates insurance. Such term does not include a group health plan.

Health maintenance organization (HMO) (as defined in section 2791(b)(3) of the PHS Act, 42 U.S.C. 300gg–91(b)(3) and used in the definition of *health plan* in this section) means a federally qualified HMO, an organization recognized as an HMO under State law, or a similar organization regulated for solvency under State law in the same manner and to the same extent as such an HMO.

Health plan means an individual or group plan that provides, or pays the cost of, medical care (as defined in section 2791(a)(2) of the PHS Act, 42 U.S.C. 300gg–91(a)(2)).

(1) **Health plan** includes the following, singly or in combination:

(i) A group health plan, as defined in this section.

(ii) A health insurance issuer, as defined in this section.

(iii) An HMO, as defined in this section.

(iv) Part A or Part B of the Medicare program under title XVIII of the Act.

(v) The Medicaid program under title XIX of the Act, 42 U.S.C. 1396, *et seq.*

(vi) The Voluntary Prescription Drug Benefit Program under Part D of title XVIII of the Act, 42 U.S.C. 1395w–101 through 1395w–152.

(vii) An issuer of a Medicare supplemental policy (as defined in section 1882(g)(1) of the Act, 42 U.S.C. 1395ss(g)(1)).

(viii) An issuer of a long-term care policy, excluding a nursing home fixed indemnity policy.

(ix) An employee welfare benefit plan or any other arrangement that is established or maintained for the purpose of offering or providing health benefits to the employees of two or more employers.

(x) The health care program for uniformed services under title 10 of the United States Code.

(xi) The veterans health care program under 38 U.S.C. chapter 17.

(xii) The Indian Health Service program under the Indian Health Care Improvement Act, 25 U.S.C. 1601, *et seq.*

(xiii) The Federal Employees Health Benefits Program under 5 U.S.C. 8902, *et seq.*

(xiv) An approved State child health plan under title XXI of the Act, providing benefits for child health assistance that meet the requirements of section 2103 of the Act, 42 U.S.C. 1397, *et seq.*

(xv) The Medicare Advantage program under Part C of title XVIII of the Act, 42 U.S.C. 1395w–21 through 1395w–28.

(xvi) A high risk pool that is a mechanism established under State law to provide health insurance coverage or comparable coverage to eligible individuals.

(xvii) Any other individual or group plan, or combination of individual or group plans, that provides or pays for the cost of medical care (as defined in section 2791(a)(2) of the PHS Act, 42 U.S.C. 300gg–91(a)(2)).

(2) **Health plan** excludes:

(i) Any policy, plan, or program to the extent that it provides, or pays for the cost of, excepted benefits that are listed in section 2791(c)(1) of the PHS Act, 42 U.S.C. 300gg–91(c)(1); and

(ii) A government-funded program (other than one listed in paragraph (1)(i)–(xvi) of this definition):

  (A) Whose principal purpose is other than providing, or paying the cost of, health care; or

  (B) Whose principal activity is:

  (1) The direct provision of health care to persons; or

(2) The making of grants to fund the direct provision of health care to persons.

Implementation specification means specific requirements or instructions for implementing a standard.

Individual means the person who is the subject of protected health information.

Individually identifiable health information is information that is a subset of health information, including demographic information collected from an individual, and:

(1) Is created or received by a health care provider, health plan, employer, or health care clearinghouse; and

(2) Relates to the past, present, or future physical or mental health or condition of an individual; the provision of health care to an individual; or the past, present, or future payment for the provision of health care to an individual; and

(i) That identifies the individual; or

(ii) With respect to which there is a reasonable basis to believe the information can be used to identify the individual.

Manifestation or *manifested* means, with respect to a disease, disorder, or pathological condition, that an individual has been or could reasonably be diagnosed with the disease, disorder, or pathological condition by a health care professional with appropriate training and expertise in the field of medicine involved. For purposes of this subchapter, a disease, disorder, or pathological condition is not manifested if the diagnosis is based principally on genetic information.

Modify or *modification* refers to a change adopted by the Secretary, through regulation, to a standard or an implementation specification.

Organized health care arrangement means:

(1) A clinically integrated care setting in which individuals typically receive health care from more than one health care provider;

(2) An organized system of health care in which more than one covered entity participates and in which the participating covered entities:

(i) Hold themselves out to the public as participating in a joint arrangement; and

(ii) Participate in joint activities that include at least one of the following:

(A) Utilization review, in which health care decisions by participating covered entities are reviewed by other participating covered entities or by a third party on their behalf;

(B) Quality assessment and improvement activities, in which treatment provided by participating covered entities is assessed by other participating covered entities or by a third party on their behalf; or

(C) Payment activities, if the financial risk for delivering health care is shared, in part or in whole, by participating covered entities through the joint arrangement and if protected health information created or received by a covered entity is reviewed by other participating covered entities or by a third party on their behalf for the purpose of administering the sharing of financial risk.

(3) A group health plan and a health insurance issuer or HMO with respect to such group health plan, but only with respect to protected health information created or received by such health insurance issuer or HMO that relates to individuals who are or who have been participants or beneficiaries in such group health plan;

(4) A group health plan and one or more other group health plans each of which are maintained by the same plan sponsor; or

(5) The group health plans described in paragraph (4) of this definition and health insurance issuers or HMOs with respect to such group health plans, but only with respect to protected health information created or received by such health insurance issuers or HMOs that relates to individuals who are or have been participants or beneficiaries in any of such group health plans.

Person means a natural person, trust or estate, partnership, corporation, professional association or corporation, or other entity, public or private.

Protected health information means individually identifiable health information:

(1) Except as provided in paragraph (2) of this definition, that is:

(i) Transmitted by electronic media;

(ii) Maintained in electronic media; or

(iii) Transmitted or maintained in any other form or medium.

(2) Protected health information excludes individually identifiable health information:

(i) In education records covered by the Family Educational Rights and Privacy Act, as amended, 20 U.S.C. 1232g;

(ii) In records described at 20 U.S.C. 1232g(a)(4)(B)(iv);

(iii) In employment records held by a covered entity in its role as employer; and

(iv) Regarding a person who has been deceased for more than 50 years.

Respondent means a covered entity or business associate upon which the Secretary has imposed, or proposes to impose, a civil money penalty.

Small health plan means a health plan with annual receipts of $5 million or less.

Standard means a rule, condition, or requirement:

(1) Describing the following information for products, systems, services, or practices:

    (i) Classification of components;

    (ii) Specification of materials, performance, or operations; or

    (iii) Delineation of procedures; or

(2) With respect to the privacy of protected health information.

Standard setting organization (SSO) means an organization accredited by the American National Standards Institute that develops and maintains standards for information transactions or data elements, or any other standard that is necessary for, or will facilitate the implementation of, this part.

State refers to one of the following:

(1) For a health plan established or regulated by Federal law, State has the meaning set forth in the applicable section of the United States Code for such health plan.

(2) For all other purposes, *State* means any of the several States, the District of Columbia, the Commonwealth of Puerto Rico, the Virgin Islands, Guam, American Samoa, and the Commonwealth of the Northern Mariana Islands.

Subcontractor means a person to whom a business associate delegates a function, activity, or service, other than in the capacity of a member of the workforce of such business associate.

Trading partner agreement means an agreement related to the exchange of information in electronic transactions, whether the agreement is distinct or part of a larger agreement, between each party to the agreement. (For example, a trading partner agreement may specify, among other things, the duties and responsibilities of each party to the agreement in conducting a standard transaction.)

Transaction means the transmission of information between two parties to carry out financial or administrative activities related to health care. It includes the following types of information transmissions:

(1) Health care claims or equivalent encounter information.

(2) Health care payment and remittance advice.

(3) Coordination of benefits.

(4) Health care claim status.

(5) Enrollment and disenrollment in a health plan.

(6) Eligibility for a health plan.

(7) Health plan premium payments.

(8) Referral certification and authorization.

(9) First report of injury.

(10) Health claims attachments.

(11) Health care electronic funds transfers (EFT) and remittance advice.

(12) Other transactions that the Secretary may prescribe by regulation.

Use means, with respect to individually identifiable health information, the sharing, employment, application, utilization, examination, or analysis of such information within an entity that maintains such information.

Violation or *violate* means, as the context may require, failure to comply with an administrative simplification provision.

Workforce means employees, volunteers, trainees, and other persons whose conduct, in the performance of work for a covered entity or business associate, is under the direct control of such covered entity or business associate, whether or not they are paid by the covered entity or business associate.

[65 FR 82798, Dec. 28, 2000, as amended at 67 FR 38019, May 31, 2002; 67 FR 53266, Aug. 14, 2002; 68 FR 8374, Feb. 20, 2003; 71 FR 8424, Feb. 16, 2006; 76 FR 40495, July 8, 2011; 77 FR 1589, Jan. 10, 2012; 78 FR 5687, Jan. 25, 2013]

§ 160.104 Modifications.

(a) Except as provided in paragraph (b) of this section, the Secretary may adopt a modification to a standard or implementation specification adopted under this subchapter no more frequently than once every 12 months.

(b) The Secretary may adopt a modification at any time during the first year after the standard or implementation specification is initially adopted, if the Secretary determines that the modification is necessary to permit compliance with the standard or implementation specification.

(c) The Secretary will establish the compliance date for any standard or implementation specification modified under this section.

(1) The compliance date for a modification is no earlier than 180 days after the effective date of the final rule in which the Secretary adopts the modification.

(2) The Secretary may consider the extent of the modification and the time needed to comply with the modification in determining the compliance date for the modification.

(3) The Secretary may extend the compliance date for small health plans, as the Secretary determines is appropriate.

[65 FR 82798, Dec. 28, 2000, as amended at 67 FR 38019, May 31, 2002]

§ 160.105 Compliance dates for implementation of new or modified standards and implementation specifications.

Except as otherwise provided, with respect to rules that adopt new standards and implementation specifications or modifications to standards and implementation specifications in this subchapter in accordance with § 160.104 that become effective after January 25, 2013, covered entities and business associates must comply with the applicable new standards and implementation specifications, or modifications to standards and implementation specifications, no later than 180 days from the effective date of any such standards or implementation specifications.

[78 FR 5689, Jan. 25, 2013]

Subpart B—Preemption of State Law

§ 160.201 Statutory basis.

The provisions of this subpart implement section 1178 of the Act, section 262 of Public Law 104–191, section 264(c) of Public Law 104–191, and section 13421(a) of Public Law 111–5.

[78 FR 5689, Jan. 25, 2013]

§ 160.202 Definitions.

For purposes of this subpart, the following terms have the following meanings:

Contrary, when used to compare a provision of State law to a standard, requirement, or implementation specification adopted under this subchapter, means:

(1) A covered entity or business associate would find it impossible to comply with both the State and Federal requirements; or

(2) The provision of State law stands as an obstacle to the accomplishment and execution of the full purposes and objectives of part C of title XI of the Act, section 264 of Public Law 104–191, or sections 13400–13424 of Public Law 111–5, as applicable.

More stringent means, in the context of a comparison of a provision of State law and a standard, requirement, or implementation specification adopted under subpart E of part 164 of this subchapter, a State law that meets one or more of the following criteria:

(1) With respect to a use or disclosure, the law prohibits or restricts a use or disclosure in circumstances under which such use or disclosure otherwise would be permitted under this subchapter, except if the disclosure is:

(i) Required by the Secretary in connection with determining whether a covered entity or business associate is in compliance with this subchapter; or

(ii) To the individual who is the subject of the individually identifiable health information.

(2) With respect to the rights of an individual, who is the subject of the individually identifiable health information, regarding access to or amendment of individually identifiable health information, permits greater rights of access or amendment, as applicable.

(3) With respect to information to be provided to an individual who is the subject of the individually identifiable health information about a use, a disclosure, rights, and remedies, provides the greater amount of information.

(4) With respect to the form, substance, or the need for express legal permission from an individual, who is the subject of the individually identifiable health information, for use or disclosure of individually identifiable health information, provides requirements that narrow the scope or duration, increase the privacy protections afforded (such as by expanding the criteria for), or reduce the coercive effect of the circumstances surrounding the express legal permission, as applicable.

(5) With respect to recordkeeping or requirements relating to accounting of disclosures, provides for the retention or reporting of more detailed information or for a longer duration.

(6) With respect to any other matter, provides greater privacy protection for the individual who is the subject of the individually identifiable health information.

Relates to the privacy of individually identifiable health information means, with respect to a State law, that the State law has the specific purpose of protecting the privacy of health information or affects the privacy of health information in a direct, clear, and substantial way.

State law means a constitution, statute, regulation, rule, common law, or other State action having the force and effect of law.

[65 FR 82798, Dec. 28, 2000, as amended at 67 FR 53266, Aug. 14, 2002; 74 FR 42767, Aug. 24, 2009; 78 FR 5689, Jan. 25, 2013]

§ 160.203 General rule and exceptions.

A standard, requirement, or implementation specification adopted under this subchapter that is contrary to a provision of State law preempts the provision of State law. This general rule applies, except if one or more of the following conditions is met:

(a) A determination is made by the Secretary under § 160.204 that the provision of State law:

(1) Is necessary:

(i) To prevent fraud and abuse related to the provision of or payment for health care;

(ii) To ensure appropriate State regulation of insurance and health plans to the extent expressly authorized by statute or regulation;

(iii) For State reporting on health care delivery or costs; or

(iv) For purposes of serving a compelling need related to public health, safety, or welfare, and, if a standard, requirement, or implementation specification under part 164 of this subchapter is at issue, if the Secretary determines that the intrusion into privacy is warranted when balanced against the need to be served; or

(2) Has as its principal purpose the regulation of the manufacture, registration, distribution, dispensing, or other control of any controlled substances (as defined in 21 U.S.C. 802), or that is deemed a controlled substance by State law.

(b) The provision of State law relates to the privacy of individually identifiable health information and is more stringent than a standard, requirement, or implementation specification adopted under subpart E of part 164 of this subchapter.

(c) The provision of State law, including State procedures established under such law, as applicable, provides for the reporting of disease or injury, child abuse, birth, or death, or for the conduct of public health surveillance, investigation, or intervention.

(d) The provision of State law requires a health plan to report, or to provide access to, information for the purpose of management audits, financial audits, program monitoring and evaluation, or the licensure or certification of facilities or individuals.

[65 FR 82798, Dec. 28, 2000, as amended at 67 FR 53266, Aug. 14, 2002]

§ 160.204 Process for requesting exception determinations.

(a) A request to except a provision of State law from preemption under § 160.203(a) may be submitted to the Secretary. A request by a State must be submitted through its chief elected official, or his or her designee. The request must be in writing and include the following information:

(1) The State law for which the exception is requested;

(2) The particular standard, requirement, or implementation specification for which the exception is requested;

(3) The part of the standard or other provision that will not be implemented based on the exception or the additional data to be collected based on the exception, as appropriate;

(4) How health care providers, health plans, and other entities would be affected by the exception;

(5) The reasons why the State law should not be preempted by the federal standard, requirement, or implementation specification, including how the State law meets one or more of the criteria at § 160.203(a); and

(6) Any other information the Secretary may request in order to make the determination.

(b) Requests for exception under this section must be submitted to the Secretary at an address that will be published in the Federal Register. Until the Secretary's determination is made, the standard, requirement, or implementation specification under this subchapter remains in effect.

(c) The Secretary's determination under this section will be made on the basis of the extent to which the information provided and other factors demonstrate that one or more of the criteria at § 160.203(a) has been met.

§ 160.205 Duration of effectiveness of exception determinations.

An exception granted under this subpart remains in effect until:

(a) Either the State law or the federal standard, requirement, or implementation specification that provided the basis for the exception is materially changed such that the ground for the exception no longer exists; or

(b) The Secretary revokes the exception, based on a determination that the ground supporting the need for the exception no longer exists.

Subpart C—Compliance and Investigations

Source: 71 FR 8424, Feb. 16, 2006, unless otherwise noted.

§ 160.300 Applicability.

This subpart applies to actions by the Secretary, covered entities, business associates, and others with respect to ascertaining the compliance by covered entities and business associates with, and the enforcement of, the applicable provisions of this part 160 and parts 162 and 164 of this subchapter.

[78 FR 5690, Jan. 25, 2013]

§ 160.302 [Reserved]

§ 160.304 Principles for achieving compliance.

(a) *Cooperation.* The Secretary will, to the extent practicable and consistent with the provisions of this subpart, seek the cooperation of covered entities and business associates in obtaining compliance with the applicable administrative simplification provisions.

(b) *Assistance.* The Secretary may provide technical assistance to covered entities and business associates to help them comply voluntarily with the applicable administrative simplification provisions.

[78 FR 5690, Jan. 25, 2013]

§ 160.306 Complaints to the Secretary.

(a) *Right to file a complaint.* A person who believes a covered entity or business associate is not complying with the administrative simplification provisions may file a complaint with the Secretary.

(b) *Requirements for filing complaints.* Complaints under this section must meet the following requirements:

(1) A complaint must be filed in writing, either on paper or electronically.

(2) A complaint must name the person that is the subject of the complaint and describe the acts or omissions believed to be in violation of the applicable administrative simplification provision(s).

(3) A complaint must be filed within 180 days of when the complainant knew or should have known that the act or omission complained of occurred, unless this time limit is waived by the Secretary for good cause shown.

(4) The Secretary may prescribe additional procedures for the filing of complaints, as well as the place and manner of filing, by notice in the Federal Register.

(c) *Investigation.*

(1) The Secretary will investigate any complaint filed under this section when a preliminary review of the facts indicates a possible violation due to willful neglect.

(2) The Secretary may investigate any other complaint filed under this section.

(3) An investigation under this section may include a review of the pertinent policies, procedures, or practices of the covered entity or business associate and of the circumstances regarding any alleged violation.

(4) At the time of the initial written communication with the covered entity or business associate about the complaint, the Secretary will describe the acts and/or omissions that are the basis of the complaint.

[71 FR 8424, Feb. 16, 2006, as amended at 78 FR 5690, Jan. 25, 2013]

§ 160.308 Compliance reviews.

(a) The Secretary will conduct a compliance review to determine whether a covered entity or business associate is complying with the applicable administrative simplification provisions when a preliminary review of the facts indicates a possible violation due to willful neglect.

(b) The Secretary may conduct a compliance review to determine whether a covered entity or business associate is complying with the applicable administrative simplification provisions in any other circumstance.

[78 FR 5690, Jan. 25, 2013]

§ 160.310 Responsibilities of covered entities and business associates.

(a) *Provide records and compliance reports.* A covered entity or business associate must keep such records and submit such compliance reports, in such time and manner and containing such information, as the Secretary may determine to be necessary to enable the Secretary to ascertain whether the covered entity or business associate has complied or is complying with the applicable administrative simplification provisions.

(b) *Cooperate with complaint investigations and compliance reviews.* A covered entity or business associate must cooperate with the Secretary, if the Secretary undertakes an investigation or compliance review of the policies, procedures, or practices of the covered entity or business associate to determine whether it is complying with the applicable administrative simplification provisions.

(c) *Permit access to information.*

(1) A covered entity or business associate must permit access by the Secretary during normal business hours to its facilities, books, records, accounts, and other sources of information, including protected health information, that are pertinent to ascertaining compliance with the applicable administrative simplification provisions. If the Secretary determines that exigent circumstances exist, such as when documents may be hidden or destroyed, a covered entity or business associate must permit access by the Secretary at any time and without notice.

(2) If any information required of a covered entity or business associate under this section is in the exclusive possession of any other agency, institution, or person and the other agency, institution, or person fails or refuses to furnish the information, the covered entity or business associate must so certify and set forth what efforts it has made to obtain the information.

(3) Protected health information obtained by the Secretary in connection with an investigation or compliance review under this subpart will not be disclosed by the Secretary, except if necessary for ascertaining or enforcing compliance with the applicable administrative simplification provisions, if otherwise required by law, or if permitted under 5 U.S.C. 552a(b)(7).

[78 FR 5690, Jan. 25, 2013]

§ 160.312 Secretarial action regarding complaints and compliance reviews.

(a) *Resolution when noncompliance is indicated.*

(1) If an investigation of a complaint pursuant to § 160.306 or a compliance review pursuant to § 160.308 indicates noncompliance, the Secretary may attempt to reach a resolution of the matter satisfactory to the Secretary by informal means. Informal means may include demonstrated compliance or a completed corrective action plan or other agreement.

(2) If the matter is resolved by informal means, the Secretary will so inform the covered entity or business associate and, if the matter arose from a complaint, the complainant, in writing.

(3) If the matter is not resolved by informal means, the Secretary will—

(i) So inform the covered entity or business associate and provide the covered entity or business associate an opportunity to submit written evidence of any mitigating factors or affirmative defenses for consideration under §§ 160.408 and 160.410 of this part. The covered entity or business associate must submit any such evidence to the Secretary within 30 days (computed in the same manner as prescribed under § 160.526 of this part) of receipt of such notification; and

(ii) If, following action pursuant to paragraph (a)(3)(i) of this section, the Secretary finds that a civil money penalty should be imposed, inform the covered entity or business associate of such finding in a notice of proposed determination in accordance with § 160.420 of this part.

(b) **Resolution when no violation is found.** If, after an investigation pursuant to § 160.306 or a compliance review pursuant to § 160.308, the Secretary determines that further action is not warranted, the Secretary will so inform the covered entity or business associate and, if the matter arose from a complaint, the complainant, in writing.

[78 FR 5690, Jan. 25, 2013]

§ 160.314 Investigational subpoenas and inquiries.

(a) The Secretary may issue subpoenas in accordance with 42 U.S.C. 405(d) and (e), 1320a–7a(j), and 1320d–5 to require the attendance and testimony of witnesses and the production of any other evidence during an investigation or compliance review pursuant to this part. For purposes of this paragraph, a person other than a natural person is termed an "entity."

(1) A subpoena issued under this paragraph must—

(i) State the name of the person (including the entity, if applicable) to whom the subpoena is addressed;

(ii) State the statutory authority for the subpoena;

(iii) Indicate the date, time, and place that the testimony will take place;

(iv) Include a reasonably specific description of any documents or items required to be produced; and

(v) If the subpoena is addressed to an entity, describe with reasonable particularity the subject matter on which testimony is required. In that event, the entity must designate one or more natural persons who will testify on its behalf, and must state as to each such person that person's name and address and the matters on which he or she will testify. The designated person must testify as to matters known or reasonably available to the entity.

(2) A subpoena under this section must be served by—

(i) Delivering a copy to the natural person named in the subpoena or to the entity named in the subpoena at its last principal place of business; or

(ii) Registered or certified mail addressed to the natural person at his or her last known dwelling place or to the entity at its last known principal place of business.

(3) A verified return by the natural person serving the subpoena setting forth the manner of service or, in the case of service by registered or certified mail, the signed return post office receipt, constitutes proof of service.

(4) Witnesses are entitled to the same fees and mileage as witnesses in the district courts of the United States (28 U.S.C. 1821 and 1825). Fees need not be paid at the time the subpoena is served.

(5) A subpoena under this section is enforceable through the district court of the United States for the district where the subpoenaed natural person resides or is found or where the entity transacts business.

(b) Investigational inquiries are non-public investigational proceedings conducted by the Secretary.

(1) Testimony at investigational inquiries will be taken under oath or affirmation.

(2) Attendance of non-witnesses is discretionary with the Secretary, except that a witness is entitled to be accompanied, represented, and advised by an attorney.

(3) Representatives of the Secretary are entitled to attend and ask questions.

(4) A witness will have the opportunity to clarify his or her answers on the record following questioning by the Secretary.

(5) Any claim of privilege must be asserted by the witness on the record.

(6) Objections must be asserted on the record. Errors of any kind that might be corrected if promptly presented will be deemed to be waived unless reasonable objection is made at the investigational inquiry. Except where the objection is on the grounds of privilege, the question will be answered on the record, subject to objection.

(7) If a witness refuses to answer any question not privileged or to produce requested documents or items, or engages in conduct likely to delay or obstruct the investigational inquiry, the Secretary may seek enforcement of the subpoena under paragraph (a)(5) of this section.

(8) The proceedings will be recorded and transcribed. The witness is entitled to a copy of the transcript, upon payment of prescribed costs, except that, for good cause, the witness may be limited to inspection of the official transcript of his or her testimony.

(9)

(i) The transcript will be submitted to the witness for signature.

(A) Where the witness will be provided a copy of the transcript, the transcript will be submitted to the witness for signature. The witness may submit to the Secretary written proposed corrections to the transcript, with such corrections attached to the transcript. If the witness does not return a signed copy of the transcript or proposed corrections within 30 days (computed in the same manner as prescribed under § 160.526 of this part) of its being submitted to him or her for signature, the witness will be deemed to have agreed that the transcript is true and accurate.

(B) Where, as provided in paragraph (b)(8) of this section, the witness is limited to inspecting the transcript, the witness will have the opportunity at the time of inspection to propose corrections to the transcript, with corrections attached to the transcript. The witness will also have the opportunity to sign the transcript. If the witness does not sign the transcript or offer corrections within 30 days (computed in the same manner as prescribed under § 160.526 of this part) of receipt of notice of the opportunity to inspect the transcript, the witness will be deemed to have agreed that the transcript is true and accurate.

(ii) The Secretary's proposed corrections to the record of transcript will be attached to the transcript.

(c) Consistent with § 160.310(c)(3), testimony and other evidence obtained in an investigational inquiry may be used by HHS in any of its activities and may be used or offered into evidence in any administrative or judicial proceeding.

§ 160.316 Refraining from intimidation or retaliation.

A covered entity or business associate may not threaten, intimidate, coerce, harass, discriminate against, or take any other retaliatory action against any individual or other person for—

(a) Filing of a complaint under § 160.306;

(b) Testifying, assisting, or participating in an investigation, compliance review, proceeding, or hearing under this part; or

(c) Opposing any act or practice made unlawful by this subchapter, provided the individual or person has a good faith belief that the practice opposed is unlawful, and the manner of opposition is reasonable and does not involve a disclosure of protected health information in violation of subpart E of part 164 of this subchapter.

[71 FR 8424, Feb. 16, 2006, as amended at 78 FR 5691, Jan. 25, 2013]

Subpart D—Imposition of Civil Money Penalties

Source: 71 FR 8426, Feb. 16, 2006, unless otherwise noted.

§ 160.400 Applicability.

This subpart applies to the imposition of a civil money penalty by the Secretary under 42 U.S.C. 1320d–5.

§ 160.401 Definitions.

As used in this subpart, the following terms have the following meanings:

Reasonable cause means an act or omission in which a covered entity or business associate knew, or by exercising reasonable diligence would have known, that the act or omission violated an administrative simplification provision, but in which the covered entity or business associate did not act with willful neglect.

Reasonable diligence means the business care and prudence expected from a person seeking to satisfy a legal requirement under similar circumstances.

Willful neglect means conscious, intentional failure or reckless indifference to the obligation to comply with the administrative simplification provision violated.

[74 FR 56130, Oct. 30, 2009, as amended at 78 FR 5691, Jan. 25, 2013]

§ 160.402 Basis for a civil money penalty.

(a) **General rule.** Subject to § 160.410, the Secretary will impose a civil money penalty upon a covered entity or business associate if the Secretary determines that the covered entity or business associate has violated an administrative simplification provision.

(b) **Violation by more than one covered entity or business associate.**

(1) Except as provided in paragraph (b)(2) of this section, if the Secretary determines that more than one covered entity or business associate was responsible for a violation, the Secretary will impose a civil money penalty against each such covered entity or business associate.

(2) A covered entity that is a member of an affiliated covered entity, in accordance with § 164.105(b) of this subchapter, is jointly and severally liable for a civil money penalty for a violation of part 164 of this subchapter based on an act or omission of the affiliated covered entity, unless it is established that another member of the affiliated covered entity was responsible for the violation.

(c) **Violation attributed to a covered entity or business associate.**

(1) A covered entity is liable, in accordance with the Federal common law of agency, for a civil money penalty for a violation based on the act or omission of any agent of the covered entity, including a workforce member or business associate, acting within the scope of the agency.

(2) A business associate is liable, in accordance with the Federal common law of agency, for a civil money penalty for a violation based on the act or omission of any agent of the business associate, including a workforce member or subcontractor, acting within the scope of the agency.

[78 FR 5691, Jan. 25, 2013]

§ 160.404 Amount of a civil money penalty.

(a) The amount of a civil money penalty will be determined in accordance with paragraph (b) of this section, and §§ 160.406, 160.408, and 160.412. These amounts were adjusted in accordance with the Federal Civil Monetary Penalty Inflation Adjustment Act of 1990, (Pub. L. 101–140), as amended by the Federal Civil Penalties Inflation Adjustment Act Improvements Act of 2015, (section 701 of Pub. L. 114–74), and appear at 45 CFR part 102. These amounts will be updated annually and published at 45 CFR part 102.

(b) The amount of a civil money penalty that may be imposed is subject to the following limitations:

(1) For violations occurring prior to February 18, 2009, the Secretary may not impose a civil money penalty—

(i) In the amount of more than $100 for each violation; or

(ii) In excess of $25,000 for identical violations during a calendar year (January 1 through the following December 31);

(2) For violations occurring on or after February 18, 2009, the Secretary may not impose a civil money penalty—

(i) For a violation in which it is established that the covered entity or business associate did not know and, by exercising reasonable diligence, would not have known that the covered entity or business associate violated such provision,

    (A) In the amount of less than $100 or more than $50,000 for each violation; or

    (B) In excess of $1,500,000 for identical violations during a calendar year (January 1 through the following December 31);

(ii) For a violation in which it is established that the violation was due to reasonable cause and not to willful neglect,

    (A) In the amount of less than $1,000 or more than $50,000 for each violation; or

    (B) In excess of $1,500,000 for identical violations during a calendar year (January 1 through the following December 31);

(iii) For a violation in which it is established that the violation was due to willful neglect and was corrected during the 30-day period beginning on the first date the covered entity or business associate liable for the penalty knew, or, by exercising reasonable diligence, would have known that the violation occurred,

    (A) In the amount of less than $10,000 or more than $50,000 for each violation; or

    (B) In excess of $1,500,000 for identical violations during a calendar year (January 1 through the following December 31);

(iv) For a violation in which it is established that the violation was due to willful neglect and was not corrected during the 30-day period beginning on the first date the covered entity or business associate liable for the penalty knew, or, by exercising reasonable diligence, would have known that the violation occurred,

    (A) In the amount of less than $50,000 for each violation; or

    (B) In excess of $1,500,000 for identical violations during a calendar year (January 1 through the following December 31).

(3) If a requirement or prohibition in one administrative simplification provision is repeated in a more general form in another administrative simplification provision in the same subpart, a civil money penalty may be imposed for a violation of only one of these administrative simplification provisions.

[71 FR 8426, Feb. 16, 2006, as amended at 74 FR 56130, Oct. 30, 2009; 78 FR 5691, Jan. 25, 2013; 81 FR 61581, Sept. 6, 2016]

§ 160.406 Violations of an identical requirement or prohibition.

The Secretary will determine the number of violations of an administrative simplification provision based on the nature of the covered entity's or business associate's obligation to act or not act under the provision that is violated, such as its obligation to act in a certain manner, or within a certain time, or to act or not act with respect to certain persons. In the case of continuing violation of a provision, a separate violation occurs each day the covered entity or business associate is in violation of the provision.

[78 FR 5691, Jan. 25, 2013]

§ 160.408 Factors considered in determining the amount of a civil money penalty.

In determining the amount of any civil money penalty, the Secretary will consider the following factors, which may be mitigating or aggravating as appropriate:

(a) The nature and extent of the violation, consideration of which may include but is not limited to:

(1) The number of individuals affected; and

(2) The time period during which the violation occurred;

(b) The nature and extent of the harm resulting from the violation, consideration of which may include but is not limited to:

(1) Whether the violation caused physical harm;

(2) Whether the violation resulted in financial harm;

(3) Whether the violation resulted in harm to an individual's reputation; and

(4) Whether the violation hindered an individual's ability to obtain health care;

(c) The history of prior compliance with the administrative simplification provisions, including violations, by the covered entity or business associate, consideration of which may include but is not limited to:

(1) Whether the current violation is the same or similar to previous indications of noncompliance;

(2) Whether and to what extent the covered entity or business associate has attempted to correct previous indications of noncompliance;

(3) How the covered entity or business associate has responded to technical assistance from the Secretary provided in the context of a compliance effort; and

(4) How the covered entity or business associate has responded to prior complaints;

(d) The financial condition of the covered entity or business associate, consideration of which may include but is not limited to:

(1) Whether the covered entity or business associate had financial difficulties that affected its ability to comply;

(2) Whether the imposition of a civil money penalty would jeopardize the ability of the covered entity or business associate to continue to provide, or to pay for, health care; and

(3) The size of the covered entity or business associate; and

(e) Such other matters as justice may require.

[78 FR 5691, Jan. 25, 2013]

§ 160.410 Affirmative defenses.

(a) The Secretary may not:

(1) Prior to February 18, 2011, impose a civil money penalty on a covered entity or business associate for an act that violates an administrative simplification provision if the covered entity or business associate establishes that the violation is punishable under 42 U.S.C. 1320d–6.

(2) On or after February 18, 2011, impose a civil money penalty on a covered entity or business associate for an act that violates an administrative simplification provision if the covered entity or business associate establishes that a penalty has been imposed under 42 U.S.C. 1320d–6 with respect to such act.

(b) For violations occurring prior to February 18, 2009, the Secretary may not impose a civil money penalty on a covered entity for a violation if the covered entity establishes that an affirmative defense exists with respect to the violation, including the following:

(1) The covered entity establishes, to the satisfaction of the Secretary, that it did not have knowledge of the violation, determined in accordance with the Federal common law of agency, and by exercising reasonable diligence, would not have known that the violation occurred; or

(2) The violation is—

(i) Due to circumstances that would make it unreasonable for the covered entity, despite the exercise of ordinary business care and prudence, to comply with the administrative simplification provision violated and is not due to willful neglect; and

(ii) Corrected during either:

(A) The 30-day period beginning on the first date the covered entity liable for the penalty knew, or by exercising reasonable diligence would have known, that the violation occurred; or

(B) Such additional period as the Secretary determines to be appropriate based on the nature and extent of the failure to comply.

(c) For violations occurring on or after February 18, 2009, the Secretary may not impose a civil money penalty on a covered entity or business associate for a violation if the covered entity or business associate establishes to the satisfaction of the Secretary that the violation is—

(1) Not due to willful neglect; and

(2) Corrected during either:

(i) The 30-day period beginning on the first date the covered entity or business associate liable for the penalty knew, or, by exercising reasonable diligence, would have known that the violation occurred; or

(ii) Such additional period as the Secretary determines to be appropriate based on the nature and extent of the failure to comply.

[78 FR 5692, Jan. 25, 2013]

§ 160.412 Waiver.

For violations described in § 160.410(b)(2) or (c) that are not corrected within the period specified under such paragraphs, the Secretary may waive the civil money penalty, in whole or in part, to the extent that the payment of the penalty would be excessive relative to the violation.

[8 FR 5692, Jan. 25, 2013]

§ 160.414 Limitations.

No action under this subpart may be entertained unless commenced by the Secretary, in accordance with § 160.420, within 6 years from the date of the occurrence of the violation.

§ 160.416 Authority to settle.

Nothing in this subpart limits the authority of the Secretary to settle any issue or case or to compromise any penalty.

§ 160.418 Penalty not exclusive.

Except as otherwise provided by 42 U.S.C. 1320d–5(b)(1) and 42 U.S.C. 299b–22(f)(3), a penalty imposed under this part is in addition to any other penalty prescribed by law.

[78 FR 5692, Jan. 25, 2013]

§ 160.420 Notice of proposed determination.

(a) If a penalty is proposed in accordance with this part, the Secretary must deliver, or send by certified mail with return receipt requested, to the respondent, written notice of the Secretary's intent to impose a penalty. This notice of proposed determination must include—

(1) Reference to the statutory basis for the penalty;

(2) A description of the findings of fact regarding the violations with respect to which the penalty is proposed (except that, in any case where the Secretary is relying upon a statistical sampling study in accordance with § 160.536 of this part, the notice must provide a copy of the study relied upon by the Secretary);

(3) The reason(s) why the violation(s) subject(s) the respondent to a penalty;

(4) The amount of the proposed penalty and a reference to the subparagraph of § 160.404 upon which it is based.

(5) Any circumstances described in § 160.408 that were considered in determining the amount of the proposed penalty; and

(6) Instructions for responding to the notice, including a statement of the respondent's right to a hearing, a statement that failure to request a hearing within 90 days permits the imposition of the proposed penalty without the right to a hearing under § 160.504 or a right of appeal under § 160.548 of this part, and the address to which the hearing request must be sent.

(b) The respondent may request a hearing before an ALJ on the proposed penalty by filing a request in accordance with § 160.504 of this part.

[71 FR 8426, Feb. 16, 2006, as amended at 74 FR 56131, Oct. 30, 2009]

§ 160.422 Failure to request a hearing.

If the respondent does not request a hearing within the time prescribed by § 160.504 of this part and the matter is not settled pursuant to § 160.416, the Secretary will impose the proposed penalty or any lesser penalty permitted by 42 U.S.C. 1320d–5. The Secretary will notify the respondent by certified mail, return receipt requested, of any penalty that has been imposed and of the means by which the respondent may satisfy the penalty, and the penalty is final on receipt of the notice. The respondent has no right to appeal a penalty under § 160.548 of this part with respect to which the respondent has not timely requested a hearing.

§ 160.424 Collection of penalty.

(a) Once a determination of the Secretary to impose a penalty has become final, the penalty will be collected by the Secretary, subject to the first sentence of 42 U.S.C. 1320a–7a(f).

(b) The penalty may be recovered in a civil action brought in the United States district court for the district where the respondent resides, is found, or is located.

(c) The amount of a penalty, when finally determined, or the amount agreed upon in compromise, may be deducted from any sum then or later owing by the United States, or by a State agency, to the respondent.

(d) Matters that were raised or that could have been raised in a hearing before an ALJ, or in an appeal under 42 U.S.C. 1320a–7a(e), may not be raised as a defense in a civil action by the United States to collect a penalty under this part.

§ 160.426 Notification of the public and other agencies.

Whenever a proposed penalty becomes final, the Secretary will notify, in such manner as the Secretary deems appropriate, the public and the following organizations and entities thereof and the reason it was imposed: the appropriate State or local medical or professional organization, the appropriate State agency or agencies administering or supervising the administration of State health care programs (as defined in 42 U.S.C. 1320a–7(h)), the appropriate utilization and quality control peer review organization, and the appropriate State or local licensing agency or organization (including the agency specified in 42 U.S.C. 1395aa(a), 1396a(a)(33)).

Subpart E—Procedures for Hearings

Source: 71 FR 8428, Feb. 16, 2006, unless otherwise noted.

§ 160.500 Applicability.

This subpart applies to hearings conducted relating to the imposition of a civil money penalty by the Secretary under 42 U.S.C. 1320d–5.

§ 160.502 Definitions.

As used in this subpart, the following term has the following meaning:

Board means the members of the HHS Departmental Appeals Board, in the Office of the Secretary, who issue decisions in panels of three.

§ 160.504 Hearing before an ALJ.

(a) A respondent may request a hearing before an ALJ. The parties to the hearing proceeding consist of—

(1) The respondent; and

(2) The officer(s) or employee(s) of HHS to whom the enforcement authority involved has been delegated.

(b) The request for a hearing must be made in writing signed by the respondent or by the respondent's attorney and sent by certified mail, return receipt requested, to the address specified in the notice of proposed determination. The request for a hearing must be mailed within 90 days after notice of the proposed determination is received by the respondent. For purposes of this section, the respondent's date of receipt of the notice of proposed determination is presumed to be 5 days after the date of the notice unless the respondent makes a reasonable showing to the contrary to the ALJ.

(c) The request for a hearing must clearly and directly admit, deny, or explain each of the findings of fact contained in the notice of proposed determination with regard to which the respondent has any knowledge. If the respondent has no knowledge of a particular finding of fact and so states, the finding shall be deemed denied. The request for a hearing must also state the circumstances or arguments that the respondent alleges constitute the grounds for any defense and the factual and legal basis for opposing the penalty, except that a respondent may raise an affirmative defense under § 160.410(b)(1) at any time.

(d) The ALJ must dismiss a hearing request where—

(1) On motion of the Secretary, the ALJ determines that the respondent's hearing request is not timely filed as required by paragraphs (b) or does not meet the requirements of paragraph (c) of this section;

(2) The respondent withdraws the request for a hearing;

(3) The respondent abandons the request for a hearing; or

(4) The respondent's hearing request fails to raise any issue that may properly be addressed in a hearing.

§ 160.506 Rights of the parties.

(a) Except as otherwise limited by this subpart, each party may—

(1) Be accompanied, represented, and advised by an attorney;

(2) Participate in any conference held by the ALJ;

(3) Conduct discovery of documents as permitted by this subpart;

(4) Agree to stipulations of fact or law that will be made part of the record;

(5) Present evidence relevant to the issues at the hearing;

(6) Present and cross-examine witnesses;

(7) Present oral arguments at the hearing as permitted by the ALJ; and

(8) Submit written briefs and proposed findings of fact and conclusions of law after the hearing.

(b) A party may appear in person or by a representative. Natural persons who appear as an attorney or other representative must conform to the standards of conduct and ethics required of practitioners before the courts of the United States.

(c) Fees for any services performed on behalf of a party by an attorney are not subject to the provisions of 42 U.S.C. 406, which authorizes the Secretary to specify or limit their fees.

§ 160.508 Authority of the ALJ.

(a) The ALJ must conduct a fair and impartial hearing, avoid delay, maintain order, and ensure that a record of the proceeding is made.

(b) The ALJ may—

(1) Set and change the date, time and place of the hearing upon reasonable notice to the parties;

(2) Continue or recess the hearing in whole or in part for a reasonable period of time;

(3) Hold conferences to identify or simplify the issues, or to consider other matters that may aid in the expeditious disposition of the proceeding;

(4) Administer oaths and affirmations;

(5) Issue subpoenas requiring the attendance of witnesses at hearings and the production of documents at or in relation to hearings;

(6) Rule on motions and other procedural matters;

(7) Regulate the scope and timing of documentary discovery as permitted by this subpart;

(8) Regulate the course of the hearing and the conduct of representatives, parties, and witnesses;

(9) Examine witnesses;

(10) Receive, rule on, exclude, or limit evidence;

(11) Upon motion of a party, take official notice of facts;

(12) Conduct any conference, argument or hearing in person or, upon agreement of the parties, by telephone; and

(13) Upon motion of a party, decide cases, in whole or in part, by summary judgment where there is no disputed issue of material fact. A summary judgment decision constitutes a hearing on the record for the purposes of this subpart.

(c) The ALJ—

(1) May not find invalid or refuse to follow Federal statutes, regulations, or Secretarial delegations of authority and must give deference to published guidance to the extent not inconsistent with statute or regulation;

(2) May not enter an order in the nature of a directed verdict;

(3) May not compel settlement negotiations;

(4) May not enjoin any act of the Secretary; or

(5) May not review the exercise of discretion by the Secretary with respect to whether to grant an extension under § 160.410(b)(2)(ii)(B) or (c)(2)(ii) of this part or to provide technical assistance under 42 U.S.C. 1320d–5(b)(2)(B).

[71 FR 8428, Feb. 16, 2006, as amended at 78 FR 34266, June 7, 2013]

§ 160.510 Ex parte contacts.

No party or person (except employees of the ALJ's office) may communicate in any way with the ALJ on any matter at issue in a case, unless on notice and opportunity for both parties to participate. This provision does not prohibit a party or person from inquiring about the status of a case or asking routine questions concerning administrative functions or procedures.

§ 160.512 Prehearing conferences.

(a) The ALJ must schedule at least one prehearing conference, and may schedule additional prehearing conferences as appropriate, upon reasonable notice, which may not be less than 14 business days, to the parties.

(b) The ALJ may use prehearing conferences to discuss the following—

(1) Simplification of the issues;

(2) The necessity or desirability of amendments to the pleadings, including the need for a more definite statement;

(3) Stipulations and admissions of fact or as to the contents and authenticity of documents;

(4) Whether the parties can agree to submission of the case on a stipulated record;

(5) Whether a party chooses to waive appearance at an oral hearing and to submit only documentary evidence (subject to the objection of the other party) and written argument;

(6) Limitation of the number of witnesses;

(7) Scheduling dates for the exchange of witness lists and of proposed exhibits;

(8) Discovery of documents as permitted by this subpart;

(9) The time and place for the hearing;

(10) The potential for the settlement of the case by the parties; and

(11) Other matters as may tend to encourage the fair, just and expeditious disposition of the proceedings, including the protection of privacy of individually identifiable health information that may be submitted into evidence or otherwise used in the proceeding, if appropriate.

(c) The ALJ must issue an order containing the matters agreed upon by the parties or ordered by the ALJ at a prehearing conference.

§ 160.514 Authority to settle.

The Secretary has exclusive authority to settle any issue or case without the consent of the ALJ.

§ 160.516 Discovery.

(a) A party may make a request to another party for production of documents for inspection and copying that are relevant and material to the issues before the ALJ.

(b) For the purpose of this section, the term "documents" includes information, reports, answers, records, accounts, papers and other data and documentary evidence. Nothing contained in this section may be interpreted to require the creation of a document, except that requested data stored in an electronic data storage system must be produced in a form accessible to the requesting party.

(c) Requests for documents, requests for admissions, written interrogatories, depositions and any forms of discovery, other than those permitted under paragraph (a) of this section, are not authorized.

(d) This section may not be construed to require the disclosure of interview reports or statements obtained by any party, or on behalf of any party, of persons who will not be called as witnesses by that party, or analyses and summaries prepared in conjunction with the investigation or litigation of the case, or any otherwise privileged documents.

(e)

(1) When a request for production of documents has been received, within 30 days the party receiving that request must either fully respond to the request, or state that the request is being objected to and the reasons for that objection. If objection is made to part of an item or category, the part must be specified. Upon receiving any objections, the party seeking production may then, within 30 days or any other time frame set by the ALJ, file a motion for an order compelling discovery. The party receiving a request for production may also file a motion for protective order any time before the date the production is due.

(2) The ALJ may grant a motion for protective order or deny a motion for an order compelling discovery if the ALJ finds that the discovery sought—

(i) Is irrelevant;

(ii) Is unduly costly or burdensome;

(iii) Will unduly delay the proceeding; or

(iv) Seeks privileged information.

(3) The ALJ may extend any of the time frames set forth in paragraph (e)(1) of this section.

(4) The burden of showing that discovery should be allowed is on the party seeking discovery.

§ 160.518 Exchange of witness lists, witness statements, and exhibits.

(a) The parties must exchange witness lists, copies of prior written statements of proposed witnesses, and copies of proposed hearing exhibits, including copies of any written statements that the party intends to offer in lieu of live testimony in accordance with § 160.538, not more than 60, and not less than 15, days before the scheduled hearing, except that if a respondent intends to introduce the evidence of a statistical expert, the respondent must provide the Secretarial party with a copy of the statistical expert's report not less than 30 days before the scheduled hearing.

(b)

(1) If, at any time, a party objects to the proposed admission of evidence not exchanged in accordance with paragraph (a) of this section, the ALJ must determine whether the failure to comply with paragraph (a) of this section should result in the exclusion of that evidence.

(2) Unless the ALJ finds that extraordinary circumstances justified the failure timely to exchange the information listed under paragraph (a) of this section, the ALJ must exclude from the party's case-in-chief—

(i) The testimony of any witness whose name does not appear on the witness list; and

(ii) Any exhibit not provided to the opposing party as specified in paragraph (a) of this section.

(3) If the ALJ finds that extraordinary circumstances existed, the ALJ must then determine whether the admission of that evidence would cause substantial prejudice to the objecting party.

(i) If the ALJ finds that there is no substantial prejudice, the evidence may be admitted.

(ii) If the ALJ finds that there is substantial prejudice, the ALJ may exclude the evidence, or, if he or she does not exclude the evidence, must postpone the hearing for such time as is necessary for the objecting party to prepare and respond to the evidence, unless the objecting party waives postponement.

(c) Unless the other party objects within a reasonable period of time before the hearing, documents exchanged in accordance with paragraph (a) of this section will be deemed to be authentic for the purpose of admissibility at the hearing.

§ 160.520 Subpoenas for attendance at hearing.

(a) A party wishing to procure the appearance and testimony of any person at the hearing may make a motion requesting the ALJ to issue a subpoena if the appearance and testimony are reasonably necessary for the presentation of a party's case.

(b) A subpoena requiring the attendance of a person in accordance with paragraph (a) of this section may also require the person (whether or not the person is a party) to produce relevant and material evidence at or before the hearing.

(c) When a subpoena is served by a respondent on a particular employee or official or particular office of HHS, the Secretary may comply by designating any knowledgeable HHS representative to appear and testify.

(d) A party seeking a subpoena must file a written motion not less than 30 days before the date fixed for the hearing, unless otherwise allowed by the ALJ for good cause shown. That motion must—

(1) Specify any evidence to be produced;

(2) Designate the witnesses; and

(3) Describe the address and location with sufficient particularity to permit those witnesses to be found.

(e) The subpoena must specify the time and place at which the witness is to appear and any evidence the witness is to produce.

(f) Within 15 days after the written motion requesting issuance of a subpoena is served, any party may file an opposition or other response.

(g) If the motion requesting issuance of a subpoena is granted, the party seeking the subpoena must serve it by delivery to the person named, or by certified mail addressed to that person at the person's last dwelling place or principal place of business.

(h) The person to whom the subpoena is directed may file with the ALJ a motion to quash the subpoena within 10 days after service.

(i) The exclusive remedy for contumacy by, or refusal to obey a subpoena duly served upon, any person is specified in 42 U.S.C. 405(e).

§ 160.522 Fees.

The party requesting a subpoena must pay the cost of the fees and mileage of any witness subpoenaed in the amounts that would be payable to a witness in a proceeding in United States District Court. A check for witness fees and mileage must accompany the subpoena when served, except that, when a subpoena is issued on behalf of the Secretary, a check for witness fees and mileage need not accompany the subpoena.

§ 160.524 Form, filing, and service of papers.

(a) *Forms.*

(1) Unless the ALJ directs the parties to do otherwise, documents filed with the ALJ must include an original and two copies.

(2) Every pleading and paper filed in the proceeding must contain a caption setting forth the title of the action, the case number, and a designation of the paper, such as motion to quash subpoena.

(3) Every pleading and paper must be signed by and must contain the address and telephone number of the party or the person on whose behalf the paper was filed, or his or her representative.

(4) Papers are considered filed when they are mailed.

(b) *Service.* A party filing a document with the ALJ or the Board must, at the time of filing, serve a copy of the document on the other party. Service upon any party of any document must be made by delivering a copy, or placing a copy of the document in the United States mail, postage prepaid and addressed, or with a private delivery service, to the party's last known address. When a party is represented by an attorney, service must be made upon the attorney in lieu of the party.

(c) *Proof of service.* A certificate of the natural person serving the document by personal delivery or by mail, setting forth the manner of service, constitutes proof of service.

§ 160.526 Computation of time.

(a) In computing any period of time under this subpart or in an order issued thereunder, the time begins with the day following the act, event or default, and includes the last day of the period unless it is a Saturday, Sunday, or legal holiday observed by the Federal Government, in which event it includes the next business day.

(b) When the period of time allowed is less than 7 days, intermediate Saturdays, Sundays, and legal holidays observed by the Federal Government must be excluded from the computation.

(c) Where a document has been served or issued by placing it in the mail, an additional 5 days must be added to the time permitted for any response. This paragraph does not apply to requests for hearing under § 160.504.

§ 160.528 Motions.

(a) An application to the ALJ for an order or ruling must be by motion. Motions must state the relief sought, the authority relied upon and the facts alleged, and must be filed with the ALJ and served on all other parties.

(b) Except for motions made during a prehearing conference or at the hearing, all motions must be in writing. The ALJ may require that oral motions be reduced to writing.

(c) Within 10 days after a written motion is served, or such other time as may be fixed by the ALJ, any party may file a response to the motion.

(d) The ALJ may not grant a written motion before the time for filing responses has expired, except upon consent of the parties or following a hearing on the motion, but may overrule or deny the motion without awaiting a response.

(e) The ALJ must make a reasonable effort to dispose of all outstanding motions before the beginning of the hearing.

§ 160.530 Sanctions.

The ALJ may sanction a person, including any party or attorney, for failing to comply with an order or procedure, for failing to defend an action or for other misconduct that interferes with the speedy, orderly or fair conduct of the hearing. The sanctions must reasonably relate to the severity and nature of the failure or misconduct. The sanctions may include—

(a) In the case of refusal to provide or permit discovery under the terms of this part, drawing negative factual inferences or treating the refusal as an admission by deeming the matter, or certain facts, to be established;

(b) Prohibiting a party from introducing certain evidence or otherwise supporting a particular claim or defense;

(c) Striking pleadings, in whole or in part;

(d) Staying the proceedings;

(e) Dismissal of the action;

(f) Entering a decision by default;

(g) Ordering the party or attorney to pay the attorney's fees and other costs caused by the failure or misconduct; and

(h) Refusing to consider any motion or other action that is not filed in a timely manner.

§ 160.532 Collateral estoppel.

When a final determination that the respondent violated an administrative simplification provision has been rendered in any proceeding in which the respondent was a party and had an opportunity to be heard, the respondent is bound by that determination in any proceeding under this part.

§ 160.534 The hearing.

(a) The ALJ must conduct a hearing on the record in order to determine whether the respondent should be found liable under this part.

(b)

(1) The respondent has the burden of going forward and the burden of persuasion with respect to any:

(i) Affirmative defense pursuant to § 160.410 of this part;

(ii) Challenge to the amount of a proposed penalty pursuant to §§ 160.404–160.408 of this part, including any factors raised as mitigating factors; or

(iii) Claim that a proposed penalty should be reduced or waived pursuant to § 160.412 of this part; and

(iv) Compliance with subpart D of part 164, as provided under § 164.414(b).

(2) The Secretary has the burden of going forward and the burden of persuasion with respect to all other issues, including issues of liability other than with respect to subpart D of part 164, and the existence of any factors considered aggravating factors in determining the amount of the proposed penalty.

(3) The burden of persuasion will be judged by a preponderance of the evidence.

(c) The hearing must be open to the public unless otherwise ordered by the ALJ for good cause shown.

(d)

(1) Subject to the 15-day rule under § 160.518(a) and the admissibility of evidence under § 160.540, either party may introduce, during its case in chief, items or information that arose or became known after the date of the issuance of the notice of proposed determination or the request for hearing, as applicable. Such items and information may not be admitted into evidence, if introduced—

(i) By the Secretary, unless they are material and relevant to the acts or omissions with respect to which the penalty is proposed in the notice of proposed determination pursuant to § 160.420 of this part, including circumstances that may increase penalties; or

(ii) By the respondent, unless they are material and relevant to an admission, denial or explanation of a finding of fact in the notice of proposed determination under § 160.420 of this part, or to a specific circumstance or argument expressly stated in the request for hearing under § 160.504, including circumstances that may reduce penalties.

(2) After both parties have presented their cases, evidence may be admitted in rebuttal even if not previously exchanged in accordance with § 160.518.

[71 FR 8428, Feb. 16, 2006, as amended at 74 FR 42767, Aug. 24, 2009; 78 FR 5692, Jan. 25, 2013]

§ 160.536 Statistical sampling.

(a) In meeting the burden of proof set forth in § 160.534, the Secretary may introduce the results of a statistical sampling study as evidence of the number of violations under § 160.406 of this part, or the factors considered in determining the amount of the civil money penalty under § 160.408 of this part. Such statistical sampling study, if based upon an appropriate sampling and computed by valid statistical methods, constitutes prima facie evidence of the number of violations and the existence of factors material to the proposed civil money penalty as described in §§ 160.406 and 160.408.

(b) Once the Secretary has made a prima facie case, as described in paragraph (a) of this section, the burden of going forward shifts to the respondent to produce evidence reasonably calculated to rebut the findings of the statistical sampling study. The Secretary will then be given the opportunity to rebut this evidence.

§ 160.538 Witnesses.

(a) Except as provided in paragraph (b) of this section, testimony at the hearing must be given orally by witnesses under oath or affirmation.

(b) At the discretion of the ALJ, testimony of witnesses other than the testimony of expert witnesses may be admitted in the form of a written statement. The ALJ may, at his or her discretion, admit prior sworn testimony of experts that has been subject to adverse examination, such as a deposition or trial testimony. Any such written statement must be provided to the other party, along with the last known address of the witness, in a manner that allows sufficient time for the other party to subpoena the witness for cross-examination at the hearing. Prior written statements of witnesses proposed to testify at the hearing must be exchanged as provided in § 160.518.

(c) The ALJ must exercise reasonable control over the mode and order of interrogating witnesses and presenting evidence so as to:

(1) Make the interrogation and presentation effective for the ascertainment of the truth;

(2) Avoid repetition or needless consumption of time; and

(3) Protect witnesses from harassment or undue embarrassment.

(d) The ALJ must permit the parties to conduct cross-examination of witnesses as may be required for a full and true disclosure of the facts.

(e) The ALJ may order witnesses excluded so that they cannot hear the testimony of other witnesses, except that the ALJ may not order to be excluded—

(1) A party who is a natural person;

(2) In the case of a party that is not a natural person, the officer or employee of the party appearing for the entity pro se or designated as the party's representative; or

(3) A natural person whose presence is shown by a party to be essential to the presentation of its case, including a person engaged in assisting the attorney for the Secretary.

§ 160.540 Evidence.

(a) The ALJ must determine the admissibility of evidence.

(b) Except as provided in this subpart, the ALJ is not bound by the Federal Rules of Evidence. However, the ALJ may apply the Federal Rules of Evidence where appropriate, for example, to exclude unreliable evidence.

54

(c) The ALJ must exclude irrelevant or immaterial evidence.

(d) Although relevant, evidence may be excluded if its probative value is substantially outweighed by the danger of unfair prejudice, confusion of the issues, or by considerations of undue delay or needless presentation of cumulative evidence.

(e) Although relevant, evidence must be excluded if it is privileged under Federal law.

(f) Evidence concerning offers of compromise or settlement are inadmissible to the extent provided in Rule 408 of the Federal Rules of Evidence.

(g) Evidence of crimes, wrongs, or acts other than those at issue in the instant case is admissible in order to show motive, opportunity, intent, knowledge, preparation, identity, lack of mistake, or existence of a scheme. This evidence is admissible regardless of whether the crimes, wrongs, or acts occurred during the statute of limitations period applicable to the acts or omissions that constitute the basis for liability in the case and regardless of whether they were referenced in the Secretary's notice of proposed determination under § 160.420 of this part.

(h) The ALJ must permit the parties to introduce rebuttal witnesses and evidence.

(i) All documents and other evidence offered or taken for the record must be open to examination by both parties, unless otherwise ordered by the ALJ for good cause shown.

§ 160.542 The record.

(a) The hearing must be recorded and transcribed. Transcripts may be obtained following the hearing from the ALJ. A party that requests a transcript of hearing proceedings must pay the cost of preparing the transcript unless, for good cause shown by the party, the payment is waived by the ALJ or the Board, as appropriate.

(b) The transcript of the testimony, exhibits, and other evidence admitted at the hearing, and all papers and requests filed in the proceeding constitute the record for decision by the ALJ and the Secretary.

(c) The record may be inspected and copied (upon payment of a reasonable fee) by any person, unless otherwise ordered by the ALJ for good cause shown.

(d) For good cause, the ALJ may order appropriate redactions made to the record.

§ 160.544 Post hearing briefs.

The ALJ may require the parties to file post-hearing briefs. In any event, any party may file a post-hearing brief. The ALJ must fix the time for filing the briefs. The time for filing may not exceed 60 days from the date the parties receive the transcript of the hearing or, if applicable, the stipulated record. The briefs may be accompanied by proposed findings of fact and conclusions of law. The ALJ may permit the parties to file reply briefs.

§ 160.546 ALJ's decision.

(a) The ALJ must issue a decision, based only on the record, which must contain findings of fact and conclusions of law.

(b) The ALJ may affirm, increase, or reduce the penalties imposed by the Secretary.

(c) The ALJ must issue the decision to both parties within 60 days after the time for submission of post-hearing briefs and reply briefs, if permitted, has expired. If the ALJ fails to meet the deadline contained in this paragraph, he or she must notify the parties of the reason for the delay and set a new deadline.

(d) Unless the decision of the ALJ is timely appealed as provided for in § 160.548, the decision of the ALJ will be final and binding on the parties 60 days from the date of service of the ALJ's decision.

§ 160.548 Appeal of the ALJ's decision.

(a) Any party may appeal the decision of the ALJ to the Board by filing a notice of appeal with the Board within 30 days of the date of service of the ALJ decision. The Board may extend the initial 30 day period for a period of time not to exceed 30 days if a party files with the Board a request for an extension within the initial 30 day period and shows good cause.

(b) If a party files a timely notice of appeal with the Board, the ALJ must forward the record of the proceeding to the Board.

(c) A notice of appeal must be accompanied by a written brief specifying exceptions to the initial decision and reasons supporting the exceptions. Any party may file a brief in opposition to the exceptions, which may raise any relevant issue not addressed in the exceptions, within 30 days of receiving the notice of appeal and the accompanying brief. The Board may permit the parties to file reply briefs.

(d) There is no right to appear personally before the Board or to appeal to the Board any interlocutory ruling by the ALJ.

(e) Except for an affirmative defense under § 160.410(a)(1) or (2) of this part, the Board may not consider any issue not raised in the parties' briefs, nor any issue in the briefs that could have been raised before the ALJ but was not.

(f) If any party demonstrates to the satisfaction of the Board that additional evidence not presented at such hearing is relevant and material and that there were reasonable grounds for the failure to adduce such evidence at the hearing, the Board may remand the matter to the ALJ for consideration of such additional evidence.

(g) The Board may decline to review the case, or may affirm, increase, reduce, reverse or remand any penalty determined by the ALJ.

(h) The standard of review on a disputed issue of fact is whether the initial decision of the ALJ is supported by substantial evidence on the whole record. The standard of review on a disputed issue of law is whether the decision is erroneous.

(i) Within 60 days after the time for submission of briefs and reply briefs, if permitted, has expired, the Board must serve on each party to the appeal a copy of the Board's decision and a statement describing the right of any respondent who is penalized to seek judicial review.

(j)

(1) The Board's decision under paragraph (i) of this section, including a decision to decline review of the initial decision, becomes the final decision of the Secretary 60 days after the date of service of the Board's decision, except with respect to a decision to remand to the ALJ or if reconsideration is requested under this paragraph.

(2) The Board will reconsider its decision only if it determines that the decision contains a clear error of fact or error of law. New evidence will not be a basis for reconsideration unless the party demonstrates that the evidence is newly discovered and was not previously available.

(3) A party may file a motion for reconsideration with the Board before the date the decision becomes final under paragraph (j)(1) of this section. A motion for reconsideration must be accompanied by a written brief specifying any alleged error of fact or law and, if the party is relying on additional evidence, explaining why the evidence was not previously available. Any party may file a brief in opposition within 15 days of receiving the motion for reconsideration and the accompanying brief unless this time limit is extended by the Board for good cause shown. Reply briefs are not permitted.

(4) The Board must rule on the motion for reconsideration not later than 30 days from the date the opposition brief is due. If the Board denies the motion, the decision issued under paragraph (i) of this section becomes the final decision of the Secretary on the date of service of the ruling. If the Board grants the motion, the Board will issue a reconsidered decision, after such procedures as the Board determines necessary to address the effect of any error. The Board's decision on reconsideration becomes the final decision of the Secretary on the date of service of the decision, except with respect to a decision to remand to the ALJ.

(5) If service of a ruling or decision issued under this section is by mail, the date of service will be deemed to be 5 days from the date of mailing.

(k)

(1) A respondent's petition for judicial review must be filed within 60 days of the date on which the decision of the Board becomes the final decision of the Secretary under paragraph (j) of this section.

(2) In compliance with 28 U.S.C. 2112(a), a copy of any petition for judicial review filed in any U.S. Court of Appeals challenging the final decision of the Secretary must be sent by certified mail, return receipt requested, to the General Counsel of HHS. The petition copy must be a copy showing that it has been time-stamped by the clerk of the court when the original was filed with the court.

(3) If the General Counsel of HHS received two or more petitions within 10 days after the final decision of the Secretary, the General Counsel will notify the U.S. Judicial Panel on Multidistrict Litigation of any petitions that were received within the 10 day period.

[71 FR 8428, Feb. 16, 2006, as amended at 78 FR 34266, June 7, 2013]

§ 160.550 Stay of the Secretary's decision.

(a) Pending judicial review, the respondent may file a request for stay of the effective date of any penalty with the ALJ. The request must be accompanied by a copy of the notice of appeal filed with the Federal court. The filing of the request automatically stays the effective date of the penalty until such time as the ALJ rules upon the request.

(b) The ALJ may not grant a respondent's request for stay of any penalty unless the respondent posts a bond or provides other adequate security.

(c) The ALJ must rule upon a respondent's request for stay within 10 days of receipt.

§ 160.552 Harmless error.

No error in either the admission or the exclusion of evidence, and no error or defect in any ruling or order or in any act done or omitted by the ALJ or by any of the parties is ground for vacating, modifying or otherwise disturbing an otherwise appropriate ruling or order or act, unless refusal to take such action appears to the ALJ or the Board inconsistent with substantial justice. The ALJ and the Board at every stage of the proceeding must disregard any error or defect in the proceeding that does not affect the substantial rights of the parties.

Intentionally Blank

45 CFR PART 162—ADMINISTRATIVE REQUIREMENTS

Authority:42 U.S.C. 1320d—1320d–9 and secs. 1104 and 10109 of Pub. L. 111–148, 124 Stat. 146–154 and 915–917.
Source:65 FR 50367, Aug. 17, 2000, unless otherwise noted.

Subpart A—General Provisions

§ 162.100 Applicability.

Covered entities (as defined in § 160.103 of this subchapter) must comply with the applicable requirements of this part.

§ 162.103 Definitions.

For purposes of this part, the following definitions apply:

Code set means any set of codes used to encode data elements, such as tables of terms, medical concepts, medical diagnostic codes, or medical procedure codes. A code set includes the codes and the descriptors of the codes.

Code set maintaining organization means an organization that creates and maintains the code sets adopted by the Secretary for use in the transactions for which standards are adopted in this part.

Covered health care provider means a health care provider that meets the definition at paragraph (3) of the definition of "covered entity" at § 160.103.

Data condition means the rule that describes the circumstances under which a covered entity must use a particular data element or segment.

Data content means all the data elements and code sets inherent to a transaction, and not related to the format of the transaction. Data elements that are related to the format are not data content.

Data element means the smallest named unit of information in a transaction.

Data set means a semantically meaningful unit of information exchanged between two parties to a transaction.

Descriptor means the text defining a code.

Designated standard maintenance organization (DSMO) means an organization designated by the Secretary under § 162.910(a).

Direct data entry means the direct entry of data (for example, using dumb terminals or web browsers) that is immediately transmitted into a health plan's computer.

Format refers to those data elements that provide or control the enveloping or hierarchical structure, or assist in identifying data content of, a transaction.

HCPCS stands for the Health [Care Financing Administration] Common Procedure Coding System.

Maintain or *maintenance* refers to activities necessary to support the use of a standard adopted by the Secretary, including technical corrections to an implementation specification, and enhancements or expansion of a code set. This term excludes the activities related to the adoption of a new standard or implementation specification, or modification to an adopted standard or implementation specification.

Maximum defined data set means all of the required data elements for a particular standard based on a specific implementation specification.

Operating rules means the necessary business rules and guidelines for the electronic exchange of information that are not defined by a standard or its implementation specifications as adopted for purposes of this part.

Segment means a group of related data elements in a transaction.

Stage 1 payment initiation means a health plan's order, instruction or authorization to its financial institution to make a health care claims payment using an electronic funds transfer (EFT) through the ACH Network.

Standard transaction means a transaction that complies with an applicable standard and associated operating rules adopted under this part.

[65 FR 50367, Aug. 17, 2000, as amended at 68 FR 8374, Feb. 20, 2003; 74 FR 3324, Jan. 16, 2009; 76 FR 40495, July 8, 2011; 77 FR 1589, Jan. 10, 2012; 77 FR 54719, Sept. 5, 2012; 84 FR 57629, Oct. 28, 2019]

Subparts B–C [Reserved]

Subpart D—Standard Unique Health Identifier for Health Care Providers

Source: 69 FR 3468, Jan. 23, 2004, unless otherwise noted.

§ 162.402 [Reserved]

§ 162.404 Compliance dates of the implementation of the standard unique health identifier for health care providers.

(a) **Health care providers.** A covered health care provider must comply with the implementation specifications in § 162.410 no later than May 23, 2007.

(b) **Health plans.** A health plan must comply with the implementation specifications in § 162.412 no later than one of the following dates:

(1) A health plan that is not a small health plan—May 23, 2007.

(2) A small health plan—May 23, 2008.

(c) *Health care clearinghouses.* A health care clearinghouse must comply with the implementation specifications in § 162.414 no later than May 23, 2007.

[69 FR 3468, Jan. 23, 2004, as amended at 77 FR 54719, Sept. 5, 2012]

§ 162.406 Standard unique health identifier for health care providers.

(a) *Standard.* The standard unique health identifier for health care providers is the National Provider Identifier (NPI). The NPI is a 10-position numeric identifier, with a check digit in the 10th position, and no intelligence about the health care provider in the number.

(b) *Required and permitted uses for the NPI.*

(1) The NPI must be used as stated in §§ 162.410, 162.412, and 162.414.

(2) The NPI may be used for any other lawful purpose.

§ 162.408 National Provider System.

National Provider System. The National Provider System (NPS) shall do the following:

(a) Assign a single, unique NPI to a health care provider, provided that—

(1) The NPS may assign an NPI to a subpart of a health care provider in accordance with paragraph (g); and

(2) The Secretary has sufficient information to permit the assignment to be made.

(b) Collect and maintain information about each health care provider that has been assigned an NPI and perform tasks necessary to update that information.

(c) If appropriate, deactivate an NPI upon receipt of appropriate information concerning the dissolution of the health care provider that is an organization, the death of the health care provider who is an individual, or other circumstances justifying deactivation.

(d) If appropriate, reactivate a deactivated NPI upon receipt of appropriate information.

(e) Not assign a deactivated NPI to any other health care provider.

(f) Disseminate NPS information upon approved requests.

(g) Assign an NPI to a subpart of a health care provider on request if the identifying data for the subpart are unique.

§ 162.410 Implementation specifications: Health care providers.

(a) A covered entity that is a covered health care provider must:

(1) Obtain, by application if necessary, an NPI from the National Provider System (NPS) for itself or for any subpart of the covered entity that would be a covered health care provider if it were a separate legal entity. A covered entity may obtain an NPI for any other subpart that qualifies for the assignment of an NPI.

(2) Use the NPI it obtained from the NPS to identify itself on all standard transactions that it conducts where its health care provider identifier is required.

(3) Disclose its NPI, when requested, to any entity that needs the NPI to identify that covered health care provider in a standard transaction.

(4) Communicate to the NPS any changes in its required data elements in the NPS within 30 days of the change.

(5) If it uses one or more business associates to conduct standard transactions on its behalf, require its business associate(s) to use its NPI and other NPIs appropriately as required by the transactions that the business associate(s) conducts on its behalf.

(6) If it has been assigned NPIs for one or more subparts, comply with the requirements of paragraphs (a)(2) through (a)(5) of this section with respect to each of those NPIs.

(b) An organization covered health care provider that has as a member, employs, or contracts with, an individual health care provider who is not a covered entity and is a prescriber, must require such health care provider to—

(1) Obtain an NPI from the National Plan and Provider Enumeration System (NPPES); and

(2) To the extent the prescriber writes a prescription while acting within the scope of the prescriber's relationship with the organization, disclose the NPI upon request to any entity that needs it to identify the prescriber in a standard transaction.

(c) A health care provider that is not a covered entity may obtain, by application if necessary, an NPI from the NPS.

[69 FR 3468, Jan. 23, 2004, as amended at 77 FR 54719, Sept. 5, 2012]

§ 162.412 Implementation specifications: Health plans.

(a) A health plan must use the NPI of any health care provider (or subpart(s), if applicable) that has been assigned an NPI to identify that health care provider on all standard transactions where that health care provider's identifier is required.

(b) A health plan may not require a health care provider that has been assigned an NPI to obtain an additional NPI.

§ 162.414 Implementation specifications: Health care clearinghouses.

A health care clearinghouse must use the NPI of any health care provider (or subpart(s), if applicable) that has been assigned an NPI to identify that health care provider on all standard transactions where that health care provider's identifier is required.

Subpart E [Reserved]

Subpart F—Standard Unique Employer Identifier

Source:67 FR 38020, May 31, 2002, unless otherwise noted.

§ 162.600 Compliance dates of the implementation of the standard unique employer identifier.

(a) *Health care providers.* Health care providers must comply with the requirements of this subpart no later than July 30, 2004.

(b) *Health plans.* A health plan must comply with the requirements of this subpart no later than one of the following dates:

(1) *Health plans other than small health plans* —July 30, 2004.

(2) *Small health plans* —August 1, 2005.

(c) *Health care clearinghouses.* Health care clearinghouses must comply with the requirements of this subpart no later than July 30, 2004.

§ 162.605 Standard unique employer identifier.

The Secretary adopts the EIN as the standard unique employer identifier provided for by 42 U.S.C. 1320d–2(b).

§ 162.610 Implementation specifications for covered entities.

(a) The standard unique employer identifier of an employer of a particular employee is the EIN that appears on that employee's IRS Form W–2, Wage and Tax Statement, from the employer.

(b) A covered entity must use the standard unique employer identifier (EIN) of the appropriate employer in standard transactions that require an employer identifier to identify a person or entity as an employer, including where situationally required.

(c) Required and permitted uses for the Employer Identifier.

(1) The Employer Identifier must be used as stated in § 162.610(b).

(2) The Employer Identifier may be used for any other lawful purpose.

[67 FR 38020, May 31, 2002, as amended at 69 FR 3469, Jan. 23, 2004]

Subparts G–H [Reserved]

Subpart I—General Provisions for Transactions

§ 162.900 [Reserved]

§ 162.910 Maintenance of standards and adoption of modifications and new standards.

(a) *Designation of DSMOs.*

(1) The Secretary may designate as a DSMO an organization that agrees to conduct, to the satisfaction of the Secretary, the following functions:

(i) Maintain standards adopted under this subchapter.

(ii) Receive and process requests for adopting a new standard or modifying an adopted standard.

(2) The Secretary designates a DSMO by notice in the Federal Register.

(b) *Maintenance of standards.* Maintenance of a standard by the appropriate DSMO constitutes maintenance of the standard for purposes of this part, if done in accordance with the processes the Secretary may require.

(c) *Process for modification of existing standards and adoption of new standards.* The Secretary considers a recommendation for a proposed modification to an existing standard, or a proposed new standard, only if the recommendation is developed through a process that provides for the following:

(1) Open public access.

(2) Coordination with other DSMOs.

(3) An appeals process for each of the following, if dissatisfied with the decision on the request:

(i) The requestor of the proposed modification.

(ii) A DSMO that participated in the review and analysis of the request for the proposed modification, or the proposed new standard.

(4) Expedited process to address content needs identified within the industry, if appropriate.

(5) Submission of the recommendation to the National Committee on Vital and Health Statistics (NCVHS).

§ 162.915 Trading partner agreements.

A covered entity must not enter into a trading partner agreement that would do any of the following:

(a) Change the definition, data condition, or use of a data element or segment in a standard or operating rule, except where necessary to implement State or Federal law, or to protect against fraud and abuse.

(b) Add any data elements or segments to the maximum defined data set.

(c) Use any code or data elements that are either marked "not used" in the standard's implementation specification or are not in the standard's implementation specification(s).

(d) Change the meaning or intent of the standard's implementation specification(s).

[65 FR 50367, Aug. 17, 2000, as amended at 76 FR 40495, July 8, 2011]

§ 162.920 Availability of implementation specifications and operating rules.

Certain material is incorporated by reference into this subpart with the approval of the Director of the Federal Register under 5 U.S.C. 552(a) and 1 CFR part 51. To enforce any edition other than that specified in this section, the Department of Health and Human Services must publish notice of change in the Federal Register and the material must be available to the public. All approved material is available for inspection at the National Archives and Records Administration (NARA). For information on the availability of this material at NARA, call (202) 714–6030, or go to: http://www.archives.gov/federal_register/code_of_federal_regulations/ibr_locations.html. The materials are also available for inspection by the public at the Centers for Medicare & Medicaid Services (CMS), 7500 Security Boulevard, Baltimore, Maryland 21244. For more information on the availability on the materials at CMS, call (410) 786–6597. The materials are also available from the sources listed below.

(a) *ASC X12N specifications and the ASC X12 Standards for Electronic Data Interchange Technical Report Type 3.* The implementation specifications for the ASC X12N and the ASC X12 Standards for Electronic Data Interchange Technical Report Type 3 (and accompanying Errata or Type 1 Errata) may be obtained from the ASC X12, 7600 Leesburg Pike, Suite 430, Falls Church, VA 22043; Telephone (703) 970–4480; and FAX (703) 970–4488. They are also available through the internet at http://www.X12.org. A fee is charged for all implementation specifications, including Technical Reports Type 3. Charging for such publications is consistent with the policies of other publishers of standards. The transaction implementation specifications are as follows:

(1) The ASC X12N 837—Health Care Claim: Dental, Version 4010, May 2000, Washington Publishing Company, 004010X097 and Addenda to Health Care Claim: Dental, Version 4010, October 2002, Washington Publishing Company, 004010X097A1, as referenced in § 162.1102 and § 162.1802.

(2) The ASC X12N 837—Health Care Claim: Professional, Volumes 1 and 2, Version 4010, May 2000, Washington Publishing Company, 004010X098 and Addenda to Health Care Claim: Professional, Volumes 1 and 2, Version 4010, October 2002, Washington Publishing Company, 004010X098A1, as referenced in § 162.1102 and § 162.1802.

(3) The ASC X12N 837—Health Care Claim: Institutional, Volumes 1 and 2, Version 4010, May 2000, Washington Publishing Company, 004010X096 and Addenda to Health Care Claim: Institutional, Volumes 1 and 2, Version 4010, October 2002, Washington Publishing Company, 004010X096A1 as referenced in § 162.1102 and § 162.1802.

(4) The ASC X12N 835—Health Care Claim Payment/Advice, Version 4010, May 2000, Washington Publishing Company, 004010X091, and Addenda to Health Care Claim Payment/Advice, Version 4010, October 2002, Washington Publishing Company, 004010X091A1 as referenced in § 162.1602.

(5) ASC X12N 834—Benefit Enrollment and Maintenance, Version 4010, May 2000, Washington Publishing Company, 004010X095 and Addenda to Benefit Enrollment and Maintenance, Version 4010, October 2002, Washington Publishing Company, 004010X095A1, as referenced in § 162.1502.

(6) The ASC X12N 820—Payroll Deducted and Other Group Premium Payment for Insurance Products, Version 4010, May 2000, Washington Publishing Company, 004010X061, and Addenda to Payroll Deducted and Other Group Premium Payment for Insurance Products, Version 4010, October 2002, Washington Publishing Company, 004010X061A1, as referenced in § 162.1702.

(7) The ASC X12N 278—Health Care Services Review—Request for Review and Response, Version 4010, May 2000, Washington Publishing Company, 004010X094 and Addenda to Health Care Services Review—Request for Review and Response, Version 4010, October 2002, Washington Publishing Company, 004010X094A1, as referenced in § 162.1302.

(8) The ASC X12N–276/277 Health Care Claim Status Request and Response, Version 4010, May 2000, Washington Publishing Company, 004010X093 and Addenda to Health Care Claim Status Request and Response, Version 4010, October 2002, Washington Publishing Company, 004010X093A1, as referenced in § 162.1402.

(9) The ASC X12N 270/271—Health Care Eligibility Benefit Inquiry and Response, Version 4010, May 2000, Washington Publishing Company, 004010X092 and Addenda to Health Care Eligibility Benefit Inquiry and Response, Version 4010, October 2002, Washington Publishing Company, 004010X092A1, as referenced in § 162.1202.

(10) The ASC X12 Standards for Electronic Data Interchange Technical Report Type 3—Health Care Claim: Dental (837), May 2006, ASC X12N/005010X224, and Type 1 Errata to Health Care Claim Dental (837), ASC X12 Standards for Electronic Data Interchange Technical Report Type 3, October 2007, ASC X12N/005010X224A1, as referenced in § 162.1102 and § 162.1802.

(11) The ASC X12 Standards for Electronic Data Interchange Technical Report Type 3—Health Care Claim: Professional (837), May 2006, ASC X12, 005010X222, as referenced in § 162.1102 and § 162.1802.

(12) The ASC X12 Standards for Electronic Data Interchange Technical Report Type 3—Health Care Claim: Institutional (837), May 2006, ASC X12/N005010X223, and Type 1 Errata to Health Care Claim: Institutional (837), ASC X12 Standards for Electronic Data Interchange Technical Report Type 3, October 2007, ASC X12N/005010X223A1, as referenced in § 162.1102 and § 162.1802.

(13) The ASC X12 Standards for Electronic Data Interchange Technical Report Type 3—Health Care Claim Payment/Advice (835), April 2006, ASC X12N/005010X221, as referenced in § 162.1602.

(14) The ASC X12 Standards for Electronic Data Interchange Technical Report Type 3—Benefit Enrollment and Maintenance (834), August 2006, ASC X12N/005010X220, as referenced in § 162.1502.

(15) The ASC X12 Standards for Electronic Data Interchange Technical Report Type 3—Payroll Deducted and Other Group Premium Payment for Insurance Products (820), February 2007, ASC X12N/005010X218, as referenced in § 162.1702.

(16) The ASC X12 Standards for Electronic Data Interchange Technical Report Type 3—Health Care Services Review—Request for Review and Response (278), May 2006, ASC X12N/005010X217, and Errata to Health Care Services Review—Request for Review and Response (278), ASC X12 Standards for Electronic Data Interchange Technical Report Type 3, April 2008, ASC X12N/005010X217E1, as referenced in § 162.1302.

(17) The ASC X12 Standards for Electronic Data Interchange Technical Report Type 3—Health Care Claim Status Request and Response (276/277), August 2006, ASC X12N/005010X212, and Errata to Health Care Claim Status Request and Response (276/277), ASC X12 Standards for Electronic Data Interchange Technical Report Type 3, April 2008, ASC X12N/005010X212E1, as referenced in § 162.1402.

(18) The ASC X12 Standards for Electronic Data Interchange Technical Report Type 3—Health Care Eligibility Benefit Inquiry and Response (270/271), April 2008, ASC X12N/005010X279, as referenced in § 162.1202.

(b) *Retail pharmacy specifications and Medicaid subrogation implementation guides.* The implementation specifications for the retail pharmacy standards and the implementation specifications for the batch standard for the Medicaid pharmacy subrogation transaction may be obtained from the National Council for Prescription Drug Programs, 9240 East Raintree Drive, Scottsdale, AZ 85260. Telephone (480) 477–1000; FAX (480) 767–1042. They are also available through the Internet at *http://www.ncpdp.org*. A fee is charged for all NCPDP Implementation Guides. Charging for such publications is consistent with the policies of other publishers of standards. The transaction implementation specifications are as follows:

(1) The Telecommunication Standard Implementation Guide Version 5, Release 1 (Version 5.1), September 1999, National Council for Prescription Drug Programs, as referenced in §§ 162.1102, 162.1202, 162.1302, 162.1602, and 162.1802.

(2) The Batch Standard Batch Implementation Guide, Version 1, Release 1 (Version 1.1), January 2000, supporting Telecommunication Standard Implementation Guide, Version 5, Release 1 (Version 5.1) for the NCPDP Data Record in the Detail Data Record, National Council for Prescription Drug Programs, as referenced in §§ 162.1102, 162.1202, 162.1302, and 162.1802.

(3) The National Council for Prescription Drug Programs (NCPDP) equivalent NCPDP Batch Standard Batch Implementation Guide, Version 1, Release 0, February 1, 1996, as referenced in §§ 162.1102, 162.1202, 162.1602, and 162.1802.

(4) The Telecommunication Standard Implementation Guide, Version D, Release 0 (Version D.0), August 2007, National Council for Prescription Drug Programs, as referenced in §§ 162.1102, 162.1202, 162.1302, and 162.1802.

(5) The Batch Standard Implementation Guide, Version 1, Release 2 (Version 1.2), January 2006, National Council for Prescription Drug Programs, as referenced in §§ 162.1102, 162.1202, 162.1302, and 162.1802.

(6) The Batch Standard Medicaid Subrogation Implementation Guide, Version 3, Release 0 (Version 3.0), July 2007, National Council for Prescription Drug Programs, as referenced in § 162.1902.

(c) Council for Affordable Quality Healthcare's (CAQH) Committee on Operating Rules for Information Exchange (CORE), 601 Pennsylvania Avenue, NW. South Building, Suite 500 Washington, DC 20004; Telephone (202) 861–1492; Fax (202) 861- 1454; E-mail *info@CAQH.org*; and Internet at *http://www.caqh.org/benefits.php*.

(1) CAQH, Committee on Operating Rules for Information Exchange, CORE Phase I Policies and Operating Rules, Approved April 2006, v5010 Update March 2011.

(i) Phase I CORE 152: Eligibility and Benefit Real Time Companion Guide Rule, version 1.1.0, March 2011, as referenced in § 162.1203.

(ii) Phase I CORE 153: Eligibility and Benefits Connectivity Rule, version 1.1.0, March 2011, as referenced in § 162.1203.

(iii) Phase I CORE 154: Eligibility and Benefits 270/271 Data Content Rule, version 1.1.0, March 2011, as referenced in § 162.1203.

(iv) Phase I CORE 155: Eligibility and Benefits Batch Response Time Rule, version 1.1.0, March 2011, as referenced in § 162.1203.

(v) Phase I CORE 156: Eligibility and Benefits Real Time Response Time Rule, version 1.1.0, March 2011, as referenced in § 162.1203.

(vi) Phase I CORE 157: Eligibility and Benefits System Availability Rule, version 1.1.0, March 2011, as referenced in § 162.1203.

(2) ACME Health Plan, HIPAA Transaction Standard Companion Guide, Refers to the Implementation Guides Based on ASC X12 version 005010, CORE v5010 Master Companion Guide Template, 005010, 1.2, (CORE v 5010 Master Companion Guide Template, 005010, 1.2), March 2011, as referenced in §§ 162.1203, 162.1403, and 162.1603.

(3) CAQH, Committee on Operating Rules for Information Exchange, CORE Phase II Policies and Operating Rules, Approved July 2008, v5010 Update March 2011.

(i) Phase II CORE 250: Claim Status Rule, version 2.1.0, March 2011, as referenced in § 162.1403.

(ii) Phase II CORE 258: Eligibility and Benefits 270/271 Normalizing Patient Last Name Rule, version 2.1.0, March 2011, as referenced in § 162.1203.

(iii) Phase II CORE 259: Eligibility and Benefits 270/271 AAA Error Code Reporting Rule, version 2.1.0, March 2011, as referenced in § 162.1203.

(iv) Phase II CORE 260: Eligibility & Benefits Data Content (270/271) Rule, version 2.1.0, March 2011, as referenced in § 162.1203.

(v) Phase II CORE 270: Connectivity Rule, version 2.2.0, March 2011, as referenced in § 162.1203 and § 162.1403.

(4) Council for Affordable Quality Healthcare (CAQH) Phase III Committee on Operating Rules for Information Exchange (CORE) EFT & ERA Operating Rule Set, Approved June 2012, as specified in this paragraph and referenced in § 162.1603.

(i) Phase III CORE 380 EFT Enrollment Data Rule, version 3.0.0, June 2012.

(ii) Phase III CORE 382 ERA Enrollment Data Rule, version 3.0.0, June 2012.

(iii) Phase III 360 CORE Uniform Use of CARCs and RARCs (835) Rule, version 3.0.0, June 2012.

(iv) CORE-required Code Combinations for CORE-defined Business Scenarios for the Phase III CORE 360 Uniform Use of Claim Adjustment Reason Codes and Remittance Advice Remark Codes (835) Rule, version 3.0.0, June 2012.

(v) Phase III CORE 370 EFT & ERA Reassociation (CCD+/835) Rule, version 3.0.0, June 2012.

(vi) Phase III CORE 350 Health Care Claim Payment/Advice (835) Infrastructure Rule, version 3.0.0, June 2012, except Requirement 4.2 titled "Health Care Claim Payment/Advice Batch Acknowledgement Requirements".

(d) The National Automated Clearing House Association (NACHA), The Electronic Payments Association, 1350 Sunrise Valle Drive, Suite 100, Herndon, Virginia 20171 (Phone) (703) 561–1100; (Fax) (703) 713–1641; Email: info@nacha.org; and Internet at http://www.nacha.org. The implementation specifications are as follows:

(1) 2011 NACHA Operating Rules & Guidelines, A Complete Guide to the Rules Governing the ACH Network, NACHA Operating Rules, Appendix One: ACH File Exchange Specifications (Operating Rule 59) as referenced in § 162.1602.

(2) 2011 NACHA Operating Rules & Guidelines, A Complete Guide to the Rules Governing the ACH Network, NACHA Operating Rules Appendix Three: ACH Record Format Specifications (Operating Rule 78), Part 3.1, Subpart 3.1.8 Sequence of Records for CCD Entries as referenced in § 162.1602.

[68 FR 8396, Feb. 20, 2003, as amended at 69 FR 18803, Apr. 9, 2004; 74 FR 3324, Jan. 16, 2009; 76 FR 40495, July 8, 2011; 77 FR 1590, Jan. 10, 2012; 77 FR 48043, Aug. 10, 2012]

§ 162.923 Requirements for covered entities.

(a) **General rule.** Except as otherwise provided in this part, if a covered entity conducts, with another covered entity that is required to comply with a transaction standard adopted under this part (or within the same covered entity), using electronic media, a transaction for which the Secretary has adopted a standard under this part, the covered entity must conduct the transaction as a standard transaction.

(b) **Exception for direct data entry transactions.** A health care provider electing to use direct data entry offered by a health plan to conduct a transaction for which a standard has been adopted under this part must use the applicable data content and data condition requirements of the standard when conducting the transaction. The health care provider is not required to use the format requirements of the standard.

(c) **Use of a business associate.** A covered entity may use a business associate, including a health care clearinghouse, to conduct a transaction covered by this part. If a covered entity chooses to use a business associate to conduct all or part of a transaction on behalf of the covered entity, the covered entity must require the business associate to do the following:

(1) Comply with all applicable requirements of this part.

(2) Require any agent or subcontractor to comply with all applicable requirements of this part.

[65 FR 50367, Aug. 17, 2000, as amended at 74 FR 3325, Jan. 16, 2009]

§ 162.925 Additional requirements for health plans.

(a) **General rules.**

(1) If an entity requests a health plan to conduct a transaction as a standard transaction, the health plan must do so.

(2) A health plan may not delay or reject a transaction, or attempt to adversely affect the other entity or the transaction, because the transaction is a standard transaction.

(3) A health plan may not reject a standard transaction on the basis that it contains data elements not needed or used by the health plan (for example, coordination of benefits information).

(4) A health plan may not offer an incentive for a health care provider to conduct a transaction covered by this part as a transaction described under the exception provided for in § 162.923(b).

(5) A health plan that operates as a health care clearinghouse, or requires an entity to use a health care clearinghouse to receive, process, or transmit a standard transaction may not charge fees or costs in excess of the fees or costs for normal telecommunications that the entity incurs when it directly transmits, or receives, a standard transaction to, or from, a health plan.

(6) During the period from March 17, 2009 through December 31, 2011, a health plan may not delay or reject a standard transaction, or attempt to adversely affect the other entity or the

transaction, on the basis that it does not comply with another adopted standard for the same period.

(b) *Coordination of benefits.* If a health plan receives a standard transaction and coordinates benefits with another health plan (or another payer), it must store the coordination of benefits data it needs to forward the standard transaction to the other health plan (or other payer).

(c) *Code sets.* A health plan must meet each of the following requirements:

(1) Accept and promptly process any standard transaction that contains codes that are valid, as provided in subpart J of this part.

(2) Keep code sets for the current billing period and appeals periods still open to processing under the terms of the health plan's coverage.

[65 FR 50367, Aug. 17, 2000, as amended at 74 FR 3325, Jan. 16, 2009]

§ 162.930 Additional rules for health care clearinghouses.

When acting as a business associate for another covered entity, a health care clearinghouse may perform the following functions:

(a) Receive a standard transaction on behalf of the covered entity and translate it into a nonstandard transaction (for example, nonstandard format and/or nonstandard data content) for transmission to the covered entity.

(b) Receive a nonstandard transaction (for example, nonstandard format and/or nonstandard data content) from the covered entity and translate it into a standard transaction for transmission on behalf of the covered entity.

§ 162.940 Exceptions from standards to permit testing of proposed modifications.

(a) *Requests for an exception.* An organization may request an exception from the use of a standard from the Secretary to test a proposed modification to that standard. For each proposed modification, the organization must meet the following requirements:

(1) *Comparison to a current standard.* Provide a detailed explanation, no more than 10 pages in length, of how the proposed modification would be a significant improvement to the current standard in terms of the following principles:

(i) Improve the efficiency and effectiveness of the health care system by leading to cost reductions for, or improvements in benefits from, electronic health care transactions.

(ii) Meet the needs of the health data standards user community, particularly health care providers, health plans, and health care clearinghouses.

(iii) Be uniform and consistent with the other standards adopted under this part and, as appropriate, with other private and public sector health data standards.

(iv) Have low additional development and implementation costs relative to the benefits of using the standard.

(v) Be supported by an ANSI-accredited SSO or other private or public organization that would maintain the standard over time.

(vi) Have timely development, testing, implementation, and updating procedures to achieve administrative simplification benefits faster.

(vii) Be technologically independent of the computer platforms and transmission protocols used in electronic health transactions, unless they are explicitly part of the standard.

(viii) Be precise, unambiguous, and as simple as possible.

(ix) Result in minimum data collection and paperwork burdens on users.

(x) Incorporate flexibility to adapt more easily to changes in the health care infrastructure (such as new services, organizations, and provider types) and information technology.

(2) *Specifications for the proposed modification.* Provide specifications for the proposed modification, including any additional system requirements.

(3) *Testing of the proposed modification.* Provide an explanation, no more than 5 pages in length, of how the organization intends to test the standard, including the number and types of health plans and health care providers expected to be involved in the test, geographical areas, and beginning and ending dates of the test.

(4) *Trading partner concurrences.* Provide written concurrences from trading partners who would agree to participate in the test.

(b) *Basis for granting an exception.* The Secretary may grant an initial exception, for a period not to exceed 3 years, based on, but not limited to, the following criteria:

(1) An assessment of whether the proposed modification demonstrates a significant improvement to the current standard.

(2) The extent and length of time of the exception.

(3) Consultations with DSMOs.

(c) *Secretary's decision on exception.* The Secretary makes a decision and notifies the organization requesting the exception whether the request is granted or denied.

(1) *Exception granted.* If the Secretary grants an exception, the notification includes the following information:

(i) The length of time for which the exception applies.

(ii) The trading partners and geographical areas the Secretary approves for testing.

(iii) Any other conditions for approving the exception.

(2) *Exception denied.* If the Secretary does not grant an exception, the notification explains the reasons the Secretary considers the proposed modification would not be a significant improvement to the current standard and any other rationale for the denial.

(d) *Organization's report on test results.* Within 90 days after the test is completed, an organization that receives an exception must submit a report on the results of the test, including a cost-benefit analysis, to a location specified by the Secretary by notice in the Federal Register.

(e) *Extension allowed.* If the report submitted in accordance with paragraph (d) of this section recommends a modification to the standard, the Secretary, on request, may grant an extension to the period granted for the exception.

Subpart J—Code Sets

§ 162.1000 General requirements.

When conducting a transaction covered by this part, a covered entity must meet the following requirements:

(a) *Medical data code sets.* Use the applicable medical data code sets described in § 162.1002 as specified in the implementation specification adopted under this part that are valid at the time the health care is furnished.

(b) *Nonmedical data code sets.* Use the nonmedical data code sets as described in the implementation specifications adopted under this part that are valid at the time the transaction is initiated.

§ 162.1002 Medical data code sets.

The Secretary adopts the following maintaining organization's code sets as the standard medical data code sets:

(a) For the period from October 16, 2002 through October 15, 2003:

(1) *International Classification of Diseases, 9th Edition, Clinical Modification, (ICD–9–CM), Volumes 1 and 2* (including The Official ICD–9–CM Guidelines for Coding and Reporting), as maintained and distributed by HHS, for the following conditions:

(i) Diseases.

(ii) Injuries.

(iii) Impairments.

(iv) Other health problems and their manifestations.

(v) Causes of injury, disease, impairment, or other health problems.

(2) *International Classification of Diseases, 9th Edition, Clinical Modification, Volume 3 Procedures* (including The Official ICD–9–CM Guidelines for Coding and Reporting), as maintained and distributed by HHS, for the following procedures or other actions taken for diseases, injuries, and impairments on hospital inpatients reported by hospitals:

(i) Prevention.

(ii) Diagnosis.

(iii) Treatment.

(iv) Management.

(3) *National Drug Codes* (NDC), as maintained and distributed by HHS, in collaboration with drug manufacturers, for the following:

(i) Drugs

(ii) Biologics.

(4) *Code on Dental Procedures and Nomenclature,* as maintained and distributed by the American Dental Association, for dental services.

(5) The combination of *Health Care Financing Administration Common Procedure Coding System (HCPCS),* as maintained and distributed by HHS, and *Current Procedural Terminology, Fourth Edition (CPT–4),* as maintained and distributed by the American Medical Association, for physician services and other health care services. These services include, but are not limited to, the following:

(i) Physician services.

(ii) Physical and occupational therapy services.

(iii) Radiologic procedures.

(iv) Clinical laboratory tests.

(v) Other medical diagnostic procedures.

(vi) Hearing and vision services.

(vii) Transportation services including ambulance.

(6) The *Health Care Financing Administration Common Procedure Coding System (HCPCS),* as maintained and distributed by HHS, for all other substances, equipment, supplies, or other items used in health care services. These items include, but are not limited to, the following:

(i) Medical supplies.

(ii) Orthotic and prosthetic devices.

(iii) Durable medical equipment.

(b) For the period on and after October 16, 2003 through September 30, 2015:

(1) The code sets specified in paragraphs (a)(1), (a)(2),(a)(4), and (a)(5) of this section.

(2) **National Drug Codes (NDC),** as maintained and distributed by HHS, for reporting the following by retail pharmacies:

(i) Drugs.

(ii) Biologics.

(3) **The Healthcare Common Procedure Coding System (HCPCS),** as maintained and distributed by HHS, for all other substances, equipment, supplies, or other items used in health care services, with the exception of drugs and biologics. These items include, but are not limited to, the following:

(i) Medical supplies.

(ii) Orthotic and prosthetic devices.

(iii) Durable medical equipment.

(c) For the period on and after October 1, 2015:

(1) The code sets specified in paragraphs (a)(4), (a)(5), (b)(2), and (b)(3) of this section.

(2) International Classification of Diseases, 10th Revision, Clinical Modification (ICD–10–CM) (including The Official ICD–10–CM Guidelines for Coding and Reporting), as maintained and distributed by HHS, for the following conditions:

(i) Diseases.

(ii) Injuries.

(iii) Impairments.

(iv) Other health problems and their manifestations.

(v) Causes of injury, disease, impairment, or other health problems.

(3) International Classification of Diseases, 10th Revision, Procedure Coding System (ICD–10–PCS) (including The Official ICD–10–PCS Guidelines for Coding and Reporting), as maintained and distributed by HHS, for the following procedures or other actions taken for diseases, injuries, and impairments on hospital inpatients reported by hospitals:

(i) Prevention.

(ii) Diagnosis.

(iii) Treatment.

(iv) Management.

[65 FR 50367, Aug. 17, 2000, as amended at 68 FR 8397, Feb. 20, 2003; 74 FR 3362, Jan. 16, 2009; 77 FR 54720, Sept. 5, 2012; 79 FR 45134, Aug. 4, 2014]

§ 162.1011 Valid code sets.

Each code set is valid within the dates specified by the organization responsible for maintaining that code set.

Subpart K—Health Care Claims or Equivalent Encounter Information

§ 162.1101 Health care claims or equivalent encounter information transaction.

The health care claims or equivalent encounter information transaction is the transmission of either of the following:

(a) A request to obtain payment, and the necessary accompanying information from a health care provider to a health plan, for health care.

(b) If there is no direct claim, because the reimbursement contract is based on a mechanism other than charges or reimbursement rates for specific services, the transaction is the transmission of encounter information for the purpose of reporting health care.

§ 162.1102 Standards for health care claims or equivalent encounter information transaction.

The Secretary adopts the following standards for the health care claims or equivalent encounter information transaction:

(a) For the period from October 16, 2003 through March 16, 2009:

(1) *Retail pharmacy drugs claims.* The National Council for Prescription Drug Programs (NCPDP) Telecommunication Standards Implementation Guide, Version 5, Release 1, September 1999, and equivalent NCPDP Batch Standards Batch Implementation Guide, Version 1, Release 1, (Version 1.1), January 2000, supporting Telecomunication Version 5.1 for the NCPDP Data Record in the Detail Data Record. (Incorporated by reference in § 162.920).

(2) *Dental, health care claims.* The ASC X12N 837—Health Care Claim: Dental, Version 4010, May 2000, Washington Publishing Company, 004010X097. and Addenda to Health Care

Claim: Dental, Version 4010, October 2002, Washington Publishing Company, 004010X097A1. (Incorporated by reference in § 162.920).

(3) **Professional health care claims.** The ASC X12N 837—Health Care Claims: Professional, Volumes 1 and 2, Version 4010, may 2000, Washington Publishing Company, 004010X098 and Addenda to Health Care Claims: Professional, Volumes 1 and 2, Version 4010, October 2002, Washington Publishing Company, 004010x098A1. (Incorporated by reference in § 162.920).

(4) **Institutional health care claims.** The ASC X12N 837—Health Care Claim: Institutional, Volumes 1 and 2, Version 4010, May 2000, Washington Publishing Company, 004010X096 and Addenda to Health Care Claim: Institutional, Volumes 1 and 2, Version 4010, October 2002, Washington Publishing Company, 004010X096A1. (Incorporated by reference in § 162.920).

(b) For the period from March 17, 2009 through December 31, 2011, both:

(1)

(i) The standards identified in paragraph (a) of this section; and

(ii) For retail pharmacy supplies and professional services claims, the following: The ASC X12N 837—Health Care Claim: Professional, Volumes 1 and 2, Version 4010, May 2000, Washington Publishing Company, 004010X096, October 2002 (Incorporated by reference in § 162.920); and

(2)

(i) **Retail pharmacy drug claims.** The Telecommunication Standard Implementation Guide, Version D, Release 0 (Version D.0), August 2007 and equivalent Batch Standard Implementation Guide, Version 1, Release 2 (Version 1.2), National Council for Prescription Drug Programs. (Incorporated by reference in § 162.920.)

(ii) **Dental health care claims.** The ASC X12 Standards for Electronic Data Interchange Technical Report Type 3— Health Care Claim: Dental (837), May 2006, ASC X12N/005010X224, and Type 1 Errata to Health Care Claim: Dental (837) ASC X12 Standards for Electronic Date Interchange Technical Report Type 3, October 2007, ASC X12N/005010X224A1. (Incorporated by reference in § 162.920.)

(iii) **Professional health care claims.** The ASC X12 Standards for Electronic Data Interchange Technical Report Type 3—Health Care Claim: Professional (837), May 2006, ASC X12N/005010X222. (Incorporated by reference in § 162.920.)

(iv) **Institutional health care claims.** The ASC X12 Standards for Electronic Data Interchange Technical Report Type 3—Health Care Claim: Institutional (837), May 2006, ASC X12N/005010X223, and Type 1 Errata to Health Care Claim: Institutional (837) ASC X12 Standards for Electronic Data Interchange Technical Report Type 3, October 2007, ASC X12N/005010X223A1. (Incorporated by reference in § 162.920.)

(v) **Retail pharmacy supplies and professional services claims.**

(A) The Telecommunication Standard, Implementation Guide Version 5, Release 1, September 1999. (Incorporated by reference in § 162.920.)

(B) The Telecommunication Standard Implementation Guide, Version D, Release 0 (Version D.0), August 2007, and equivalent Batch Standard Implementation Guide, Version 1, Release 2 (Version 1.2), National Council for Prescription Drug Programs (Incorporated by reference in § 162.920); and

(C) The ASC X12 Standards for Electronic Data Interchange Technical Report Type 3—Health Care Claim: Professional (837), May 2006, ASC X12N/005010X222. (Incorporated by reference in § 162.920.)

(c) For the period on and after the January 1, 2012, the standards identified in paragraph (b)(2) of this section, except the standard identified in paragraph (b)(2)(v)(A) of this section.

(d) For the period on and after September 21, 2020, the Quantity Prescribed (460–ET) field, as set forth in the Telecommunication Standard Implementation Guide, Version D, Release 0 (Version D.0), August 2007 and equivalent Batch Standard Implementation Guide, Version 1, Release 2 (Version 1.2), National Council for Prescription Drug Programs, must be treated as required where the transmission meets both of the following:

(1) Is for a Schedule II drug, as defined in 21 CFR 1308.12.

(2) Uses the standard identified in paragraph (b)(2)(i) of this section.

[68 FR 8397, Feb. 20, 2003; 68 FR 11445, Mar. 10, 2003, as amended at 74 FR 3325, Jan. 16, 2009; 85 FR 4242, Jan. 24, 2020]

Subpart L—Eligibility for a Health Plan

§ 162.1201 Eligibility for a health plan transaction.

The eligibility for a health plan transaction is the transmission of either of the following:

(a) An inquiry from a health care provider to a health plan, or from one health plan to another health plan, to obtain any of the following information about a benefit plan for an enrollee:

(1) Eligibility to receive health care under the health plan.

(2) Coverage of health care under the health plan.

(3) Benefits associated with the benefit plan.

(b) A response from a health plan to a health care provider's (or another health plan's) inquiry described in paragraph (a) of this section.

§ 162.1202 Standards for eligibility for a health plan transaction.

The Secretary adopts the following standards for the eligibility for a health plan transaction:

(a) For the period from October 16, 2003 through March 16, 2009:

(1) *Retail pharmacy drugs.* The National Council for Prescription Drug Programs Telecommunication Standard Implementation Guide, Version 5, Release 1 (Version 5.1), September 1999, and equivalent NCPDP Batch Standard Batch Implementation Guide, Version 1, Release 1 (Version 1.1), January 2000 supporting Telecommunications Standard Implementation Guide, Version 5, Release 1 (Version 5.1) for the NCPDP Data Record in the Detail Data Record. (Incorporated by reference in § 162.920).

(2) *Dental, professional, and institutional health care eligibility benefit inquiry and response.* The ASC X12N 270/271—Health Care Eligibility Benefit Inquiry and Response, Version 4010, May 2000, Washington Publishing Company, 004010X092 and Addenda to Health Care Eligibility Benefit Inquiry and Response, Version 4010, October 2002, Washington Publishing Company, 004010X092A1. (Incorporated by reference in § 162.920).

(b) For the period from March 17, 2009 through December 31, 2011 both:

(1) The standards identified in paragraph (a) of this section; and

(2)

(i) *Retail pharmacy drugs.* The Telecommunication Standard Implementation Guide Version D, Release 0 (Version D.0), August 2007, and equivalent Batch Standard Implementation Guide, Version 1, Release 2 (Version 1.2), National Council for Prescription Drug Programs. (Incorporated by reference in § 162.920.)

(ii) *Dental, professional, and institutional health care eligibility benefit inquiry and response.* The ASC X12 Standards for Electronic Data Interchange Technical Report Type 3—Health Care Eligibility Benefit Inquiry and Response (270/271), April 2008, ASC X12N/005010X279. (Incorporated by reference in § 162.920.)

(c) For the period on and after January 1, 2012, the standards identified in paragraph (b)(2) of this section.

[68 FR 8398, Feb. 20, 2003; 68 FR 11445, Mar. 10, 2003, as amended at 74 FR 3326, Jan. 16, 2009]

§ 162.1203 Operating rules for eligibility for a health plan transaction.

On and after January 1, 2013, the Secretary adopts the following:

(a) Except as specified in paragraph (b) of this section, the following CAQH CORE Phase I and Phase II operating rules (updated for Version 5010) for the eligibility for a health plan transaction:

(1) Phase I CORE 152: Eligibility and Benefit Real Time Companion Guide Rule, version 1.1.0, March 2011, and CORE v5010 Master Companion Guide Template. (Incorporated by reference in § 162.920).

(2) Phase I CORE 153: Eligibility and Benefits Connectivity Rule, version 1.1.0, March 2011. (Incorporated by reference in § 162.920).

(3) Phase I CORE 154: Eligibility and Benefits 270/271 Data Content Rule, version 1.1.0, March 2011. (Incorporated by reference in § 162.920).

(4) Phase I CORE 155: Eligibility and Benefits Batch Response Time Rule, version 1.1.0, March 2011. (Incorporated by reference in § 162.920).

(5) Phase I CORE 156: Eligibility and Benefits Real Time Response Rule, version 1.1.0, March 2011. (Incorporated by reference in § 162.920).

(6) Phase I CORE 157: Eligibility and Benefits System Availability Rule, version 1.1.0, March 2011. (Incorporated by reference in § 162.920).

(7) Phase II CORE 258: Eligibility and Benefits 270/271 Normalizing Patient Last Name Rule, version 2.1.0, March 2011. (Incorporated by reference in § 162.920).

(8) Phase II CORE 259: Eligibility and Benefits 270/271 AAA Error Code Reporting Rule, version 2.1.0. (Incorporated by reference in § 162.920).

(9) Phase II CORE 260: Eligibility & Benefits Data Content (270/271) Rule, version 2.1.0, March 2011. (Incorporated by reference in § 162.920).

(10) Phase II CORE 270: Connectivity Rule, version 2.2.0, March 2011. (Incorporated by reference in § 162.920).

(b) Excluding where the CAQH CORE rules reference and pertain to acknowledgements and CORE certification.

[76 FR 40496, July 8, 2011]

Subpart M—Referral Certification and Authorization

§ 162.1301 Referral certification and authorization transaction.

The referral certification and authorization transaction is any of the following transmissions:

(a) A request from a health care provider to a health plan for the review of health care to obtain an authorization for the health care.

(b) A request from a health care provider to a health plan to obtain authorization for referring an individual to another health care provider.

(c) A response from a health plan to a health care provider to a request described in paragraph (a) or paragraph (b) of this section.

[74 FR 3326, Jan. 16, 2009]

§ 162.1302 Standards for referral certification and authorization transaction.

The Secretary adopts the following standards for the referral certification and authorization transaction:

(a) For the period from October 16, 2003 through March 16, 2009:

(1) *Retail pharmacy drug referral certification and authorization.* The NCPDP Telecommunication Standard Implementation Guide, Version 5, Release 1 (Version 5.1), September 1999, and equivalent NCPDP Batch Standard Batch Implementation Guide, Version 1, Release 1 (Version 1.1), January 2000, supporting Telecommunications Standard Implementation Guide, Version 5, Release 1 (Version 5.1) for the NCPDP Data Record in the Detail Data Record. (Incorporated by reference in § 162.920).

(2) *Dental, professional, and institutional referral certification and authorization.* The ASC X12N 278—Health Care Services Review—Request for Review and Response, Version 4010, May 2000, Washington Publishing Company, 004010X094 and Addenda to Health Care Services Review—Request for Review and Response, Version 4010, October 2002, Washington Publishing Company, 004010X094A1. (Incorporated by reference in § 162.920).

(b) For the period from March 17, 2009 through December 31, 2011 both—

(1) The standards identified in paragraph (a) of this section; and

(2)

(i) *Retail pharmacy drugs.* The Telecommunication Standard Implementation Guide Version D, Release 0 (Version D.0), August 2007, and equivalent Batch Standard Implementation Guide, Version 1, Release 2 (Version 1.2), National Council for Prescription Drug Programs. (Incorporated by reference in § 162.920.)

(ii) *Dental, professional, and institutional request for review and response.* The ASC X12 Standards for Electronic Data Interchange Technical Report Type 3—Health Care Services Review—Request for Review and Response (278), May 2006, ASC X12N/005010X217, and Errata to Health Care Services Review-—Request for Review and Response (278), ASC X12 Standards for Electronic Data Interchange Technical Report Type 3, April 2008, ASC X12N/005010X217E1. (Incorporated by reference in § 162.920.)

(c) For the period on and after January 1, 2012, the standards identified in paragraph (b)(2) of this section.

(d) For the period on and after September 21, 2020, the Quantity Prescribed (460–ET) field, as set forth in the Telecommunication Standard Implementation Guide, Version D, Release 0 (Version D.0), August 2007 and equivalent Batch Standard Implementation Guide, Version 1, Release 2 (Version 1.2), National Council for Prescription Drug Programs, must be treated as required where the transmission meets both of the following:

(1) Is for a Schedule II drug, as defined in 21 CFR 1308.12.

(2) Uses the standard identified in paragraph (b)(2)(i) of this section.

[68 FR 8398, Feb. 20, 2003, as amended at 74 FR 3326, Jan. 16, 2009; 85 FR 4242, Jan. 24, 2020]

Subpart N—Health Care Claim Status

§ 162.1401 Health care claim status transaction.

The health care claim status transaction is the transmission of either of the following:

(a) An inquiry from a health care provider to a health plan to determine the status of a health care claim.

(b) A response from a health plan to a health care provider about the status of a health care claim.

[74 FR 3326, Jan. 16, 2009]

§ 162.1402 Standards for health care claim status transaction.

The Secretary adopts the following standards for the health care claim status transaction:

(a) For the period from October 16, 2003 through March 16, 2009: The ASC X12N–276/277 Health Care Claim Status Request and Response, Version 4010, May 2000, Washington Publishing Company, 004010X093 and Addenda to Health Care Claim Status Request and Response, Version 4010, October 2002, Washington Publishing Company, 004010X093A1. (Incorporated by reference in § 162.920.)

(b) For the period from March 17, 2009 through December 31, 2011, both:

(1) The standard identified in paragraph (a) of this section; and

(2) The ASC X12 Standards for Electronic Data Interchange Technical Report Type 3—Health Care Claim Status Request and Response (276/277), August 2006, ASC X12N/005010X212, and Errata to Health Care Claim Status Request and Response (276/277), ASC X12 Standards for Electronic Data Interchange Technical Report Type 3, April 2008, ASC X12N/005010X212E1. (Incorporated by reference in § 162.920.)

(c) For the period on and after January 1, 2012, the standard identified in paragraph (b)(2) of this section.

[74 FR 3326, Jan. 16, 2009]

§ 162.1403 Operating rules for health care claim status transaction.

On and after January 1, 2013, the Secretary adopts the following:

(a) Except as specified in paragraph (b) of this section, the following CAQH CORE Phase II operating rules (updated for Version 5010) for the health care claim status transaction:

(1) Phase II CORE 250: Claim Status Rule, version 2.1.0, March 2011, and CORE v5010 Master Companion Guide, 00510, 1.2, March 2011. (Incorporated by reference in § 162.920).

(2) Phase II CORE 270: Connectivity Rule, version 2.2.0, March 2011. (Incorporated by reference in § 162.920).

(b) Excluding where the CAQH CORE rules reference and pertain to acknowledgements and CORE certification.

[76 FR 40496, July 8, 2011]

Subpart O—Enrollment and Disenrollment in a Health Plan

§ 162.1501 Enrollment and disenrollment in a health plan transaction.

The enrollment and disenrollment in a health plan transaction is the transmission of subscriber enrollment information from the sponsor of the insurance coverage, benefits, or policy, to a health plan to establish or terminate insurance coverage.

[74 FR 3327, Jan. 16, 2009]

§ 162.1502 Standards for enrollment and disenrollment in a health plan transaction.

The Secretary adopts the following standards for enrollment and disenrollment in a health plan transaction.

(a) For the period from October 16, 2003 through March 16, 2009: ASC X12N 834—Benefit Enrollment and Maintenance, Version 4010, May 2000, Washington Publishing Company, 004010X095 and Addenda to Benefit Enrollment and Maintenance, Version 4010, October 2002, Washington Publishing Company, 004010X095A1. (Incorporated by reference in § 162.920.)

(b) For the period from March 17, 2009 through December 31, 2011, both:

(1) The standard identified in paragraph (a) of this section; and

(2) The ASC X12 Standards for Electronic Data Interchange Technical Report Type 3—Benefit Enrollment and Maintenance (834), August 2006, ASC X12N/005010X220 (Incorporated by reference in § 162.920)

(c) For the period on and after January 1, 2012, the standard identified in paragraph (b)(2) of this section.

[74 FR 3327, Jan. 16, 2009]

Subpart P—Health Care Electronic Funds Transfers (EFT) and Remittance Advice

§ 162.1601 Health care electronic funds transfers (EFT) and remittance advice transaction.

The health care electronic funds transfers (EFT) and remittance advice transaction is the transmission of either of the following for health care:

(a) The transmission of any of the following from a health plan to a health care provider:

(1) Payment.

(2) Information about the transfer of funds.

(3) Payment processing information.

(b) The transmission of either of the following from a health plan to a health care provider:

(1) Explanation of benefits.

(2) Remittance advice.

[65 FR 50367, Aug. 17, 2000, as amended at 77 FR 1590, Jan. 10, 2012; 77 FR 48043, Aug. 10, 2012]

§ 162.1602 Standards for health care electronic funds transfers (EFT) and remittance advice transaction.

The Secretary adopts the following standards:

(a) For the period from October 16, 2003 through March 16, 2009: Health care claims and remittance advice. The ASC X12N 835—Health Care Claim Payment/Advice, Version 4010, May 2000, Washington Publishing Company, 004010X091, and Addenda to Health Care Claim Payment/Advice, Version 4010, October 2002, Washington Publishing Company, 004010X091A1. (Incorporated by reference in § 162.920.)

(b) For the period from March 17, 2009 through December 31, 2011, both of the following standards:

(1) The standard identified in paragraph (a) of this section.

(2) The ASC X12 Standards for Electronic Data Interchange Technical Report Type 3—Health Care Claim Payment/Advice (835), April 2006, ASC X12N/005010X221. (Incorporated by reference in § 162.920.)

(c) For the period from January 1, 2012 through December 31, 2013, the standard identified in paragraph (b)(2) of this section.

(d) For the period on and after January 1, 2014, the following standards:

(1) Except when transmissions as described in § 162.1601(a) and (b) are contained within the same transmission, for Stage 1 Payment Initiation transmissions described in § 162.1601(a), all of the following standards:

(i) The National Automated Clearing House Association (NACHA) Corporate Credit or Deposit Entry with Addenda Record (CCD+) implementation specifications as contained in the 2011 NACHA Operating Rules & Guidelines, A Complete Guide to the Rules Governing the ACH Network as follows (incorporated by reference in § 162.920)—

(A) NACHA Operating Rules, Appendix One: ACH File Exchange Specifications; and

(B) NACHA Operating Rules, Appendix Three: ACH Record Format Specifications, Subpart 3.1.8 Sequence of Records for CCD Entries.

(ii) For the CCD Addenda Record ("7"), field 3, of the standard identified in 1602(d)(1)(i), the Accredited Standards Committee (ASC) X12 Standards for Electronic Data Interchange Technical Report Type 3, "Health Care Claim Payment/Advice (835), April 2006: Section 2.4: 835 Segment Detail: "TRN Reassociation Trace Number," Washington Publishing Company, 005010X221 (Incorporated by reference in § 162.920).

(2) For transmissions described in § 162.1601(b), including when transmissions as described in § 162.1601(a) and (b) are contained within the same transmission, the ASC X12 Standards for Electronic Data Interchange Technical Report Type 3, "Health Care Claim Payment/Advice (835), April 2006, ASC X12N/005010X221. (Incorporated by reference in § 162.920).

[77 FR 1590, Jan. 10, 2012]

§ 162.1603 Operating rules for health care electronic funds transfers (EFT) and remittance advice transaction.

On and after January 1, 2014, the Secretary adopts the following for the health care electronic funds transfers (EFT) and remittance advice transaction:

(a) The Phase III CORE EFT & ERA Operating Rule Set, Approved June 2012 (Incorporated by reference in § 162.920) which includes the following rules:

(1) Phase III CORE 380 EFT Enrollment Data Rule, version 3.0.0, June 2012.

(2) Phase III CORE 382 ERA Enrollment Data Rule, version 3.0.0, June 2012.

(3) Phase III 360 CORE Uniform Use of CARCs and RARCs (835) Rule, version 3.0.0, June 2012.

(4) CORE-required Code Combinations for CORE-defined Business Scenarios for the Phase III CORE 360 Uniform Use of Claim Adjustment Reason Codes and Remittance Advice Remark Codes (835) Rule, version 3.0.0, June 2012.

(5) Phase III CORE 370 EFT & ERA Reassociation (CCD+/835) Rule, version 3.0.0, June 2012.

(6) Phase III CORE 350 Health Care Claim Payment/Advice (835) Infrastructure Rule, version 3.0.0, June 2012, except Requirement 4.2 titled "Health Care Claim Payment/Advice Batch Acknowledgement Requirements".

(b) ACME Health Plan, CORE v5010 Master Companion Guide Template, 005010, 1.2, March 2011 (incorporated by reference in § 162.920), as required by the Phase III CORE 350 Health Care Claim Payment/Advice (835) Infrastructure Rule, version 3.0.0, June 2012.

[77 FR 48043, Aug. 10, 2012]

Subpart Q—Health Plan Premium Payments

§ 162.1701 Health plan premium payments transaction.

The health plan premium payment transaction is the transmission of any of the following from the entity that is arranging for the provision of health care or is providing health care coverage payments for an individual to a health plan:

(a) Payment.

(b) Information about the transfer of funds.

(c) Detailed remittance information about individuals for whom premiums are being paid.

(d) Payment processing information to transmit health care premium payments including any of the following:

(1) Payroll deductions.

(2) Other group premium payments.

(3) Associated group premium payment information.

§ 162.1702 Standards for health plan premium payments transaction.

The Secretary adopts the following standards for the health plan premium payments transaction:

(a) For the period from October 16, 2003 through March 16, 2009: The ASC X12N 820—Payroll Deducted and Other Group Premium Payment for Insurance Products, Version 4010, May 2000, Washington Publishing Company, 004010X061, and Addenda to Payroll Deducted and Other Group Premium Payment for Insurance Products, Version 4010, October 2002, Washington Publishing Company, 004010X061A1. (Incorporated by reference in § 162.920.)

(b) For the period from March 17, 2009 through December 31, 2011, both:

(1) The standard identified in paragraph (a) of this section, and

(2) The ASC X12 Standards for Electronic Data Interchange Technical Report Type 3—Payroll Deducted and Other Group Premium Payment for Insurance Products (820), February 2007, ASC X12N/005010X218. (Incorporated by reference in § 162.920.)

(c) For the period on and after January 1, 2012, the standard identified in paragraph (b)(2) of this section.

[74 FR 3327, Jan. 16, 2009]

Subpart R—Coordination of Benefits

§ 162.1801 Coordination of benefits transaction.

The coordination of benefits transaction is the transmission from any entity to a health plan for the purpose of determining the relative payment responsibilities of the health plan, of either of the following for health care:

(a) Claims.

(b) Payment information.

§ 162.1802 Standards for coordination of benefits information transaction.

The Secretary adopts the following standards for the coordination of benefits information transaction.

(a) For the period from October 16, 2003 through March 16, 2009:

(1) *Retail pharmacy drug claims.* The National Council for Prescription Drug Programs Telecommunication Standard Implementation Guide, Version 5, Release 1 (Version 5.1), September 1999, and equivalent NCPDP Batch Standard Batch Implementation Guide, Version 1, Release 1 (Version 1.1), January 2000, supporting Telecommunications Standard Implementation Guide, Version 5, Release 1 (Version 5.1) for the NCPDP Data Record in the Detail Data Record. (Incorporated by reference in § 162.920).

(2) *Dental health care claims.* The ASC X12N 837—Health Care Claim: Dental, Version 4010, May 2000, Washington Publishing Company, 004010X097 and Addenda to Health Care Claim: Dental, Version 4010, October 2002, Washington Publishing Company, 004010X097A1. (Incorporated by reference in § 162.920).

(3) *Professional health care claims.* The ASC X12N 837—Health Care Claim: Professional, Volumes 1 and 2, Version 4010, May 2000, Washington Publishing Company, 004010X098 and Addenda to Health Care Claim: Professional, Volumes 1 and 2, Version 4010, October 2002, Washington Publishing Company, 004010X098A1. (Incorporated by reference in § 162.920).

(4) *Institutional health care claims.* The ASC X12N 837—Health Care Claim: Institutional, Volumes 1 and 2, Version 4010, May 2000, Washington Publishing Company, 004010X096 and

Addenda to Health Care Claim: Institutional, Volumes 1 and 2, Version 4010, October 2002, Washington Publishing Company, 004010X096A1. (Incorporated by reference in § 162.920).

(b) For the period from March 17, 2009 through December 31, 2011, both:

(1) The standards identified in paragraph (a) of this section; and

(2)

(i) *Retail pharmacy drug claims.* The Telecommunication Standard Implementation Guide, Version D, Release 0 (Version D.0), August 2007, and equivalent Batch Standard Implementation Guide, Version 1, Release 2 (Version 1.2), National Council for Prescription Drug Programs. (Incorporated by reference in § 162.920.)

(ii) The ASC X12 Standards for Electronic Data Interchange Technical Report Type 3— Health Care Claim: Dental (837), May 2006, ASC X12N/005010X224, and Type 1 Errata to Health Care Claim: Dental (837), ASC X12 Standards for Electronic Date Interchange Technical Report Type 3, October 2007, ASC X12N/005010X224A1. (Incorporated by reference in § 162.920.)

(iii) The ASC X12 Standards for Electronic Data Interchange Technical Report Type 3— Health Care Claim: Professional (837), May 2006, ASC X12N/005010X222. (Incorporated by reference in § 162.920.)

(iv) The ASC X12 Standards for Electronic Data Interchange Technical Report Type 3— Health Care Claim: Institutional (837), May 2006, ASC X12N/005010X223, and Type 1 Errata to Health Care Claim: Institutional (837), ASC X12 Standards for Electronic Data Interchange Technical Report Type 3, October 2007, ASC X12N/005010X223A1. (Incorporated by reference in § 162.920.)

(c) For the period on and after January 1, 2012, the standards identified in paragraph (b)(2) of this section.

(d) For the period on and after September 21, 2020, the Quantity Prescribed (460–ET) field, as set forth in the Telecommunication Standard Implementation Guide, Version D, Release 0 (Version D.0), August 2007 and equivalent Batch Standard Implementation Guide, Version 1, Release 2 (Version 1.2), National Council for Prescription Drug Programs, must be treated as required where the transmission meets both of the following:

(1) Is for a Schedule II drug, as defined in 21 CFR 1308.12.

(2) Uses the standard identified in paragraph (b)(2)(i) of this section.

[68 FR 8399, Feb. 20, 2003, as amended at 74 FR 3327, Jan. 16, 2009; 85 FR 4242, Jan. 24, 2020]

Subpart S—Medicaid Pharmacy Subrogation

Source: 74 FR 3328, Jan. 16, 2009, unless otherwise noted.

§ 162.1901 Medicaid pharmacy subrogation transaction.

The Medicaid pharmacy subrogation transaction is the transmission of a claim from a Medicaid agency to a payer for the purpose of seeking reimbursement from the responsible health plan for a pharmacy claim the State has paid on behalf of a Medicaid recipient.

§ 162.1902 Standard for Medicaid pharmacy subrogation transaction.

The Secretary adopts the Batch Standard Medicaid Subrogation Implementation Guide, Version 3, Release 0 (Version 3.0), July 2007, National Council for Prescription Drug Programs, as referenced in § 162.1902 (Incorporated by reference at § 162.920):

(a) For the period on and after January 1, 2012, for covered entities that are not small health plans;

(b) For the period on and after January 1, 2013 for small health plans.

Intentionally Blank

45 CFR PART 164—SECURITY AND PRIVACY

Authority:42 U.S.C. 1302(a); 42 U.S.C. 1320d–1320d–9; sec. 264, Pub. L. 104–191, 110 Stat. 2033–2034 (42 U.S.C. 1320d–2(note)); and secs. 13400–13424, Pub. L. 111–5, 123 Stat. 258–279.
Source:65 FR 82802, Dec. 28, 2000, unless otherwise noted.

Subpart A—General Provisions

§ 164.102 Statutory basis.

The provisions of this part are adopted pursuant to the Secretary's authority to prescribe standards, requirements, and implementation specifications under part C of title XI of the Act, section 264 of Public Law 104–191, and sections 13400–13424 of Public Law 111–5.

[78 FR 5692, Jan. 25, 2013]

§ 164.103 Definitions.

As used in this part, the following terms have the following meanings:

Common control exists if an entity has the power, directly or indirectly, significantly to influence or direct the actions or policies of another entity.

Common ownership exists if an entity or entities possess an ownership or equity interest of 5 percent or more in another entity.

Covered functions means those functions of a covered entity the performance of which makes the entity a health plan, health care provider, or health care clearinghouse.

Health care component means a component or combination of components of a hybrid entity designated by the hybrid entity in accordance with § 164.105(a)(2)(iii)(D).

Hybrid entity means a single legal entity:

(1) That is a covered entity;

(2) Whose business activities include both covered and non-covered functions; and

(3) That designates health care components in accordance with paragraph § 164.105(a)(2)(iii)(D).

Law enforcement official means an officer or employee of any agency or authority of the United States, a State, a territory, a political subdivision of a State or territory, or an Indian tribe, who is empowered by law to:

(1) Investigate or conduct an official inquiry into a potential violation of law; or

(2) Prosecute or otherwise conduct a criminal, civil, or administrative proceeding arising from an alleged violation of law.

Plan sponsor is defined as defined at section 3(16)(B) of ERISA, 29 U.S.C. 1002(16)(B).

Required by law means a mandate contained in law that compels an entity to make a use or disclosure of protected health information and that is enforceable in a court of law. *Required by law* includes, but is not limited to, court orders and court-ordered warrants; subpoenas or summons issued by a court, grand jury, a governmental or tribal inspector general, or an administrative body authorized to require the production of information; a civil or an authorized investigative demand; Medicare conditions of participation with respect to health care providers participating in the program; and statutes or regulations that require the production of information, including statutes or regulations that require such information if payment is sought under a government program providing public benefits.

[68 FR 8374, Feb. 20, 2003, as amended at 74 FR 42767, Aug. 24, 2009; 78 FR 34266, June 7, 2013]

§ 164.104 Applicability.

(a) Except as otherwise provided, the standards, requirements, and implementation specifications adopted under this part apply to the following entities:

(1) A health plan.

(2) A health care clearinghouse.

(3) A health care provider who transmits any health information in electronic form in connection with a transaction covered by this subchapter.

(b) Where provided, the standards, requirements, and implementation specifications adopted under this part apply to a business associate.

[68 FR 8375, Feb. 20, 2003, as amended at 78 FR 5692, Jan. 25, 2013]

§ 164.105 Organizational requirements.

(a)

(1) *Standard: Health care component.* If a covered entity is a hybrid entity, the requirements of this part, other than the requirements of this section, §§ 164.314, and 164.504, apply only to the health care component(s) of the entity, as specified in this section.

(2) *Implementation specifications:*

(i) *Application of other provisions.* In applying a provision of this part, other than the requirements of this section, §§ 164.314, and 164.504, to a hybrid entity:

(A) A reference in such provision to a "covered entity" refers to a health care component of the covered entity;

(B) A reference in such provision to a "health plan," "covered health care provider," or "health care clearinghouse," refers to a health care component of the covered entity if such health care component performs the functions of a health plan, health care provider, or health care clearinghouse, as applicable;

(C) A reference in such provision to "protected health information" refers to protected health information that is created or received by or on behalf of the health care component of the covered entity; and

(D) A reference in such provision to "electronic protected health information" refers to electronic protected health information that is created, received, maintained, or transmitted by or on behalf of the health care component of the covered entity.

(ii) *Safeguard requirements.* The covered entity that is a hybrid entity must ensure that a health care component of the entity complies with the applicable requirements of this part. In particular, and without limiting this requirement, such covered entity must ensure that:

(A) Its health care component does not disclose protected health information to another component of the covered entity in circumstances in which subpart E of this part would prohibit such disclosure if the health care component and the other component were separate and distinct legal entities;

(B) Its health care component protects electronic protected health information with respect to another component of the covered entity to the same extent that it would be required under subpart C of this part to protect such information if the health care component and the other component were separate and distinct legal entities;

(C) If a person performs duties for both the health care component in the capacity of a member of the workforce of such component and for another component of the entity in the same capacity with respect to that component, such workforce member must not use or disclose protected health information created or received in the course of or incident to the member's work for the health care component in a way prohibited by subpart E of this part.

(iii) *Responsibilities of the covered entity.* A covered entity that is a hybrid entity has the following responsibilities:

(A) For purposes of subpart C of part 160 of this subchapter, pertaining to compliance and enforcement, the covered entity has the responsibility of complying with this part.

(B) The covered entity is responsible for complying with §§ 164.316(a) and 164.530(i), pertaining to the implementation of policies and procedures to ensure compliance with applicable requirements of this part, including the safeguard requirements in paragraph (a)(2)(ii) of this section.

(C) The covered entity is responsible for complying with §§ 164.314 and 164.504 regarding business associate arrangements and other organizational requirements.

(D) The covered entity is responsible for designating the components that are part of one or more health care components of the covered entity and documenting the designation in accordance with paragraph (c) of this section, provided that, if the covered entity designates one or more health care components, it must include any component that would meet the definition of a covered entity or business associate if it were a separate legal entity. Health care component(s) also may include a component only to the extent that it performs covered functions.

(b)

(1) **Standard: Affiliated covered entities.** Legally separate covered entities that are affiliated may designate themselves as a single covered entity for purposes of this part.

(2) **Implementation specifications** —

(i) **Requirements for designation of an affiliated covered entity.**

(A) Legally separate covered entities may designate themselves (including any health care component of such covered entity) as a single affiliated covered entity, for purposes of this part, if all of the covered entities designated are under common ownership or control.

(B) The designation of an affiliated covered entity must be documented and the documentation maintained as required by paragraph (c) of this section.

(ii) **Safeguard requirements.** An affiliated covered entity must ensure that it complies with the applicable requirements of this part, including, if the affiliated covered entity combines the functions of a health plan, health care provider, or health care clearinghouse, §§ 164.308(a)(4)(ii)(A) and 164.504(g), as applicable.

(c)

(1) **Standard: Documentation.** A covered entity must maintain a written or electronic record of a designation as required by paragraphs (a) or (b) of this section.

(2) **Implementation specification: Retention period.** A covered entity must retain the documentation as required by paragraph (c)(1) of this section for 6 years from the date of its creation or the date when it last was in effect, whichever is later.

[68 FR 8375, Feb. 20, 2003, as amended at 78 FR 5692, Jan. 25, 2013]

§ 164.106 Relationship to other parts.

In complying with the requirements of this part, covered entities and, where provided, business associates, are required to comply with the applicable provisions of parts 160 and 162 of this subchapter.

[78 FR 5693, Jan. 25, 2013]

Subpart B [Reserved]

Subpart C—Security Standards for the Protection of Electronic Protected Health Information

Authority: 42 U.S.C. 1320d–2 and 1320d–4; sec. 13401, Pub. L. 111–5, 123 Stat. 260.

Source:68 FR 8376, Feb. 20, 2003, unless otherwise noted.

§ 164.302 Applicability.

A covered entity or business associate must comply with the applicable standards, implementation specifications, and requirements of this subpart with respect to electronic protected health information of a covered entity.

[78 FR 5693, Jan. 25, 2013]

§ 164.304 Definitions.

As used in this subpart, the following terms have the following meanings:

Access means the ability or the means necessary to read, write, modify, or communicate data/information or otherwise use any system resource. (This definition applies to "access" as used in this subpart, not as used in subparts D or E of this part.)

Administrative safeguards are administrative actions, and policies and procedures, to manage the selection, development, implementation, and maintenance of security measures to protect electronic protected health information and to manage the conduct of the covered entity's or business associate's workforce in relation to the protection of that information.

Authentication means the corroboration that a person is the one claimed.

Availability means the property that data or information is accessible and useable upon demand by an authorized person.

Confidentiality means the property that data or information is not made available or disclosed to unauthorized persons or processes.

Encryption means the use of an algorithmic process to transform data into a form in which there is a low probability of assigning meaning without use of a confidential process or key.

Facility means the physical premises and the interior and exterior of a building(s).

Information system means an interconnected set of information resources under the same direct management control that shares common functionality. A system normally includes hardware, software, information, data, applications, communications, and people.

Integrity means the property that data or information have not been altered or destroyed in an unauthorized manner.

Malicious software means software, for example, a virus, designed to damage or disrupt a system.

Password means confidential authentication information composed of a string of characters.

Physical safeguards are physical measures, policies, and procedures to protect a covered entity's or business associate's electronic information systems and related buildings and equipment, from natural and environmental hazards, and unauthorized intrusion.

Security or Security measures encompass all of the administrative, physical, and technical safeguards in an information system.

Security incident means the attempted or successful unauthorized access, use, disclosure, modification, or destruction of information or interference with system operations in an information system.

Technical safeguards means the technology and the policy and procedures for its use that protect electronic protected health information and control access to it.

User means a person or entity with authorized access.

Workstation means an electronic computing device, for example, a laptop or desktop computer, or any other device that performs similar functions, and electronic media stored in its immediate environment.

[68 FR 8376, Feb. 20, 2003, as amended at 74 FR 42767, Aug. 24, 2009; 78 FR 5693, Jan. 25, 2013]

§ 164.306 Security standards: General rules.

(a) *General requirements.* Covered entities and business associates must do the following:

(1) Ensure the confidentiality, integrity, and availability of all electronic protected health information the covered entity or business associate creates, receives, maintains, or transmits.

(2) Protect against any reasonably anticipated threats or hazards to the security or integrity of such information.

(3) Protect against any reasonably anticipated uses or disclosures of such information that are not permitted or required under subpart E of this part.

(4) Ensure compliance with this subpart by its workforce.

(b) *Flexibility of approach.*

(1) Covered entities and business associates may use any security measures that allow the covered entity or business associate to reasonably and appropriately implement the standards and implementation specifications as specified in this subpart.

(2) In deciding which security measures to use, a covered entity or business associate must take into account the following factors:

(i) The size, complexity, and capabilities of the covered entity or business associate.

(ii) The covered entity's or the business associate's technical infrastructure, hardware, and software security capabilities.

(iii) The costs of security measures.

(iv) The probability and criticality of potential risks to electronic protected health information.

(c) **Standards.** A covered entity or business associate must comply with the applicable standards as provided in this section and in §§ 164.308, 164.310, 164.312, 164.314 and 164.316 with respect to all electronic protected health information.

(d) **Implementation specifications.** In this subpart:

(1) Implementation specifications are required or addressable. If an implementation specification is required, the word "Required" appears in parentheses after the title of the implementation specification. If an implementation specification is addressable, the word "Addressable" appears in parentheses after the title of the implementation specification.

(2) When a standard adopted in § 164.308, § 164.310, § 164.312, § 164.314, or § 164.316 includes required implementation specifications, a covered entity or business associate must implement the implementation specifications.

(3) When a standard adopted in § 164.308, § 164.310, § 164.312, § 164.314, or § 164.316 includes addressable implementation specifications, a covered entity or business associate must—

(i) Assess whether each implementation specification is a reasonable and appropriate safeguard in its environment, when analyzed with reference to the likely contribution to protecting electronic protected health information; and

(ii) As applicable to the covered entity or business associate—

(A) Implement the implementation specification if reasonable and appropriate; or

(B) If implementing the implementation specification is not reasonable and appropriate—

(1) Document why it would not be reasonable and appropriate to implement the implementation specification; and

(2) Implement an equivalent alternative measure if reasonable and appropriate.

(e) **Maintenance.** A covered entity or business associate must review and modify the security measures implemented under this subpart as needed to continue provision of reasonable and appropriate protection of electronic protected health information, and update documentation of such security measures in accordance with § 164.316(b)(2)(iii).

[68 FR 8376, Feb. 20, 2003; 68 FR 17153, Apr. 8, 2003; 78 FR 5693, Jan. 25, 2013]

§ 164.308 Administrative safeguards.

(a) A covered entity or business associate must, in accordance with § 164.306:

(1)

(i) *Standard: Security management process.* Implement policies and procedures to prevent, detect, contain, and correct security violations.

(ii) *Implementation specifications:*

(A) *Risk analysis (Required).* Conduct an accurate and thorough assessment of the potential risks and vulnerabilities to the confidentiality, integrity, and availability of electronic protected health information held by the covered entity or business associate.

(B) *Risk management (Required).* Implement security measures sufficient to reduce risks and vulnerabilities to a reasonable and appropriate level to comply with § 164.306(a).

(C) *Sanction policy (Required).* Apply appropriate sanctions against workforce members who fail to comply with the security policies and procedures of the covered entity or business associate.

(D) *Information system activity review (Required).* Implement procedures to regularly review records of information system activity, such as audit logs, access reports, and security incident tracking reports.

(2) *Standard: Assigned security responsibility.* Identify the security official who is responsible for the development and implementation of the policies and procedures required by this subpart for the covered entity or business associate.

(3)

(i) *Standard: Workforce security.* Implement policies and procedures to ensure that all members of its workforce have appropriate access to electronic protected health information, as provided under paragraph (a)(4) of this section, and to prevent those workforce members who do not have access under paragraph (a)(4) of this section from obtaining access to electronic protected health information.

(ii) *Implementation specifications:*

(A) *Authorization and/or supervision (Addressable).* Implement procedures for the authorization and/or supervision of workforce members who work with electronic protected health information or in locations where it might be accessed.

(B) *Workforce clearance procedure (Addressable).* Implement procedures to determine that the access of a workforce member to electronic protected health information is appropriate.

(C) *Termination procedures (Addressable).* Implement procedures for terminating access to electronic protected health information when the employment of, or other arrangement with, a workforce member ends or as required by determinations made as specified in paragraph (a)(3)(ii)(B) of this section.

(4)

(i) *Standard: Information access management.* Implement policies and procedures for authorizing access to electronic protected health information that are consistent with the applicable requirements of subpart E of this part.

(ii) *Implementation specifications:*

(A) *Isolating health care clearinghouse functions (Required).* If a health care clearinghouse is part of a larger organization, the clearinghouse must implement policies and procedures that protect the electronic protected health information of the clearinghouse from unauthorized access by the larger organization.

(B) *Access authorization (Addressable).* Implement policies and procedures for granting access to electronic protected health information, for example, through access to a workstation, transaction, program, process, or other mechanism.

(C) *Access establishment and modification (Addressable).* Implement policies and procedures that, based upon the covered entity's or the business associate's access authorization policies, establish, document, review, and modify a user's right of access to a workstation, transaction, program, or process.

(5)

(i) *Standard: Security awareness and training.* Implement a security awareness and training program for all members of its workforce (including management).

(ii) *Implementation specifications.* Implement:

(A) *Security reminders (Addressable).* Periodic security updates.

(B) *Protection from malicious software (Addressable).* Procedures for guarding against, detecting, and reporting malicious software.

(C) *Log-in monitoring (Addressable).* Procedures for monitoring log-in attempts and reporting discrepancies.

(D) *Password management (Addressable).* Procedures for creating, changing, and safeguarding passwords.

(6)

(i) *Standard: Security incident procedures.* Implement policies and procedures to address security incidents.

(ii) *Implementation specification: Response and reporting (Required).* Identify and respond to suspected or known security incidents; mitigate, to the extent practicable, harmful effects of security incidents that are known to the covered entity or business associate; and document security incidents and their outcomes.

(7)

(i) *Standard: Contingency plan.* Establish (and implement as needed) policies and procedures for responding to an emergency or other occurrence (for example, fire, vandalism, system failure, and natural disaster) that damages systems that contain electronic protected health information.

(ii) *Implementation specifications:*

(A) *Data backup plan (Required).* Establish and implement procedures to create and maintain retrievable exact copies of electronic protected health information.

(B) *Disaster recovery plan (Required).* Establish (and implement as needed) procedures to restore any loss of data.

(C) *Emergency mode operation plan (Required).* Establish (and implement as needed) procedures to enable continuation of critical business processes for protection of the security of electronic protected health information while operating in emergency mode.

(D) *Testing and revision procedures (Addressable).* Implement procedures for periodic testing and revision of contingency plans.

(E) *Applications and data criticality analysis (Addressable).* Assess the relative criticality of specific applications and data in support of other contingency plan components.

(8) *Standard: Evaluation.* Perform a periodic technical and nontechnical evaluation, based initially upon the standards implemented under this rule and, subsequently, in response to environmental or operational changes affecting the security of electronic protected health information, that establishes the extent to which a covered entity's or business associate's security policies and procedures meet the requirements of this subpart.

(b)

(1) *Business associate contracts and other arrangements.* A covered entity may permit a business associate to create, receive, maintain, or transmit electronic protected health information on the covered entity's behalf only if the covered entity obtains satisfactory assurances, in accordance with § 164.314(a), that the business associate will appropriately safeguard the information. A covered entity is not required to obtain such satisfactory assurances from a business associate that is a subcontractor.

(2) A business associate may permit a business associate that is a subcontractor to create, receive, maintain, or transmit electronic protected health information on its behalf only if the business associate obtains satisfactory assurances, in accordance with § 164.314(a), that the subcontractor will appropriately safeguard the information.

(3) *Implementation specifications: Written contract or other arrangement (Required).* Document the satisfactory assurances required by paragraph (b)(1) or (b)(2) of this section through a written contract or other arrangement with the business associate that meets the applicable requirements of § 164.314(a).

[68 FR 8376, Feb. 20, 2003, as amended at 78 FR 5694, Jan. 25, 2013]

§ 164.310 Physical safeguards.

A covered entity or business associate must, in accordance with § 164.306:

(a)

(1) *Standard: Facility access controls.* Implement policies and procedures to limit physical access to its electronic information systems and the facility or facilities in which they are housed, while ensuring that properly authorized access is allowed.

(2) *Implementation specifications:*

(i) *Contingency operations (Addressable).* Establish (and implement as needed) procedures that allow facility access in support of restoration of lost data under the disaster recovery plan and emergency mode operations plan in the event of an emergency.

(ii) *Facility security plan (Addressable).* Implement policies and procedures to safeguard the facility and the equipment therein from unauthorized physical access, tampering, and theft.

(iii) *Access control and validation procedures (Addressable).* Implement procedures to control and validate a person's access to facilities based on their role or function, including visitor control, and control of access to software programs for testing and revision.

(iv) *Maintenance records (Addressable).* Implement policies and procedures to document repairs and modifications to the physical components of a facility which are related to security (for example, hardware, walls, doors, and locks).

(b) *Standard: Workstation use.* Implement policies and procedures that specify the proper functions to be performed, the manner in which those functions are to be performed, and the physical attributes of the surroundings of a specific workstation or class of workstation that can access electronic protected health information.

(c) *Standard: Workstation security.* Implement physical safeguards for all workstations that access electronic protected health information, to restrict access to authorized users.

(d)

(1) *Standard: Device and media controls.* Implement policies and procedures that govern the receipt and removal of hardware and electronic media that contain electronic protected health information into and out of a facility, and the movement of these items within the facility.

(2) *Implementation specifications:*

(i) **Disposal (Required).** Implement policies and procedures to address the final disposition of electronic protected health information, and/or the hardware or electronic media on which it is stored.

(ii) **Media re-use (Required).** Implement procedures for removal of electronic protected health information from electronic media before the media are made available for re-use.

(iii) **Accountability (Addressable).** Maintain a record of the movements of hardware and electronic media and any person responsible therefore.

(iv) **Data backup and storage (Addressable).** Create a retrievable, exact copy of electronic protected health information, when needed, before movement of equipment.

[68 FR 8376, Feb. 20, 2003, as amended at 78 FR 5694, Jan. 25, 2013]

§ 164.312 Technical safeguards.

A covered entity or business associate must, in accordance with § 164.306:

(a)

(1) **Standard: Access control.** Implement technical policies and procedures for electronic information systems that maintain electronic protected health information to allow access only to those persons or software programs that have been granted access rights as specified in § 164.308(a)(4).

(2) **Implementation specifications:**

(i) **Unique user identification (Required).** Assign a unique name and/or number for identifying and tracking user identity.

(ii) **Emergency access procedure (Required).** Establish (and implement as needed) procedures for obtaining necessary electronic protected health information during an emergency.

(iii) **Automatic logoff (Addressable).** Implement electronic procedures that terminate an electronic session after a predetermined time of inactivity.

(iv) **Encryption and decryption (Addressable).** Implement a mechanism to encrypt and decrypt electronic protected health information.

(b) **Standard: Audit controls.** Implement hardware, software, and/or procedural mechanisms that record and examine activity in information systems that contain or use electronic protected health information.

(c)

(1) **Standard: Integrity.** Implement policies and procedures to protect electronic protected health information from improper alteration or destruction.

(2) *Implementation specification: Mechanism to authenticate electronic protected health information (Addressable).* Implement electronic mechanisms to corroborate that electronic protected health information has not been altered or destroyed in an unauthorized manner.

(d) *Standard: Person or entity authentication.* Implement procedures to verify that a person or entity seeking access to electronic protected health information is the one claimed.

(e)

(1) *Standard: Transmission security.* Implement technical security measures to guard against unauthorized access to electronic protected health information that is being transmitted over an electronic communications network.

(2) *Implementation specifications:*

(i) *Integrity controls (Addressable).* Implement security measures to ensure that electronically transmitted electronic protected health information is not improperly modified without detection until disposed of.

(ii) *Encryption (Addressable).* Implement a mechanism to encrypt electronic protected health information whenever deemed appropriate.

[68 FR 8376, Feb. 20, 2003, as amended at 78 FR 5694, Jan. 25, 2013]

§ 164.314 Organizational requirements.

(a)

(1) *Standard: Business associate contracts or other arrangements.* The contract or other arrangement required by § 164.308(b)(3) must meet the requirements of paragraph (a)(2)(i), (a)(2)(ii), or (a)(2)(iii) of this section, as applicable.

(2) *Implementation specifications (Required)* —

(i) *Business associate contracts.* The contract must provide that the business associate will—

(A) Comply with the applicable requirements of this subpart;

(B) In accordance with § 164.308(b)(2), ensure that any subcontractors that create, receive, maintain, or transmit electronic protected health information on behalf of the business associate agree to comply with the applicable requirements of this subpart by entering into a contract or other arrangement that complies with this section; and

(C) Report to the covered entity any security incident of which it becomes aware, including breaches of unsecured protected health information as required by § 164.410.

(ii) *Other arrangements.* The covered entity is in compliance with paragraph (a)(1) of this section if it has another arrangement in place that meets the requirements of § 164.504(e)(3).

(iii) *Business associate contracts with subcontractors.* The requirements of paragraphs (a)(2)(i) and (a)(2)(ii) of this section apply to the contract or other arrangement between a business associate and a subcontractor required by § 164.308(b)(4) in the same manner as such requirements apply to contracts or other arrangements between a covered entity and business associate.

(b)

(1) *Standard: Requirements for group health plans.* Except when the only electronic protected health information disclosed to a plan sponsor is disclosed pursuant to § 164.504(f)(1)(ii) or (iii), or as authorized under § 164.508, a group health plan must ensure that its plan documents provide that the plan sponsor will reasonably and appropriately safeguard electronic protected health information created, received, maintained, or transmitted to or by the plan sponsor on behalf of the group health plan.

(2) *Implementation specifications (Required).* The plan documents of the group health plan must be amended to incorporate provisions to require the plan sponsor to—

(i) Implement administrative, physical, and technical safeguards that reasonably and appropriately protect the confidentiality, integrity, and availability of the electronic protected health information that it creates, receives, maintains, or transmits on behalf of the group health plan;

(ii) Ensure that the adequate separation required by § 164.504(f)(2)(iii) is supported by reasonable and appropriate security measures;

(iii) Ensure that any agent to whom it provides this information agrees to implement reasonable and appropriate security measures to protect the information; and

(iv) Report to the group health plan any security incident of which it becomes aware.

[68 FR 8376, Feb. 20, 2003, as amended at 78 FR 5694, Jan. 25, 2013; 78 FR 34266, June 7, 2013]

§ 164.316 Policies and procedures and documentation requirements.

A covered entity or business associate must, in accordance with § 164.306:

(a) *Standard: Policies and procedures.* Implement reasonable and appropriate policies and procedures to comply with the standards, implementation specifications, or other requirements of this subpart, taking into account those factors specified in § 164.306(b)(2)(i), (ii), (iii), and (iv). This standard is not to be construed to permit or excuse an action that violates any other standard, implementation specification, or other requirements of this subpart. A covered entity or business associate may change its policies and procedures at any time, provided that the changes are documented and are implemented in accordance with this subpart.

(b)

(1) *Standard: Documentation.*

(i) Maintain the policies and procedures implemented to comply with this subpart in written (which may be electronic) form; and

(ii) If an action, activity or assessment is required by this subpart to be documented, maintain a written (which may be electronic) record of the action, activity, or assessment.

(2) *Implementation specifications:*

(i) *Time limit (Required).* Retain the documentation required by paragraph (b)(1) of this section for 6 years from the date of its creation or the date when it last was in effect, whichever is later.

(ii) *Availability (Required).* Make documentation available to those persons responsible for implementing the procedures to which the documentation pertains.

(iii) *Updates (Required).* Review documentation periodically, and update as needed, in response to environmental or operational changes affecting the security of the electronic protected health information.

[68 FR 8376, Feb. 20, 2003, as amended at 78 FR 5695, Jan. 25, 2013]

§ 164.318 Compliance dates for the initial implementation of the security standards.

(a) *Health plan.*

(1) A health plan that is not a small health plan must comply with the applicable requirements of this subpart no later than April 20, 2005.

(2) A small health plan must comply with the applicable requirements of this subpart no later than April 20, 2006.

(b) *Health care clearinghouse.* A health care clearinghouse must comply with the applicable requirements of this subpart no later than April 20, 2005.

(c) *Health care provider.* A covered health care provider must comply with the applicable requirements of this subpart no later than April 20, 2005.

Appendix A to Subpart C of Part 164—Security Standards: Matrix

Standards	Sections	Implementation Specifications (R) = Required, (A) = Addressable
Administrative Safeguards		
Security Management Process	164.308(a)(1)	Risk Analysis (R)
		Risk Management (R)
		Sanction Policy (R)
		Information System Activity Review (R)

Standards	Sections	Implementation Specifications (R) = Required, (A) = Addressable
Assigned Security Responsibility	164.308(a)(2)	(R)
Workforce Security	164.308(a)(3)	Authorization and/or Supervision (A)
		Workforce Clearance Procedure
		Termination Procedures (A)
Information Access Management	164.308(a)(4)	Isolating Health care Clearinghouse Function (R)
		Access Authorization (A)
		Access Establishment and Modification (A)
Security Awareness and Training	164.308(a)(5)	Security Reminders (A)
		Protection from Malicious Software (A)
		Log-in Monitoring (A)
		Password Management (A)
Security Incident Procedures	164.308(a)(6)	Response and Reporting (R)
Contingency Plan	164.308(a)(7)	Data Backup Plan (R)
		Disaster Recovery Plan (R)
		Emergency Mode Operation Plan (R)
		Testing and Revision Procedure (A)
		Applications and Data Criticality Analysis (A)
Evaluation	164.308(a)(8)	(R)
Business Associate Contracts and Other Arrangement	164.308(b)(1)	Written Contract or Other Arrangement (R)
Physical Safeguards		
Facility Access Controls	164.310(a)(1)	Contingency Operations (A)
		Facility Security Plan (A)
		Access Control and Validation Procedures (A)
		Maintenance Records (A)
Workstation Use	164.310(b)	(R)
Workstation Security	164.310(c)	(R)
Device and Media Controls	164.310(d)(1)	Disposal (R)
		Media Re-use (R)
		Accountability (A)
		Data Backup and Storage (A)
Technical Safeguards (see § 164.312)		
Access Control	164.312(a)(1)	Unique User Identification (R)
		Emergency Access Procedure (R)
		Automatic Logoff (A)
		Encryption and Decryption (A)
Audit Controls	164.312(b)	(R)
Integrity	164.312(c)(1)	Mechanism to Authenticate Electronic Protected Health Information (A)

Standards	Sections	Implementation Specifications (R) = Required, (A) = Addressable
Person or Entity Authentication	164.312(d) (R)	
Transmission Security	164.312(e)(1)	Integrity Controls (A)
		Encryption (A)

Subpart D—Notification in the Case of Breach of Unsecured Protected Health Information

Source:74 FR 42767, Aug. 24, 2009, unless otherwise noted.

§ 164.400 Applicability.

The requirements of this subpart shall apply with respect to breaches of protected health information occurring on or after September 23, 2009.

§ 164.402 Definitions.

As used in this subpart, the following terms have the following meanings:

Breach means the acquisition, access, use, or disclosure of protected health information in a manner not permitted under subpart E of this part which compromises the security or privacy of the protected health information.

(1) Breach excludes:

(i) Any unintentional acquisition, access, or use of protected health information by a workforce member or person acting under the authority of a covered entity or a business associate, if such acquisition, access, or use was made in good faith and within the scope of authority and does not result in further use or disclosure in a manner not permitted under subpart E of this part.

(ii) Any inadvertent disclosure by a person who is authorized to access protected health information at a covered entity or business associate to another person authorized to access protected health information at the same covered entity or business associate, or organized health care arrangement in which the covered entity participates, and the information received as a result of such disclosure is not further used or disclosed in a manner not permitted under subpart E of this part.

(iii) A disclosure of protected health information where a covered entity or business associate has a good faith belief that an unauthorized person to whom the disclosure was made would not reasonably have been able to retain such information.

(2) Except as provided in paragraph (1) of this definition, an acquisition, access, use, or disclosure of protected health information in a manner not permitted under subpart E is presumed to be a breach unless the covered entity or business associate, as applicable, demonstrates that there is a low probability that the protected health information has been compromised based on a risk assessment of at least the following factors:

(i) The nature and extent of the protected health information involved, including the types of identifiers and the likelihood of re-identification;

(ii) The unauthorized person who used the protected health information or to whom the disclosure was made;

(iii) Whether the protected health information was actually acquired or viewed; and

(iv) The extent to which the risk to the protected health information has been mitigated.

Unsecured protected health information means protected health information that is not rendered unusable, unreadable, or indecipherable to unauthorized persons through the use of a technology or methodology specified by the Secretary in the guidance issued under section 13402(h)(2) of Public Law 111–5.

[78 FR 5695, Jan. 25, 2013]

§ 164.404 Notification to individuals.

(a) *Standard* —

(1) *General rule.* A covered entity shall, following the discovery of a breach of unsecured protected health information, notify each individual whose unsecured protected health information has been, or is reasonably believed by the covered entity to have been, accessed, acquired, used, or disclosed as a result of such breach.

(2) *Breaches treated as discovered.* For purposes of paragraph (a)(1) of this section, §§ 164.406(a), and 164.408(a), a breach shall be treated as discovered by a covered entity as of the first day on which such breach is known to the covered entity, or, by exercising reasonable diligence would have been known to the covered entity. A covered entity shall be deemed to have knowledge of a breach if such breach is known, or by exercising reasonable diligence would have been known, to any person, other than the person committing the breach, who is a workforce member or agent of the covered entity (determined in accordance with the federal common law of agency).

(b) *Implementation specification: Timeliness of notification.* Except as provided in § 164.412, a covered entity shall provide the notification required by paragraph (a) of this section without unreasonable delay and in no case later than 60 calendar days after discovery of a breach.

(c) *Implementation specifications: Content of notification* —

(1) *Elements.* The notification required by paragraph (a) of this section shall include, to the extent possible:

(A) A brief description of what happened, including the date of the breach and the date of the discovery of the breach, if known;

(B) A description of the types of unsecured protected health information that were involved in the breach (such as whether full name, social security number, date of birth, home address, account number, diagnosis, disability code, or other types of information were involved);

(C) Any steps individuals should take to protect themselves from potential harm resulting from the breach;

(D) A brief description of what the covered entity involved is doing to investigate the breach, to mitigate harm to individuals, and to protect against any further breaches; and

(E) Contact procedures for individuals to ask questions or learn additional information, which shall include a toll-free telephone number, an e-mail address, Web site, or postal address.

(2) **Plain language requirement.** The notification required by paragraph (a) of this section shall be written in plain language.

(d) **Implementation specifications: Methods of individual notification.** The notification required by paragraph (a) of this section shall be provided in the following form:

(1) **Written notice.** (i) Written notification by first-class mail to the individual at the last known address of the individual or, if the individual agrees to electronic notice and such agreement has not been withdrawn, by electronic mail. The notification may be provided in one or more mailings as information is available.

(ii) If the covered entity knows the individual is deceased and has the address of the next of kin or personal representative of the individual (as specified under § 164.502(g)(4) of subpart E), written notification by first-class mail to either the next of kin or personal representative of the individual. The notification may be provided in one or more mailings as information is available.

(2) **Substitute notice.** In the case in which there is insufficient or out-of-date contact information that precludes written notification to the individual under paragraph (d)(1)(i) of this section, a substitute form of notice reasonably calculated to reach the individual shall be provided. Substitute notice need not be provided in the case in which there is insufficient or out-of-date contact information that precludes written notification to the next of kin or personal representative of the individual under paragraph (d)(1)(ii).

(i) In the case in which there is insufficient or out-of-date contact information for fewer than 10 individuals, then such substitute notice may be provided by an alternative form of written notice, telephone, or other means.

(ii) In the case in which there is insufficient or out-of-date contact information for 10 or more individuals, then such substitute notice shall:

(A) Be in the form of either a conspicuous posting for a period of 90 days on the home page of the Web site of the covered entity involved, or conspicuous notice in major print or broadcast media in geographic areas where the individuals affected by the breach likely reside; and

(B) Include a toll-free phone number that remains active for at least 90 days where an individual can learn whether the individual's unsecured protected health information may be included in the breach.

(3) **Additional notice in urgent situations.** In any case deemed by the covered entity to require urgency because of possible imminent misuse of unsecured protected health

information, the covered entity may provide information to individuals by telephone or other means, as appropriate, in addition to notice provided under paragraph (d)(1) of this section.

§ 164.406 Notification to the media.

(a) *Standard.* For a breach of unsecured protected health information involving more than 500 residents of a State or jurisdiction, a covered entity shall, following the discovery of the breach as provided in § 164.404(a)(2), notify prominent media outlets serving the State or jurisdiction.

(b) *Implementation specification: Timeliness of notification.* Except as provided in § 164.412, a covered entity shall provide the notification required by paragraph (a) of this section without unreasonable delay and in no case later than 60 calendar days after discovery of a breach.

(c) *Implementation specifications: Content of notification.* The notification required by paragraph (a) of this section shall meet the requirements of § 164.404(c).

[74 FR 42767, Aug. 24, 2009, as amended at 78 FR 5695, Jan. 25, 2013]

§ 164.408 Notification to the Secretary.

(a) *Standard.* A covered entity shall, following the discovery of a breach of unsecured protected health information as provided in § 164.404(a)(2), notify the Secretary.

(b) *Implementation specifications: Breaches involving 500 or more individuals.* For breaches of unsecured protected health information involving 500 or more individuals, a covered entity shall, except as provided in § 164.412, provide the notification required by paragraph (a) of this section contemporaneously with the notice required by § 164.404(a) and in the manner specified on the HHS Web site.

(c) *Implementation specifications: Breaches involving less than 500 individuals.* For breaches of unsecured protected health information involving less than 500 individuals, a covered entity shall maintain a log or other documentation of such breaches and, not later than 60 days after the end of each calendar year, provide the notification required by paragraph (a) of this section for breaches discovered during the preceding calendar year, in the manner specified on the HHS web site.

[74 FR 42767, Aug. 24, 2009, as amended at 78 FR 5695, Jan. 25, 2013]

§ 164.410 Notification by a business associate.

(a) *Standard* —

(1) *General rule.* A business associate shall, following the discovery of a breach of unsecured protected health information, notify the covered entity of such breach.

(2) *Breaches treated as discovered.* For purposes of paragraph (a)(1) of this section, a breach shall be treated as discovered by a business associate as of the first day on which such breach is known to the business associate or, by exercising reasonable diligence, would have been known to the business associate. A business associate shall be deemed to have knowledge of a breach if

the breach is known, or by exercising reasonable diligence would have been known, to any person, other than the person committing the breach, who is an employee, officer, or other agent of the business associate (determined in accordance with the Federal common law of agency).

(b) *Implementation specifications: Timeliness of notification.* Except as provided in § 164.412, a business associate shall provide the notification required by paragraph (a) of this section without unreasonable delay and in no case later than 60 calendar days after discovery of a breach.

(c) *Implementation specifications: Content of notification.*

(1) The notification required by paragraph (a) of this section shall include, to the extent possible, the identification of each individual whose unsecured protected health information has been, or is reasonably believed by the business associate to have been, accessed, acquired, used, or disclosed during the breach.

(2) A business associate shall provide the covered entity with any other available information that the covered entity is required to include in notification to the individual under § 164.404(c) at the time of the notification required by paragraph (a) of this section or promptly thereafter as information becomes available.

[74 FR 42767, Aug. 24, 2009, as amended at 78 FR 5695, Jan. 25, 2013]

§ 164.412 Law enforcement delay.

If a law enforcement official states to a covered entity or business associate that a notification, notice, or posting required under this subpart would impede a criminal investigation or cause damage to national security, a covered entity or business associate shall:

(a) If the statement is in writing and specifies the time for which a delay is required, delay such notification, notice, or posting for the time period specified by the official; or

(b) If the statement is made orally, document the statement, including the identity of the official making the statement, and delay the notification, notice, or posting temporarily and no longer than 30 days from the date of the oral statement, unless a written statement as described in paragraph (a) of this section is submitted during that time.

§ 164.414 Administrative requirements and burden of proof.

(a) *Administrative requirements.* A covered entity is required to comply with the administrative requirements of § 164.530(b), (d), (e), (g), (h), (i), and (j) with respect to the requirements of this subpart.

(b) *Burden of proof.* In the event of a use or disclosure in violation of subpart E, the covered entity or business associate, as applicable, shall have the burden of demonstrating that all notifications were made as required by this subpart or that the use or disclosure did not constitute a breach, as defined at § 164.402.

Subpart E—Privacy of Individually Identifiable Health Information

Authority:42 U.S.C. 1320d–2, 1320d–4, and 1320d–9; sec. 264 of Pub. L. 104–191, 110 Stat. 2033–2034 (42 U.S.C. 1320d–2 (note)); and secs. 13400–13424, Pub. L. 111–5, 123 Stat. 258–279.

§ 164.500 Applicability.

(a) Except as otherwise provided herein, the standards, requirements, and implementation specifications of this subpart apply to covered entities with respect to protected health information.

(b) Health care clearinghouses must comply with the standards, requirements, and implementation specifications as follows:

(1) When a health care clearinghouse creates or receives protected health information as a business associate of another covered entity, the clearinghouse must comply with:

(i) Section 164.500 relating to applicability;

(ii) Section 164.501 relating to definitions;

(iii) Section 164.502 relating to uses and disclosures of protected health information, except that a clearinghouse is prohibited from using or disclosing protected health information other than as permitted in the business associate contract under which it created or received the protected health information;

(iv) Section 164.504 relating to the organizational requirements for covered entities;

(v) Section 164.512 relating to uses and disclosures for which individual authorization or an opportunity to agree or object is not required, except that a clearinghouse is prohibited from using or disclosing protected health information other than as permitted in the business associate contract under which it created or received the protected health information;

(vi) Section 164.532 relating to transition requirements; and

(vii) Section 164.534 relating to compliance dates for initial implementation of the privacy standards.

(2) When a health care clearinghouse creates or receives protected health information other than as a business associate of a covered entity, the clearinghouse must comply with all of the standards, requirements, and implementation specifications of this subpart.

(c) Where provided, the standards, requirements, and implementation specifications adopted under this subpart apply to a business associate with respect to the protected health information of a covered entity.

(d) The standards, requirements, and implementation specifications of this subpart do not apply to the Department of Defense or to any other federal agency, or non-governmental organization acting on its behalf, when providing health care to overseas foreign national beneficiaries.

[65 FR 82802, Dec. 28, 2000, as amended at 67 FR 53266, Aug. 14, 2002; 68 FR 8381, Feb. 20, 2003; 78 FR 5695, Jan. 25, 2013]

§ 164.501 Definitions.

As used in this subpart, the following terms have the following meanings:

Correctional institution means any penal or correctional facility, jail, reformatory, detention center, work farm, halfway house, or residential community program center operated by, or under contract to, the United States, a State, a territory, a political subdivision of a State or territory, or an Indian tribe, for the confinement or rehabilitation of persons charged with or convicted of a criminal offense or other persons held in lawful custody. *Other persons* held in lawful custody includes juvenile offenders adjudicated delinquent, aliens detained awaiting deportation, persons committed to mental institutions through the criminal justice system, witnesses, or others awaiting charges or trial.

Data aggregation means, with respect to protected health information created or received by a business associate in its capacity as the business associate of a covered entity, the combining of such protected health information by the business associate with the protected health information received by the business associate in its capacity as a business associate of another covered entity, to permit data analyses that relate to the health care operations of the respective covered entities.

Designated record set means:

(1) A group of records maintained by or for a covered entity that is:

(i) The medical records and billing records about individuals maintained by or for a covered health care provider;

(ii) The enrollment, payment, claims adjudication, and case or medical management record systems maintained by or for a health plan; or

(iii) Used, in whole or in part, by or for the covered entity to make decisions about individuals.

(2) For purposes of this paragraph, the term record means any item, collection, or grouping of information that includes protected health information and is maintained, collected, used, or disseminated by or for a covered entity.

Direct treatment relationship means a treatment relationship between an individual and a health care provider that is not an indirect treatment relationship.

Health care operations means any of the following activities of the covered entity to the extent that the activities are related to covered functions:

(1) Conducting quality assessment and improvement activities, including outcomes evaluation and development of clinical guidelines, provided that the obtaining of generalizable knowledge is not the primary purpose of any studies resulting from such activities; patient safety activities (as defined in 42 CFR 3.20); population-based activities relating to improving health or reducing health care costs, protocol development, case management and care coordination, contacting of

health care providers and patients with information about treatment alternatives; and related functions that do not include treatment;

(2) Reviewing the competence or qualifications of health care professionals, evaluating practitioner and provider performance, health plan performance, conducting training programs in which students, trainees, or practitioners in areas of health care learn under supervision to practice or improve their skills as health care providers, training of non-health care professionals, accreditation, certification, licensing, or credentialing activities;

(3) Except as prohibited under § 164.502(a)(5)(i), underwriting, enrollment, premium rating, and other activities related to the creation, renewal, or replacement of a contract of health insurance or health benefits, and ceding, securing, or placing a contract for reinsurance of risk relating to claims for health care (including stop-loss insurance and excess of loss insurance), provided that the requirements of § 164.514(g) are met, if applicable;

(4) Conducting or arranging for medical review, legal services, and auditing functions, including fraud and abuse detection and compliance programs;

(5) Business planning and development, such as conducting cost-management and planning-related analyses related to managing and operating the entity, including formulary development and administration, development or improvement of methods of payment or coverage policies; and

(6) Business management and general administrative activities of the entity, including, but not limited to:

(i) Management activities relating to implementation of and compliance with the requirements of this subchapter;

(ii) Customer service, including the provision of data analyses for policy holders, plan sponsors, or other customers, provided that protected health information is not disclosed to such policy holder, plan sponsor, or customer.

(iii) Resolution of internal grievances;

(iv) The sale, transfer, merger, or consolidation of all or part of the covered entity with another covered entity, or an entity that following such activity will become a covered entity and due diligence related to such activity; and

(v) Consistent with the applicable requirements of § 164.514, creating de-identified health information or a limited data set, and fundraising for the benefit of the covered entity.

Health oversight agency means an agency or authority of the United States, a State, a territory, a political subdivision of a State or territory, or an Indian tribe, or a person or entity acting under a grant of authority from or contract with such public agency, including the employees or agents of such public agency or its contractors or persons or entities to whom it has granted authority, that is authorized by law to oversee the health care system (whether public or private) or government programs in which health information is necessary to determine eligibility or compliance, or to enforce civil rights laws for which health information is relevant.

Indirect treatment relationship means a relationship between an individual and a health care provider in which:

(1) The health care provider delivers health care to the individual based on the orders of another health care provider; and

(2) The health care provider typically provides services or products, or reports the diagnosis or results associated with the health care, directly to another health care provider, who provides the services or products or reports to the individual.

Inmate means a person incarcerated in or otherwise confined to a correctional institution.

Marketing:

(1) Except as provided in paragraph (2) of this definition, marketing means to make a communication about a product or service that encourages recipients of the communication to purchase or use the product or service.

(2) Marketing does not include a communication made:

(i) To provide refill reminders or otherwise communicate about a drug or biologic that is currently being prescribed for the individual, only if any financial remuneration received by the covered entity in exchange for making the communication is reasonably related to the covered entity's cost of making the communication.

(ii) For the following treatment and health care operations purposes, except where the covered entity receives financial remuneration in exchange for making the communication:

(A) For treatment of an individual by a health care provider, including case management or care coordination for the individual, or to direct or recommend alternative treatments, therapies, health care providers, or settings of care to the individual;

(B) To describe a health-related product or service (or payment for such product or service) that is provided by, or included in a plan of benefits of, the covered entity making the communication, including communications about: the entities participating in a health care provider network or health plan network; replacement of, or enhancements to, a health plan; and health-related products or services available only to a health plan enrollee that add value to, but are not part of, a plan of benefits; or

(C) For case management or care coordination, contacting of individuals with information about treatment alternatives, and related functions to the extent these activities do not fall within the definition of treatment.

(3) **Financial remuneration** means direct or indirect payment from or on behalf of a third party whose product or service is being described. Direct or indirect payment does not include any payment for treatment of an individual.

Payment means:

(1) The activities undertaken by:

(i) Except as prohibited under § 164.502(a)(5)(i), a health plan to obtain premiums or to determine or fulfill its responsibility for coverage and provision of benefits under the health plan; or

(ii) A health care provider or health plan to obtain or provide reimbursement for the provision of health care; and

(2) The activities in paragraph (1) of this definition relate to the individual to whom health care is provided and include, but are not limited to:

(i) Determinations of eligibility or coverage (including coordination of benefits or the determination of cost sharing amounts), and adjudication or subrogation of health benefit claims;

(ii) Risk adjusting amounts due based on enrollee health status and demographic characteristics;

(iii) Billing, claims management, collection activities, obtaining payment under a contract for reinsurance (including stop-loss insurance and excess of loss insurance), and related health care data processing;

(iv) Review of health care services with respect to medical necessity, coverage under a health plan, appropriateness of care, or justification of charges;

(v) Utilization review activities, including precertification and preauthorization of services, concurrent and retrospective review of services; and

(vi) Disclosure to consumer reporting agencies of any of the following protected health information relating to collection of premiums or reimbursement:

(A) Name and address;

(B) Date of birth;

(C) Social security number;

(D) Payment history;

(E) Account number; and

(F) Name and address of the health care provider and/or health plan.

Psychotherapy notes means notes recorded (in any medium) by a health care provider who is a mental health professional documenting or analyzing the contents of conversation during a private counseling session or a group, joint, or family counseling session and that are separated from the rest of the individual's medical record. *Psychotherapy notes* excludes medication prescription and monitoring, counseling session start and stop times, the modalities and frequencies of treatment furnished, results of clinical tests, and any summary of the following items: Diagnosis, functional status, the treatment plan, symptoms, prognosis, and progress to date.

Public health authority means an agency or authority of the United States, a State, a territory, a political subdivision of a State or territory, or an Indian tribe, or a person or entity acting under a grant of authority from or contract with such public agency, including the employees or agents of such public agency or its contractors or persons or entities to whom it has granted authority, that is responsible for public health matters as part of its official mandate.

Research means a systematic investigation, including research development, testing, and evaluation, designed to develop or contribute to generalizable knowledge.

Treatment means the provision, coordination, or management of health care and related services by one or more health care providers, including the coordination or management of health care by a health care provider with a third party; consultation between health care providers relating to a patient; or the referral of a patient for health care from one health care provider to another.

[65 FR 82802, Dec. 28, 2000, as amended at 67 FR 53266, Aug. 14, 2002; 68 FR 8381, Feb. 20, 2003; 74 FR 42769, Aug. 24, 2009; 78 FR 5695, Jan. 25, 2013]

§ 164.502 Uses and disclosures of protected health information: General rules.

(a) **Standard.** A covered entity or business associate may not use or disclose protected health information, except as permitted or required by this subpart or by subpart C of part 160 of this subchapter.

(1) **Covered entities: Permitted uses and disclosures.** A covered entity is permitted to use or disclose protected health information as follows:

(i) To the individual;

(ii) For treatment, payment, or health care operations, as permitted by and in compliance with § 164.506;

(iii) Incident to a use or disclosure otherwise permitted or required by this subpart, provided that the covered entity has complied with the applicable requirements of §§ 164.502(b), 164.514(d), and 164.530(c) with respect to such otherwise permitted or required use or disclosure;

(iv) Except for uses and disclosures prohibited under § 164.502(a)(5)(i), pursuant to and in compliance with a valid authorization under § 164.508;

(v) Pursuant to an agreement under, or as otherwise permitted by, § 164.510; and

(vi) As permitted by and in compliance with this section, § 164.512, § 164.514(e), (f), or (g).

(2) **Covered entities: Required disclosures.** A covered entity is required to disclose protected health information:

(i) To an individual, when requested under, and required by § 164.524 or § 164.528; and

(ii) When required by the Secretary under subpart C of part 160 of this subchapter to investigate or determine the covered entity's compliance with this subchapter.

(3) **Business associates: Permitted uses and disclosures.** A business associate may use or disclose protected health information only as permitted or required by its business associate contract or other arrangement pursuant to § 164.504(e) or as required by law. The business associate may not use or disclose protected health information in a manner that would violate the requirements of this subpart, if done by the covered entity, except for the purposes specified under § 164.504(e)(2)(i)(A) or (B) if such uses or disclosures are permitted by its contract or other arrangement.

(4) **Business associates: Required uses and disclosures.** A business associate is required to disclose protected health information:

(i) When required by the Secretary under subpart C of part 160 of this subchapter to investigate or determine the business associate's compliance with this subchapter.

(ii) To the covered entity, individual, or individual's designee, as necessary to satisfy a covered entity's obligations under § 164.524(c)(2)(ii) and (3)(ii) with respect to an individual's request for an electronic copy of protected health information.

(5) **Prohibited uses and disclosures —**

(i) **Use and disclosure of genetic information for underwriting purposes:**
Notwithstanding any other provision of this subpart, a health plan, excluding an issuer of a long-term care policy falling within paragraph (1)(viii) of the definition of *health plan,* shall not use or disclose protected health information that is genetic information for underwriting purposes. For purposes of paragraph (a)(5)(i) of this section, underwriting purposes means, with respect to a health plan:

(A) Except as provided in paragraph (a)(5)(i)(B) of this section:

(*1*) Rules for, or determination of, eligibility (including enrollment and continued eligibility) for, or determination of, benefits under the plan, coverage, or policy (including changes in deductibles or other cost-sharing mechanisms in return for activities such as completing a health risk assessment or participating in a wellness program);

(*2*) The computation of premium or contribution amounts under the plan, coverage, or policy (including discounts, rebates, payments in kind, or other premium differential mechanisms in return for activities such as completing a health risk assessment or participating in a wellness program);

(*3*) The application of any pre-existing condition exclusion under the plan, coverage, or policy; and

(*4*) Other activities related to the creation, renewal, or replacement of a contract of health insurance or health benefits.

(B) Underwriting purposes does not include determinations of medical appropriateness where an individual seeks a benefit under the plan, coverage, or policy.

(ii) *Sale of protected health information:*

(A) Except pursuant to and in compliance with § 164.508(a)(4), a covered entity or business associate may not sell protected health information.

(B) For purposes of this paragraph, sale of protected health information means:

(1) Except as provided in paragraph (a)(5)(ii)(B)(2) of this section, a disclosure of protected health information by a covered entity or business associate, if applicable, where the covered entity or business associate directly or indirectly receives remuneration from or on behalf of the recipient of the protected health information in exchange for the protected health information.

(2) Sale of protected health information does not include a disclosure of protected health information:

(i) For public health purposes pursuant to § 164.512(b) or § 164.514(e);

(ii) For research purposes pursuant to § 164.512(i) or § 164.514(e), where the only remuneration received by the covered entity or business associate is a reasonable cost-based fee to cover the cost to prepare and transmit the protected health information for such purposes;

(iii) For treatment and payment purposes pursuant to § 164.506(a);

(iv) For the sale, transfer, merger, or consolidation of all or part of the covered entity and for related due diligence as described in paragraph (6)(iv) of the definition of health care operations and pursuant to § 164.506(a);

(v) To or by a business associate for activities that the business associate undertakes on behalf of a covered entity, or on behalf of a business associate in the case of a subcontractor, pursuant to §§ 164.502(e) and 164.504(e), and the only remuneration provided is by the covered entity to the business associate, or by the business associate to the subcontractor, if applicable, for the performance of such activities;

(vi) To an individual, when requested under § 164.524 or § 164.528;

(vii) Required by law as permitted under § 164.512(a); and

(viii) For any other purpose permitted by and in accordance with the applicable requirements of this subpart, where the only remuneration received by the covered entity or business associate is a reasonable, cost-based fee to cover the cost to prepare and transmit the protected health information for such purpose or a fee otherwise expressly permitted by other law.

(b) **Standard: Minimum necessary** — *Minimum necessary applies.* When using or disclosing protected health information or when requesting protected health information from another covered entity or business associate, a covered entity or business associate must make reasonable efforts to limit protected health information to the minimum necessary to accomplish the intended purpose of the use, disclosure, or request.

(2) *Minimum necessary does not apply.* This requirement does not apply to:

(i) Disclosures to or requests by a health care provider for treatment;

(ii) Uses or disclosures made to the individual, as permitted under paragraph (a)(1)(i) of this section or as required by paragraph (a)(2)(i) of this section;

(iii) Uses or disclosures made pursuant to an authorization under § 164.508;

(iv) Disclosures made to the Secretary in accordance with subpart C of part 160 of this subchapter;

(v) Uses or disclosures that are required by law, as described by § 164.512(a); and

(vi) Uses or disclosures that are required for compliance with applicable requirements of this subchapter.

(c) *Standard: Uses and disclosures of protected health information subject to an agreed upon restriction.* A covered entity that has agreed to a restriction pursuant to § 164.522(a)(1) may not use or disclose the protected health information covered by the restriction in violation of such restriction, except as otherwise provided in § 164.522(a).

(d) *Standard: Uses and disclosures of de-identified protected health information* —

(1) *Uses and disclosures to create de-identified information.* A covered entity may use protected health information to create information that is not individually identifiable health information or disclose protected health information only to a business associate for such purpose, whether or not the de-identified information is to be used by the covered entity.

(2) *Uses and disclosures of de-identified information.* Health information that meets the standard and implementation specifications for de-identification under § 164.514(a) and (b) is considered not to be individually identifiable health information, *i.e.,* de-identified. The requirements of this subpart do not apply to information that has been de-identified in accordance with the applicable requirements of § 164.514, provided that:

(i) Disclosure of a code or other means of record identification designed to enable coded or otherwise de-identified information to be re-identified constitutes disclosure of protected health information; and

(ii) If de-identified information is re-identified, a covered entity may use or disclose such re-identified information only as permitted or required by this subpart.

(e)

(1) *Standard: Disclosures to business associates.*

(i) A covered entity may disclose protected health information to a business associate and may allow a business associate to create, receive, maintain, or transmit protected health information on its behalf, if the covered entity obtains satisfactory assurance that the business associate will appropriately safeguard the information. A covered entity is not required to obtain such satisfactory assurances from a business associate that is a subcontractor.

(ii) A business associate may disclose protected health information to a business associate that is a subcontractor and may allow the subcontractor to create, receive, maintain, or transmit protected health information on its behalf, if the business associate obtains satisfactory assurances, in accordance with § 164.504(e)(1)(i), that the subcontractor will appropriately safeguard the information.

(2) *Implementation specification: Documentation.* The satisfactory assurances required by paragraph (e)(1) of this section must be documented through a written contract or other written agreement or arrangement with the business associate that meets the applicable requirements of § 164.504(e).

(f) *Standard: Deceased individuals.* A covered entity must comply with the requirements of this subpart with respect to the protected health information of a deceased individual for a period of 50 years following the death of the individual.

(g)

(1) *Standard: Personal representatives.* As specified in this paragraph, a covered entity must, except as provided in paragraphs (g)(3) and (g)(5) of this section, treat a personal representative as the individual for purposes of this subchapter.

(2) *Implementation specification: Adults and emancipated minors.* If under applicable law a person has authority to act on behalf of an individual who is an adult or an emancipated minor in making decisions related to health care, a covered entity must treat such person as a personal representative under this subchapter, with respect to protected health information relevant to such personal representation.

(3)

(i) *Implementation specification: Unemancipated minors.* If under applicable law a parent, guardian, or other person acting *in loco parentis* has authority to act on behalf of an individual who is an unemancipated minor in making decisions related to health care, a covered entity must treat such person as a personal representative under this subchapter, with respect to protected health information relevant to such personal representation, except that such person may not be a personal representative of an unemancipated minor, and the minor has the authority to act as an individual, with respect to protected health information pertaining to a health care service, if:

(A) The minor consents to such health care service; no other consent to such health care service is required by law, regardless of whether the consent of another person has also been obtained; and the minor has not requested that such person be treated as the personal representative;

(B) The minor may lawfully obtain such health care service without the consent of a parent, guardian, or other person acting *in loco parentis,* and the minor, a court, or another person authorized by law consents to such health care service; or

(C) A parent, guardian, or other person acting *in loco parentis* assents to an agreement of confidentiality between a covered health care provider and the minor with respect to such health care service.

(ii) Notwithstanding the provisions of paragraph (g)(3)(i) of this section:

(A) If, and to the extent, permitted or required by an applicable provision of State or other law, including applicable case law, a covered entity may disclose, or provide access in accordance with § 164.524 to, protected health information about an unemancipated minor to a parent, guardian, or other person acting *in loco parentis*;

(B) If, and to the extent, prohibited by an applicable provision of State or other law, including applicable case law, a covered entity may not disclose, or provide access in accordance with § 164.524 to, protected health information about an unemancipated minor to a parent, guardian, or other person acting *in loco parentis*; and

(C) Where the parent, guardian, or other person acting *in loco parentis,* is not the personal representative under paragraphs (g)(3)(i)(A), (B), or (C) of this section and where there is no applicable access provision under State or other law, including case law, a covered entity may provide or deny access under § 164.524 to a parent, guardian, or other person acting *in loco parentis,* if such action is consistent with State or other applicable law, provided that such decision must be made by a licensed health care professional, in the exercise of professional judgment.

(4) *Implementation specification: Deceased individuals.* If under applicable law an executor, administrator, or other person has authority to act on behalf of a deceased individual or of the individual's estate, a covered entity must treat such person as a personal representative under this subchapter, with respect to protected health information relevant to such personal representation.

(5) *Implementation specification: Abuse, neglect, endangerment situations.* Notwithstanding a State law or any requirement of this paragraph to the contrary, a covered entity may elect not to treat a person as the personal representative of an individual if:

(i) The covered entity has a reasonable belief that:

(A) The individual has been or may be subjected to domestic violence, abuse, or neglect by such person; or

(B) Treating such person as the personal representative could endanger the individual; and

(ii) The covered entity, in the exercise of professional judgment, decides that it is not in the best interest of the individual to treat the person as the individual's personal representative.

(h) *Standard: Confidential communications.* A covered health care provider or health plan must comply with the applicable requirements of § 164.522(b) in communicating protected health information.

(i) *Standard: Uses and disclosures consistent with notice.* A covered entity that is required by § 164.520 to have a notice may not use or disclose protected health information in a manner inconsistent with such notice. A covered entity that is required by § 164.520(b)(1)(iii) to include a specific statement in its notice if it intends to engage in an activity listed in § 164.520(b)(1)(iii)(A)–(C), may not use or disclose protected health information for such activities, unless the required statement is included in the notice.

(j) **Standard: Disclosures by whistleblowers and workforce member crime victims —**

(1) **Disclosures by whistleblowers.** A covered entity is not considered to have violated the requirements of this subpart if a member of its workforce or a business associate discloses protected health information, provided that:

(i) The workforce member or business associate believes in good faith that the covered entity has engaged in conduct that is unlawful or otherwise violates professional or clinical standards, or that the care, services, or conditions provided by the covered entity potentially endangers one or more patients, workers, or the public; and

(ii) The disclosure is to:

(A) A health oversight agency or public health authority authorized by law to investigate or otherwise oversee the relevant conduct or conditions of the covered entity or to an appropriate health care accreditation organization for the purpose of reporting the allegation of failure to meet professional standards or misconduct by the covered entity; or

(B) An attorney retained by or on behalf of the workforce member or business associate for the purpose of determining the legal options of the workforce member or business associate with regard to the conduct described in paragraph (j)(1)(i) of this section.

(2) **Disclosures by workforce members who are victims of a crime.** A covered entity is not considered to have violated the requirements of this subpart if a member of its workforce who is the victim of a criminal act discloses protected health information to a law enforcement official, provided that:

(i) The protected health information disclosed is about the suspected perpetrator of the criminal act; and

(ii) The protected health information disclosed is limited to the information listed in § 164.512(f)(2)(i).

[65 FR 82802, Dec. 28, 2000, as amended at 67 FR 53267, Aug. 14, 2002; 78 FR 5696, Jan. 25, 2013]

§ 164.504 Uses and disclosures: Organizational requirements.

(a) **Definitions.** As used in this section:

Plan administration functions means administration functions performed by the plan sponsor of a group health plan on behalf of the group health plan and excludes functions performed by the plan sponsor in connection with any other benefit or benefit plan of the plan sponsor.

Summary health information means information, that may be individually identifiable health information, and:

(1) That summarizes the claims history, claims expenses, or type of claims experienced by individuals for whom a plan sponsor has provided health benefits under a group health plan; and

(2) From which the information described at § 164.514(b)(2)(i) has been deleted, except that the geographic information described in § 164.514(b)(2)(i)(B) need only be aggregated to the level of a five digit zip code.

(b)–(d) [Reserved]

(e)

  (1) *Standard: Business associate contracts.*

    (i) The contract or other arrangement required by § 164.502(e)(2) must meet the requirements of paragraph (e)(2), (e)(3), or (e)(5) of this section, as applicable.

    (ii) A covered entity is not in compliance with the standards in § 164.502(e) and this paragraph, if the covered entity knew of a pattern of activity or practice of the business associate that constituted a material breach or violation of the business associate's obligation under the contract or other arrangement, unless the covered entity took reasonable steps to cure the breach or end the violation, as applicable, and, if such steps were unsuccessful, terminated the contract or arrangement, if feasible.

    (iii) A business associate is not in compliance with the standards in § 164.502(e) and this paragraph, if the business associate knew of a pattern of activity or practice of a subcontractor that constituted a material breach or violation of the subcontractor's obligation under the contract or other arrangement, unless the business associate took reasonable steps to cure the breach or end the violation, as applicable, and, if such steps were unsuccessful, terminated the contract or arrangement, if feasible.

  (2) *Implementation specifications: Business associate contracts.* A contract between the covered entity and a business associate must:

    (i) Establish the permitted and required uses and disclosures of protected health information by the business associate. The contract may not authorize the business associate to use or further disclose the information in a manner that would violate the requirements of this subpart, if done by the covered entity, except that:

      (A) The contract may permit the business associate to use and disclose protected health information for the proper management and administration of the business associate, as provided in paragraph (e)(4) of this section; and

      (B) The contract may permit the business associate to provide data aggregation services relating to the health care operations of the covered entity.

    (ii) Provide that the business associate will:

      (A) Not use or further disclose the information other than as permitted or required by the contract or as required by law;

(B) Use appropriate safeguards and comply, where applicable, with subpart C of this part with respect to electronic protected health information, to prevent use or disclosure of the information other than as provided for by its contract;

(C) Report to the covered entity any use or disclosure of the information not provided for by its contract of which it becomes aware, including breaches of unsecured protected health information as required by § 164.410;

(D) In accordance with § 164.502(e)(1)(ii), ensure that any subcontractors that create, receive, maintain, or transmit protected health information on behalf of the business associate agree to the same restrictions and conditions that apply to the business associate with respect to such information;

(E) Make available protected health information in accordance with § 164.524;

(F) Make available protected health information for amendment and incorporate any amendments to protected health information in accordance with § 164.526;

(G) Make available the information required to provide an accounting of disclosures in accordance with § 164.528;

(H) To the extent the business associate is to carry out a covered entity's obligation under this subpart, comply with the requirements of this subpart that apply to the covered entity in the performance of such obligation.

(I) Make its internal practices, books, and records relating to the use and disclosure of protected health information received from, or created or received by the business associate on behalf of, the covered entity available to the Secretary for purposes of determining the covered entity's compliance with this subpart; and

(J) At termination of the contract, if feasible, return or destroy all protected health information received from, or created or received by the business associate on behalf of, the covered entity that the business associate still maintains in any form and retain no copies of such information or, if such return or destruction is not feasible, extend the protections of the contract to the information and limit further uses and disclosures to those purposes that make the return or destruction of the information infeasible.

(iii) Authorize termination of the contract by the covered entity, if the covered entity determines that the business associate has violated a material term of the contract.

(3) *Implementation specifications: Other arrangements.*

(i) If a covered entity and its business associate are both governmental entities:

(A) The covered entity may comply with this paragraph and § 164.314(a)(1), if applicable, by entering into a memorandum of understanding with the business associate that contains terms that accomplish the objectives of paragraph (e)(2) of this section and § 164.314(a)(2), if applicable.

(B) The covered entity may comply with this paragraph and § 164.314(a)(1), if applicable, if other law (including regulations adopted by the covered entity or its business associate) contains requirements applicable to the business associate that accomplish the objectives of paragraph (e)(2) of this section and § 164.314(a)(2), if applicable.

(ii) If a business associate is required by law to perform a function or activity on behalf of a covered entity or to provide a service described in the definition of business associate in § 160.103 of this subchapter to a covered entity, such covered entity may disclose protected health information to the business associate to the extent necessary to comply with the legal mandate without meeting the requirements of this paragraph and § 164.314(a)(1), if applicable, provided that the covered entity attempts in good faith to obtain satisfactory assurances as required by paragraph (e)(2) of this section and § 164.314(a)(1), if applicable, and, if such attempt fails, documents the attempt and the reasons that such assurances cannot be obtained.

(iii) The covered entity may omit from its other arrangements the termination authorization required by paragraph (e)(2)(iii) of this section, if such authorization is inconsistent with the statutory obligations of the covered entity or its business associate.

(iv) A covered entity may comply with this paragraph and § 164.314(a)(1) if the covered entity discloses only a limited data set to a business associate for the business associate to carry out a health care operations function and the covered entity has a data use agreement with the business associate that complies with §§ 164.514(e)(4) and 164.314(a)(1), if applicable.

(4) *Implementation specifications: Other requirements for contracts and other arrangements.*

(i) The contract or other arrangement between the covered entity and the business associate may permit the business associate to use the protected health information received by the business associate in its capacity as a business associate to the covered entity, if necessary:

(A) For the proper management and administration of the business associate; or

(B) To carry out the legal responsibilities of the business associate.

(ii) The contract or other arrangement between the covered entity and the business associate may permit the business associate to disclose the protected health information received by the business associate in its capacity as a business associate for the purposes described in paragraph (e)(4)(i) of this section, if:

(A) The disclosure is required by law; or

(B)

(*1*) The business associate obtains reasonable assurances from the person to whom the information is disclosed that it will be held confidentially and used or further disclosed only as required by law or for the purposes for which it was disclosed to the person; and

(*2*) The person notifies the business associate of any instances of which it is aware in which the confidentiality of the information has been breached.

(5) *Implementation specifications: Business associate contracts with subcontractors.* The requirements of § 164.504(e)(2) through (e)(4) apply to the contract or other arrangement required by § 164.502(e)(1)(ii) between a business associate and a business associate that is a subcontractor in the same manner as such requirements apply to contracts or other arrangements between a covered entity and business associate.

(f)

(1) *Standard: Requirements for group health plans.*

(i) Except as provided under paragraph (f)(1)(ii) or (iii) of this section or as otherwise authorized under § 164.508, a group health plan, in order to disclose protected health information to the plan sponsor or to provide for or permit the disclosure of protected health information to the plan sponsor by a health insurance issuer or HMO with respect to the group health plan, must ensure that the plan documents restrict uses and disclosures of such information by the plan sponsor consistent with the requirements of this subpart.

(ii) Except as prohibited by § 164.502(a)(5)(i), the group health plan, or a health insurance issuer or HMO with respect to the group health plan, may disclose summary health information to the plan sponsor, if the plan sponsor requests the summary health information for purposes of:

(A) Obtaining premium bids from health plans for providing health insurance coverage under the group health plan; or

(B) Modifying, amending, or terminating the group health plan.

(iii) The group health plan, or a health insurance issuer or HMO with respect to the group health plan, may disclose to the plan sponsor information on whether the individual is participating in the group health plan, or is enrolled in or has disenrolled from a health insurance issuer or HMO offered by the plan.

(2) *Implementation specifications: Requirements for plan documents.* The plan documents of the group health plan must be amended to incorporate provisions to:

(i) Establish the permitted and required uses and disclosures of such information by the plan sponsor, provided that such permitted and required uses and disclosures may not be inconsistent with this subpart.

(ii) Provide that the group health plan will disclose protected health information to the plan sponsor only upon receipt of a certification by the plan sponsor that the plan documents have been amended to incorporate the following provisions and that the plan sponsor agrees to:

(A) Not use or further disclose the information other than as permitted or required by the plan documents or as required by law;

(B) Ensure that any agents to whom it provides protected health information received from the group health plan agree to the same restrictions and conditions that apply to the plan sponsor with respect to such information;

(C) Not use or disclose the information for employment-related actions and decisions or in connection with any other benefit or employee benefit plan of the plan sponsor;

(D) Report to the group health plan any use or disclosure of the information that is inconsistent with the uses or disclosures provided for of which it becomes aware;

(E) Make available protected health information in accordance with § 164.524;

(F) Make available protected health information for amendment and incorporate any amendments to protected health information in accordance with § 164.526;

(G) Make available the information required to provide an accounting of disclosures in accordance with § 164.528;

(H) Make its internal practices, books, and records relating to the use and disclosure of protected health information received from the group health plan available to the Secretary for purposes of determining compliance by the group health plan with this subpart;

(I) If feasible, return or destroy all protected health information received from the group health plan that the sponsor still maintains in any form and retain no copies of such information when no longer needed for the purpose for which disclosure was made, except that, if such return or destruction is not feasible, limit further uses and disclosures to those purposes that make the return or destruction of the information infeasible; and

(J) Ensure that the adequate separation required in paragraph (f)(2)(iii) of this section is established.

(iii) Provide for adequate separation between the group health plan and the plan sponsor. The plan documents must:

(A) Describe those employees or classes of employees or other persons under the control of the plan sponsor to be given access to the protected health information to be disclosed, provided that any employee or person who receives protected health information relating to payment under, health care operations of, or other matters pertaining to the group health plan in the ordinary course of business must be included in such description;

(B) Restrict the access to and use by such employees and other persons described in paragraph (f)(2)(iii)(A) of this section to the plan administration functions that the plan sponsor performs for the group health plan; and

(C) Provide an effective mechanism for resolving any issues of noncompliance by persons described in paragraph (f)(2)(iii)(A) of this section with the plan document provisions required by this paragraph.

(3) **_Implementation specifications: Uses and disclosures._** A group health plan may:

(i) Disclose protected health information to a plan sponsor to carry out plan administration functions that the plan sponsor performs only consistent with the provisions of paragraph (f)(2) of this section;

(ii) Not permit a health insurance issuer or HMO with respect to the group health plan to disclose protected health information to the plan sponsor except as permitted by this paragraph;

(iii) Not disclose and may not permit a health insurance issuer or HMO to disclose protected health information to a plan sponsor as otherwise permitted by this paragraph unless a statement required by § 164.520(b)(1)(iii)(C) is included in the appropriate notice; and

(iv) Not disclose protected health information to the plan sponsor for the purpose of employment-related actions or decisions or in connection with any other benefit or employee benefit plan of the plan sponsor.

(g) *Standard: Requirements for a covered entity with multiple covered functions.*

(1) A covered entity that performs multiple covered functions that would make the entity any combination of a health plan, a covered health care provider, and a health care clearinghouse, must comply with the standards, requirements, and implementation specifications of this subpart, as applicable to the health plan, health care provider, or health care clearinghouse covered functions performed.

(2) A covered entity that performs multiple covered functions may use or disclose the protected health information of individuals who receive the covered entity's health plan or health care provider services, but not both, only for purposes related to the appropriate function being performed.

[65 FR 82802, Dec. 28, 2000, as amended at 67 FR 53267, Aug. 14, 2002; 68 FR 8381, Feb. 20, 2003; 78 FR 5697, Jan. 25, 2013]

§ 164.506 Uses and disclosures to carry out treatment, payment, or health care operations.

(a) *Standard: Permitted uses and disclosures.* Except with respect to uses or disclosures that require an authorization under § 164.508(a)(2) through (4) or that are prohibited under § 164.502(a)(5)(i), a covered entity may use or disclose protected health information for treatment, payment, or health care operations as set forth in paragraph (c) of this section, provided that such use or disclosure is consistent with other applicable requirements of this subpart.

(b) *Standard: Consent for uses and disclosures permitted.*

(1) A covered entity may obtain consent of the individual to use or disclose protected health information to carry out treatment, payment, or health care operations.

(2) Consent, under paragraph (b) of this section, shall not be effective to permit a use or disclosure of protected health information when an authorization, under § 164.508, is required or when another condition must be met for such use or disclosure to be permissible under this subpart.

(c) *Implementation specifications: Treatment, payment, or health care operations.*

(1) A covered entity may use or disclose protected health information for its own treatment, payment, or health care operations.

(2) A covered entity may disclose protected health information for treatment activities of a health care provider.

(3) A covered entity may disclose protected health information to another covered entity or a health care provider for the payment activities of the entity that receives the information.

(4) A covered entity may disclose protected health information to another covered entity for health care operations activities of the entity that receives the information, if each entity either has or had a relationship with the individual who is the subject of the protected health information being requested, the protected health information pertains to such relationship, and the disclosure is:

(i) For a purpose listed in paragraph (1) or (2) of the definition of health care operations; or

(ii) For the purpose of health care fraud and abuse detection or compliance.

(5) A covered entity that participates in an organized health care arrangement may disclose protected health information about an individual to other participants in the organized health care arrangement for any health care operations activities of the organized health care arrangement.

[67 FR 53268, Aug. 14, 2002, as amended at 78 FR 5698, Jan. 25, 2013]

§ 164.508 Uses and disclosures for which an authorization is required.

(a) *Standard: Authorizations for uses and disclosures —*

(1) *Authorization required: General rule.* Except as otherwise permitted or required by this subchapter, a covered entity may not use or disclose protected health information without an authorization that is valid under this section. When a covered entity obtains or receives a valid authorization for its use or disclosure of protected health information, such use or disclosure must be consistent with such authorization.

(2) *Authorization required: Psychotherapy notes.* Notwithstanding any provision of this subpart, other than the transition provisions in § 164.532, a covered entity must obtain an authorization for any use or disclosure of psychotherapy notes, except:

(i) To carry out the following treatment, payment, or health care operations:

(A) Use by the originator of the psychotherapy notes for treatment;

(B) Use or disclosure by the covered entity for its own training programs in which students, trainees, or practitioners in mental health learn under supervision to practice or improve their skills in group, joint, family, or individual counseling; or

(C) Use or disclosure by the covered entity to defend itself in a legal action or other proceeding brought by the individual; and

(ii) A use or disclosure that is required by § 164.502(a)(2)(ii) or permitted by § 164.512(a); § 164.512(d) with respect to the oversight of the originator of the psychotherapy notes; § 164.512(g)(1); or § 164.512(j)(1)(i).

(3) *Authorization required: Marketing.*

(i) Notwithstanding any provision of this subpart, other than the transition provisions in § 164.532, a covered entity must obtain an authorization for any use or disclosure of protected health information for marketing, except if the communication is in the form of:

(A) A face-to-face communication made by a covered entity to an individual; or

(B) A promotional gift of nominal value provided by the covered entity.

(ii) If the marketing involves financial remuneration, as defined in paragraph (3) of the definition of marketing at § 164.501, to the covered entity from a third party, the authorization must state that such remuneration is involved.

(4) *Authorization required: Sale of protected health information.*

(i) Notwithstanding any provision of this subpart, other than the transition provisions in § 164.532, a covered entity must obtain an authorization for any disclosure of protected health information which is a sale of protected health information, as defined in § 164.501 of this subpart.

(ii) Such authorization must state that the disclosure will result in remuneration to the covered entity.

(b) *Implementation specifications: General requirements —*

(1) *Valid authorizations.*

(i) A valid authorization is a document that meets the requirements in paragraphs (a)(3)(ii), (a)(4)(ii), (c)(1), and (c)(2) of this section, as applicable.

(ii) A valid authorization may contain elements or information in addition to the elements required by this section, provided that such additional elements or information are not inconsistent with the elements required by this section.

(2) *Defective authorizations.* An authorization is not valid, if the document submitted has any of the following defects:

(i) The expiration date has passed or the expiration event is known by the covered entity to have occurred;

(ii) The authorization has not been filled out completely, with respect to an element described by paragraph (c) of this section, if applicable;

(iii) The authorization is known by the covered entity to have been revoked;

(iv) The authorization violates paragraph (b)(3) or (4) of this section, if applicable;

(v) Any material information in the authorization is known by the covered entity to be false.

(3) **Compound authorizations.** An authorization for use or disclosure of protected health information may not be combined with any other document to create a compound authorization, except as follows:

(i) An authorization for the use or disclosure of protected health information for a research study may be combined with any other type of written permission for the same or another research study. This exception includes combining an authorization for the use or disclosure of protected health information for a research study with another authorization for the same research study, with an authorization for the creation or maintenance of a research database or repository, or with a consent to participate in research. Where a covered health care provider has conditioned the provision of research-related treatment on the provision of one of the authorizations, as permitted under paragraph (b)(4)(i) of this section, any compound authorization created under this paragraph must clearly differentiate between the conditioned and unconditioned components and provide the individual with an opportunity to opt in to the research activities described in the unconditioned authorization.

(ii) An authorization for a use or disclosure of psychotherapy notes may only be combined with another authorization for a use or disclosure of psychotherapy notes.

(iii) An authorization under this section, other than an authorization for a use or disclosure of psychotherapy notes, may be combined with any other such authorization under this section, except when a covered entity has conditioned the provision of treatment, payment, enrollment in the health plan, or eligibility for benefits under paragraph (b)(4) of this section on the provision of one of the authorizations. The prohibition in this paragraph on combining authorizations where one authorization conditions the provision of treatment, payment, enrollment in a health plan, or eligibility for benefits under paragraph (b)(4) of this section does not apply to a compound authorization created in accordance with paragraph (b)(3)(i) of this section.

(4) **Prohibition on conditioning of authorizations.** A covered entity may not condition the provision to an individual of treatment, payment, enrollment in the health plan, or eligibility for benefits on the provision of an authorization, except:

(i) A covered health care provider may condition the provision of research-related treatment on provision of an authorization for the use or disclosure of protected health information for such research under this section;

(ii) A health plan may condition enrollment in the health plan or eligibility for benefits on provision of an authorization requested by the health plan prior to an individual's enrollment in the health plan, if:

(A) The authorization sought is for the health plan's eligibility or enrollment determinations relating to the individual or for its underwriting or risk rating determinations; and

(B) The authorization is not for a use or disclosure of psychotherapy notes under paragraph (a)(2) of this section; and

(iii) A covered entity may condition the provision of health care that is solely for the purpose of creating protected health information for disclosure to a third party on provision of an authorization for the disclosure of the protected health information to such third party.

(5) **Revocation of authorizations.** An individual may revoke an authorization provided under this section at any time, provided that the revocation is in writing, except to the extent that:

(i) The covered entity has taken action in reliance thereon; or

(ii) If the authorization was obtained as a condition of obtaining insurance coverage, other law provides the insurer with the right to contest a claim under the policy or the policy itself.

(6) **Documentation.** A covered entity must document and retain any signed authorization under this section as required by § 164.530(j).

(c) *Implementation specifications: Core elements and requirements —*

(1) **Core elements.** A valid authorization under this section must contain at least the following elements:

(i) A description of the information to be used or disclosed that identifies the information in a specific and meaningful fashion.

(ii) The name or other specific identification of the person(s), or class of persons, authorized to make the requested use or disclosure.

(iii) The name or other specific identification of the person(s), or class of persons, to whom the covered entity may make the requested use or disclosure.

(iv) A description of each purpose of the requested use or disclosure. The statement "at the request of the individual" is a sufficient description of the purpose when an individual initiates the authorization and does not, or elects not to, provide a statement of the purpose.

(v) An expiration date or an expiration event that relates to the individual or the purpose of the use or disclosure. The statement "end of the research study," "none," or similar language is sufficient if the authorization is for a use or disclosure of protected health information for research, including for the creation and maintenance of a research database or research repository.

(vi) Signature of the individual and date. If the authorization is signed by a personal representative of the individual, a description of such representative's authority to act for the individual must also be provided.

(2) **Required statements.** In addition to the core elements, the authorization must contain statements adequate to place the individual on notice of all of the following:

(i) The individual's right to revoke the authorization in writing, and either:

(A) The exceptions to the right to revoke and a description of how the individual may revoke the authorization; or

(B) To the extent that the information in paragraph (c)(2)(i)(A) of this section is included in the notice required by § 164.520, a reference to the covered entity's notice.

(ii) The ability or inability to condition treatment, payment, enrollment or eligibility for benefits on the authorization, by stating either:

(A) The covered entity may not condition treatment, payment, enrollment or eligibility for benefits on whether the individual signs the authorization when the prohibition on conditioning of authorizations in paragraph (b)(4) of this section applies; or

(B) The consequences to the individual of a refusal to sign the authorization when, in accordance with paragraph (b)(4) of this section, the covered entity can condition treatment, enrollment in the health plan, or eligibility for benefits on failure to obtain such authorization.

(iii) The potential for information disclosed pursuant to the authorization to be subject to redisclosure by the recipient and no longer be protected by this subpart.

(3) *Plain language requirement.* The authorization must be written in plain language.

(4) *Copy to the individual.* If a covered entity seeks an authorization from an individual for a use or disclosure of protected health information, the covered entity must provide the individual with a copy of the signed authorization.

[67 FR 53268, Aug. 14, 2002, as amended at 78 FR 5699, Jan. 25, 2013]

§ 164.510 Uses and disclosures requiring an opportunity for the individual to agree or to object.

A covered entity may use or disclose protected health information, provided that the individual is informed in advance of the use or disclosure and has the opportunity to agree to or prohibit or restrict the use or disclosure, in accordance with the applicable requirements of this section. The covered entity may orally inform the individual of and obtain the individual's oral agreement or objection to a use or disclosure permitted by this section.

(a) *Standard: Use and disclosure for facility directories* —

(1) *Permitted uses and disclosure.* Except when an objection is expressed in accordance with paragraphs (a)(2) or (3) of this section, a covered health care provider may:

(i) Use the following protected health information to maintain a directory of individuals in its facility:

(A) The individual's name;

(B) The individual's location in the covered health care provider's facility;

(C) The individual's condition described in general terms that does not communicate specific medical information about the individual; and

(D) The individual's religious affiliation; and

(ii) Use or disclose for directory purposes such information:

(A) To members of the clergy; or

(B) Except for religious affiliation, to other persons who ask for the individual by name.

(2) **Opportunity to object.** A covered health care provider must inform an individual of the protected health information that it may include in a directory and the persons to whom it may disclose such information (including disclosures to clergy of information regarding religious affiliation) and provide the individual with the opportunity to restrict or prohibit some or all of the uses or disclosures permitted by paragraph (a)(1) of this section.

(3) **Emergency circumstances.**

(i) If the opportunity to object to uses or disclosures required by paragraph (a)(2) of this section cannot practicably be provided because of the individual's incapacity or an emergency treatment circumstance, a covered health care provider may use or disclose some or all of the protected health information permitted by paragraph (a)(1) of this section for the facility's directory, if such disclosure is:

(A) Consistent with a prior expressed preference of the individual, if any, that is known to the covered health care provider; and

(B) In the individual's best interest as determined by the covered health care provider, in the exercise of professional judgment.

(ii) The covered health care provider must inform the individual and provide an opportunity to object to uses or disclosures for directory purposes as required by paragraph (a)(2) of this section when it becomes practicable to do so.

(b) **Standard: Uses and disclosures for involvement in the individual's care and notification purposes —**

(1) **Permitted uses and disclosures.**

(i) A covered entity may, in accordance with paragraphs (b)(2), (b)(3), or (b)(5) of this section, disclose to a family member, other relative, or a close personal friend of the individual, or any other person identified by the individual, the protected health information directly relevant to such person's involvement with the individual's health care or payment related to the individual's health care.

(ii) A covered entity may use or disclose protected health information to notify, or assist in the notification of (including identifying or locating), a family member, a personal representative of the individual, or another person responsible for the care of the individual of the individual's location, general condition, or death. Any such use or disclosure of protected health information for such notification purposes must be in accordance with paragraphs (b)(2), (b)(3), (b)(4), or (b)(5) of this section, as applicable.

(2) *Uses and disclosures with the individual present.* If the individual is present for, or otherwise available prior to, a use or disclosure permitted by paragraph (b)(1) of this section and has the capacity to make health care decisions, the covered entity may use or disclose the protected health information if it:

(i) Obtains the individual's agreement;

(ii) Provides the individual with the opportunity to object to the disclosure, and the individual does not express an objection; or

(iii) Reasonably infers from the circumstances, based on the exercise of professional judgment, that the individual does not object to the disclosure.

(3) *Limited uses and disclosures when the individual is not present.* If the individual is not present, or the opportunity to agree or object to the use or disclosure cannot practicably be provided because of the individual's incapacity or an emergency circumstance, the covered entity may, in the exercise of professional judgment, determine whether the disclosure is in the best interests of the individual and, if so, disclose only the protected health information that is directly relevant to the person's involvement with the individual's care or payment related to the individual's health care or needed for notification purposes. A covered entity may use professional judgment and its experience with common practice to make reasonable inferences of the individual's best interest in allowing a person to act on behalf of the individual to pick up filled prescriptions, medical supplies, X-rays, or other similar forms of protected health information.

(4) *Uses and disclosures for disaster relief purposes.* A covered entity may use or disclose protected health information to a public or private entity authorized by law or by its charter to assist in disaster relief efforts, for the purpose of coordinating with such entities the uses or disclosures permitted by paragraph (b)(1)(ii) of this section. The requirements in paragraphs (b)(2), (b)(3), or (b)(5) of this section apply to such uses and disclosures to the extent that the covered entity, in the exercise of professional judgment, determines that the requirements do not interfere with the ability to respond to the emergency circumstances.

(5) *Uses and disclosures when the individual is deceased.* If the individual is deceased, a covered entity may disclose to a family member, or other persons identified in paragraph (b)(1) of this section who were involved in the individual's care or payment for health care prior to the individual's death, protected health information of the individual that is relevant to such person's involvement, unless doing so is inconsistent with any prior expressed preference of the individual that is known to the covered entity.

[65 FR 82802, Dec. 28, 2000, as amended at 67 FR 53270, Aug. 14, 2002; 78 FR 5699, Jan. 25, 2013]

§ 164.512 Uses and disclosures for which an authorization or opportunity to agree or object is not required.

A covered entity may use or disclose protected health information without the written authorization of the individual, as described in § 164.508, or the opportunity for the individual to agree or object as described in § 164.510, in the situations covered by this section, subject to the applicable requirements of this section. When the covered entity is required by this section to inform the individual of, or when the individual may agree to, a use or disclosure permitted by this section, the covered entity's information and the individual's agreement may be given orally.

(a) **Standard: Uses and disclosures required by law.**

(1) A covered entity may use or disclose protected health information to the extent that such use or disclosure is required by law and the use or disclosure complies with and is limited to the relevant requirements of such law.

(2) A covered entity must meet the requirements described in paragraph (c), (e), or (f) of this section for uses or disclosures required by law.

(b) **Standard: Uses and disclosures for public health activities —**

(1) **Permitted uses and disclosures.** A covered entity may use or disclose protected health information for the public health activities and purposes described in this paragraph to:

(i) A public health authority that is authorized by law to collect or receive such information for the purpose of preventing or controlling disease, injury, or disability, including, but not limited to, the reporting of disease, injury, vital events such as birth or death, and the conduct of public health surveillance, public health investigations, and public health interventions; or, at the direction of a public health authority, to an official of a foreign government agency that is acting in collaboration with a public health authority;

(ii) A public health authority or other appropriate government authority authorized by law to receive reports of child abuse or neglect;

(iii) A person subject to the jurisdiction of the Food and Drug Administration (FDA) with respect to an FDA-regulated product or activity for which that person has responsibility, for the purpose of activities related to the quality, safety or effectiveness of such FDA-regulated product or activity. Such purposes include:

(A) To collect or report adverse events (or similar activities with respect to food or dietary supplements), product defects or problems (including problems with the use or labeling of a product), or biological product deviations;

(B) To track FDA-regulated products;

(C) To enable product recalls, repairs, or replacement, or lookback (including locating and notifying individuals who have received products that have been recalled, withdrawn, or are the subject of lookback); or

(D) To conduct post marketing surveillance;

(iv) A person who may have been exposed to a communicable disease or may otherwise be at risk of contracting or spreading a disease or condition, if the covered entity or public health authority is authorized by law to notify such person as necessary in the conduct of a public health intervention or investigation; or

(v) An employer, about an individual who is a member of the workforce of the employer, if:

(A) The covered entity is a covered health care provider who provides health care to the individual at the request of the employer:

    (*1*) To conduct an evaluation relating to medical surveillance of the workplace; or

    (*2*) To evaluate whether the individual has a work-related illness or injury;

(B) The protected health information that is disclosed consists of findings concerning a work-related illness or injury or a workplace-related medical surveillance;

(C) The employer needs such findings in order to comply with its obligations, under 29 CFR parts 1904 through 1928, 30 CFR parts 50 through 90, or under state law having a similar purpose, to record such illness or injury or to carry out responsibilities for workplace medical surveillance; and

(D) The covered health care provider provides written notice to the individual that protected health information relating to the medical surveillance of the workplace and work-related illnesses and injuries is disclosed to the employer:

    (*1*) By giving a copy of the notice to the individual at the time the health care is provided; or

    (*2*) If the health care is provided on the work site of the employer, by posting the notice in a prominent place at the location where the health care is provided.

(vi) A school, about an individual who is a student or prospective student of the school, if:

    (A) The protected health information that is disclosed is limited to proof of immunization;

    (B) The school is required by State or other law to have such proof of immunization prior to admitting the individual; and

    (C) The covered entity obtains and documents the agreement to the disclosure from either:

        (*1*) A parent, guardian, or other person acting *in loco parentis* of the individual, if the individual is an unemancipated minor; or

        (*2*) The individual, if the individual is an adult or emancipated minor.

(2) **Permitted uses.** If the covered entity also is a public health authority, the covered entity is permitted to use protected health information in all cases in which it is permitted to disclose such information for public health activities under paragraph (b)(1) of this section.

(c) **Standard: Disclosures about victims of abuse, neglect or domestic violence —**

(1) **Permitted disclosures.** Except for reports of child abuse or neglect permitted by paragraph (b)(1)(ii) of this section, a covered entity may disclose protected health information about an individual whom the covered entity reasonably believes to be a victim of abuse, neglect, or domestic violence to a government authority, including a social service or protective services agency, authorized by law to receive reports of such abuse, neglect, or domestic violence:

(i) To the extent the disclosure is required by law and the disclosure complies with and is limited to the relevant requirements of such law;

(ii) If the individual agrees to the disclosure; or

(iii) To the extent the disclosure is expressly authorized by statute or regulation and:

(A) The covered entity, in the exercise of professional judgment, believes the disclosure is necessary to prevent serious harm to the individual or other potential victims; or

(B) If the individual is unable to agree because of incapacity, a law enforcement or other public official authorized to receive the report represents that the protected health information for which disclosure is sought is not intended to be used against the individual and that an immediate enforcement activity that depends upon the disclosure would be materially and adversely affected by waiting until the individual is able to agree to the disclosure.

(2) **Informing the individual.** A covered entity that makes a disclosure permitted by paragraph (c)(1) of this section must promptly inform the individual that such a report has been or will be made, except if:

(i) The covered entity, in the exercise of professional judgment, believes informing the individual would place the individual at risk of serious harm; or

(ii) The covered entity would be informing a personal representative, and the covered entity reasonably believes the personal representative is responsible for the abuse, neglect, or other injury, and that informing such person would not be in the best interests of the individual as determined by the covered entity, in the exercise of professional judgment.

(d) **Standard: Uses and disclosures for health oversight activities —**

(1) **Permitted disclosures.** A covered entity may disclose protected health information to a health oversight agency for oversight activities authorized by law, including audits; civil, administrative, or criminal investigations; inspections; licensure or disciplinary actions; civil, administrative, or criminal proceedings or actions; or other activities necessary for appropriate oversight of:

(i) The health care system;

(ii) Government benefit programs for which health information is relevant to beneficiary eligibility;

(iii) Entities subject to government regulatory programs for which health information is necessary for determining compliance with program standards; or

(iv) Entities subject to civil rights laws for which health information is necessary for determining compliance.

(2) **Exception to health oversight activities.** For the purpose of the disclosures permitted by paragraph (d)(1) of this section, a health oversight activity does not include an investigation or

other activity in which the individual is the subject of the investigation or activity and such investigation or other activity does not arise out of and is not directly related to:

(i) The receipt of health care;

(ii) A claim for public benefits related to health; or

(iii) Qualification for, or receipt of, public benefits or services when a patient's health is integral to the claim for public benefits or services.

(3) *Joint activities or investigations.* Notwithstanding paragraph (d)(2) of this section, if a health oversight activity or investigation is conducted in conjunction with an oversight activity or investigation relating to a claim for public benefits not related to health, the joint activity or investigation is considered a health oversight activity for purposes of paragraph (d) of this section.

(4) *Permitted uses.* If a covered entity also is a health oversight agency, the covered entity may use protected health information for health oversight activities as permitted by paragraph (d) of this section.

(e) *Standard: Disclosures for judicial and administrative proceedings —*

(1) *Permitted disclosures.* A covered entity may disclose protected health information in the course of any judicial or administrative proceeding:

(i) In response to an order of a court or administrative tribunal, provided that the covered entity discloses only the protected health information expressly authorized by such order; or

(ii) In response to a subpoena, discovery request, or other lawful process, that is not accompanied by an order of a court or administrative tribunal, if:

(A) The covered entity receives satisfactory assurance, as described in paragraph (e)(1)(iii) of this section, from the party seeking the information that reasonable efforts have been made by such party to ensure that the individual who is the subject of the protected health information that has been requested has been given notice of the request; or

(B) The covered entity receives satisfactory assurance, as described in paragraph (e)(1)(iv) of this section, from the party seeking the information that reasonable efforts have been made by such party to secure a qualified protective order that meets the requirements of paragraph (e)(1)(v) of this section.

(iii) For the purposes of paragraph (e)(1)(ii)(A) of this section, a covered entity receives satisfactory assurances from a party seeking protected health information if the covered entity receives from such party a written statement and accompanying documentation demonstrating that:

(A) The party requesting such information has made a good faith attempt to provide written notice to the individual (or, if the individual's location is unknown, to mail a notice to the individual's last known address);

(B) The notice included sufficient information about the litigation or proceeding in which the protected health information is requested to permit the individual to raise an objection to the court or administrative tribunal; and

(C) The time for the individual to raise objections to the court or administrative tribunal has elapsed, and:

(1) No objections were filed; or

(2) All objections filed by the individual have been resolved by the court or the administrative tribunal and the disclosures being sought are consistent with such resolution.

(iv) For the purposes of paragraph (e)(1)(ii)(B) of this section, a covered entity receives satisfactory assurances from a party seeking protected health information, if the covered entity receives from such party a written statement and accompanying documentation demonstrating that:

(A) The parties to the dispute giving rise to the request for information have agreed to a qualified protective order and have presented it to the court or administrative tribunal with jurisdiction over the dispute; or

(B) The party seeking the protected health information has requested a qualified protective order from such court or administrative tribunal.

(v) For purposes of paragraph (e)(1) of this section, a qualified protective order means, with respect to protected health information requested under paragraph (e)(1)(ii) of this section, an order of a court or of an administrative tribunal or a stipulation by the parties to the litigation or administrative proceeding that:

(A) Prohibits the parties from using or disclosing the protected health information for any purpose other than the litigation or proceeding for which such information was requested; and

(B) Requires the return to the covered entity or destruction of the protected health information (including all copies made) at the end of the litigation or proceeding.

(vi) Notwithstanding paragraph (e)(1)(ii) of this section, a covered entity may disclose protected health information in response to lawful process described in paragraph (e)(1)(ii) of this section without receiving satisfactory assurance under paragraph (e)(1)(ii)(A) or (B) of this section, if the covered entity makes reasonable efforts to provide notice to the individual sufficient to meet the requirements of paragraph (e)(1)(iii) of this section or to seek a qualified protective order sufficient to meet the requirements of paragraph (e)(1)(v) of this section.

(2) **Other uses and disclosures under this section.** The provisions of this paragraph do not supersede other provisions of this section that otherwise permit or restrict uses or disclosures of protected health information.

(f) *Standard: Disclosures for law enforcement purposes.* A covered entity may disclose protected health information for a law enforcement purpose to a law enforcement official if the conditions in paragraphs (f)(1) through (f)(6) of this section are met, as applicable.

(1) *Permitted disclosures: Pursuant to process and as otherwise required by law.* A covered entity may disclose protected health information:

(i) As required by law including laws that require the reporting of certain types of wounds or other physical injuries, except for laws subject to paragraph (b)(1)(ii) or (c)(1)(i) of this section; or

(ii) In compliance with and as limited by the relevant requirements of:

(A) A court order or court-ordered warrant, or a subpoena or summons issued by a judicial officer;

(B) A grand jury subpoena; or

(C) An administrative request, including an administrative subpoena or summons, a civil or an authorized investigative demand, or similar process authorized under law, provided that:

(*1*) The information sought is relevant and material to a legitimate law enforcement inquiry;

(*2*) The request is specific and limited in scope to the extent reasonably practicable in light of the purpose for which the information is sought; and

(*3*) De-identified information could not reasonably be used.

(2) *Permitted disclosures: Limited information for identification and location purposes.* Except for disclosures required by law as permitted by paragraph (f)(1) of this section, a covered entity may disclose protected health information in response to a law enforcement official's request for such information for the purpose of identifying or locating a suspect, fugitive, material witness, or missing person, provided that:

(i) The covered entity may disclose only the following information:

(A) Name and address;

(B) Date and place of birth;

(C) Social security number;

(D) ABO blood type and rh factor;

(E) Type of injury;

(F) Date and time of treatment;

(G) Date and time of death, if applicable; and

(H) A description of distinguishing physical characteristics, including height, weight, gender, race, hair and eye color, presence or absence of facial hair (beard or moustache), scars, and tattoos.

(ii) Except as permitted by paragraph (f)(2)(i) of this section, the covered entity may not disclose for the purposes of identification or location under paragraph (f)(2) of this section any protected health information related to the individual's DNA or DNA analysis, dental records, or typing, samples or analysis of body fluids or tissue.

(3) *Permitted disclosure: Victims of a crime.* Except for disclosures required by law as permitted by paragraph (f)(1) of this section, a covered entity may disclose protected health information in response to a law enforcement official's request for such information about an individual who is or is suspected to be a victim of a crime, other than disclosures that are subject to paragraph (b) or (c) of this section, if:

(i) The individual agrees to the disclosure; or

(ii) The covered entity is unable to obtain the individual's agreement because of incapacity or other emergency circumstance, provided that:

(A) The law enforcement official represents that such information is needed to determine whether a violation of law by a person other than the victim has occurred, and such information is not intended to be used against the victim;

(B) The law enforcement official represents that immediate law enforcement activity that depends upon the disclosure would be materially and adversely affected by waiting until the individual is able to agree to the disclosure; and

(C) The disclosure is in the best interests of the individual as determined by the covered entity, in the exercise of professional judgment.

(4) *Permitted disclosure: Decedents.* A covered entity may disclose protected health information about an individual who has died to a law enforcement official for the purpose of alerting law enforcement of the death of the individual if the covered entity has a suspicion that such death may have resulted from criminal conduct.

(5) *Permitted disclosure: Crime on premises.* A covered entity may disclose to a law enforcement official protected health information that the covered entity believes in good faith constitutes evidence of criminal conduct that occurred on the premises of the covered entity.

(6) *Permitted disclosure: Reporting crime in emergencies.*

(i) A covered health care provider providing emergency health care in response to a medical emergency, other than such emergency on the premises of the covered health care provider, may disclose protected health information to a law enforcement official if such disclosure appears necessary to alert law enforcement to:

(A) The commission and nature of a crime;

(B) The location of such crime or of the victim(s) of such crime; and

(C) The identity, description, and location of the perpetrator of such crime.

(ii) If a covered health care provider believes that the medical emergency described in paragraph (f)(6)(i) of this section is the result of abuse, neglect, or domestic violence of the individual in need of emergency health care, paragraph (f)(6)(i) of this section does not apply and any disclosure to a law enforcement official for law enforcement purposes is subject to paragraph (c) of this section.

(g) **Standard: Uses and disclosures about decedents** —

(1) **Coroners and medical examiners.** A covered entity may disclose protected health information to a coroner or medical examiner for the purpose of identifying a deceased person, determining a cause of death, or other duties as authorized by law. A covered entity that also performs the duties of a coroner or medical examiner may use protected health information for the purposes described in this paragraph.

(2) **Funeral directors.** A covered entity may disclose protected health information to funeral directors, consistent with applicable law, as necessary to carry out their duties with respect to the decedent. If necessary for funeral directors to carry out their duties, the covered entity may disclose the protected health information prior to, and in reasonable anticipation of, the individual's death.

(h) **Standard: Uses and disclosures for cadaveric organ, eye or tissue donation purposes.** A covered entity may use or disclose protected health information to organ procurement organizations or other entities engaged in the procurement, banking, or transplantation of cadaveric organs, eyes, or tissue for the purpose of facilitating organ, eye or tissue donation and transplantation.

(i) **Standard: Uses and disclosures for research purposes** —

(1) **Permitted uses and disclosures.** A covered entity may use or disclose protected health information for research, regardless of the source of funding of the research, provided that:

(i) **Board approval of a waiver of authorization.** The covered entity obtains documentation that an alteration to or waiver, in whole or in part, of the individual authorization required by § 164.508 for use or disclosure of protected health information has been approved by either:

(A) An Institutional Review Board (IRB), established in accordance with 7 CFR lc.107, 10 CFR 745.107, 14 CFR 1230.107, 15 CFR 27.107, 16 CFR 1028.107, 21 CFR 56.107, 22 CFR 225.107, 24 CFR 60.107, 28 CFR 46.107, 32 CFR 219.107, 34 CFR 97.107, 38 CFR 16.107, 40 CFR 26.107, 45 CFR 46.107, 45 CFR 690.107, or 49 CFR 11.107; or

(B) A privacy board that:

(1) Has members with varying backgrounds and appropriate professional competency as necessary to review the effect of the research protocol on the individual's privacy rights and related interests;

(*2*) Includes at least one member who is not affiliated with the covered entity, not affiliated with any entity conducting or sponsoring the research, and not related to any person who is affiliated with any of such entities; and

(*3*) Does not have any member participating in a review of any project in which the member has a conflict of interest.

(ii) **Reviews preparatory to research.** The covered entity obtains from the researcher representations that:

(A) Use or disclosure is sought solely to review protected health information as necessary to prepare a research protocol or for similar purposes preparatory to research;

(B) No protected health information is to be removed from the covered entity by the researcher in the course of the review; and

(C) The protected health information for which use or access is sought is necessary for the research purposes.

(iii) **Research on decedent's information.** The covered entity obtains from the researcher:

(A) Representation that the use or disclosure sought is solely for research on the protected health information of decedents;

(B) Documentation, at the request of the covered entity, of the death of such individuals; and

(C) Representation that the protected health information for which use or disclosure is sought is necessary for the research purposes.

(2) **Documentation of waiver approval.** For a use or disclosure to be permitted based on documentation of approval of an alteration or waiver, under paragraph (i)(1)(i) of this section, the documentation must include all of the following:

(i) **Identification and date of action.** A statement identifying the IRB or privacy board and the date on which the alteration or waiver of authorization was approved;

(ii) **Waiver criteria.** A statement that the IRB or privacy board has determined that the alteration or waiver, in whole or in part, of authorization satisfies the following criteria:

(A) The use or disclosure of protected health information involves no more than a minimal risk to the privacy of individuals, based on, at least, the presence of the following elements;

(*1*) An adequate plan to protect the identifiers from improper use and disclosure;

(*2*) An adequate plan to destroy the identifiers at the earliest opportunity consistent with conduct of the research, unless there is a health or research justification for retaining the identifiers or such retention is otherwise required by law; and

(*3*) Adequate written assurances that the protected health information will not be reused or disclosed to any other person or entity, except as required by law, for authorized oversight of the research study, or for other research for which the use or disclosure of protected health information would be permitted by this subpart;

(B) The research could not practicably be conducted without the waiver or alteration; and

(C) The research could not practicably be conducted without access to and use of the protected health information.

(iii) *Protected health information needed.* A brief description of the protected health information for which use or access has been determined to be necessary by the institutional review board or privacy board, pursuant to paragraph (i)(2)(ii)(C) of this section;

(iv) *Review and approval procedures.* A statement that the alteration or waiver of authorization has been reviewed and approved under either normal or expedited review procedures, as follows:

(A) An IRB must follow the requirements of the Common Rule, including the normal review procedures (7 CFR 1c.108(b), 10 CFR 745.108(b), 14 CFR 1230.108(b), 15 CFR 27.108(b), 16 CFR 1028.108(b), 21 CFR 56.108(b), 22 CFR 225.108(b), 24 CFR 60.108(b), 28 CFR 46.108(b), 32 CFR 219.108(b), 34 CFR 97.108(b), 38 CFR 16.108(b), 40 CFR 26.108(b), 45 CFR 46.108(b), 45 CFR 690.108(b), or 49 CFR 11.108(b)) or the expedited review procedures (7 CFR 1c.110, 10 CFR 745.110, 14 CFR 1230.110, 15 CFR 27.110, 16 CFR 1028.110, 21 CFR 56.110, 22 CFR 225.110, 24 CFR 60.110, 28 CFR 46.110, 32 CFR 219.110, 34 CFR 97.110, 38 CFR 16.110, 40 CFR 26.110, 45 CFR 46.110, 45 CFR 690.110, or 49 CFR 11.110);

(B) A privacy board must review the proposed research at convened meetings at which a majority of the privacy board members are present, including at least one member who satisfies the criterion stated in paragraph (i)(1)(i)(B)(2) of this section, and the alteration or waiver of authorization must be approved by the majority of the privacy board members present at the meeting, unless the privacy board elects to use an expedited review procedure in accordance with paragraph (i)(2)(iv)(C) of this section;

(C) A privacy board may use an expedited review procedure if the research involves no more than minimal risk to the privacy of the individuals who are the subject of the protected health information for which use or disclosure is being sought. If the privacy board elects to use an expedited review procedure, the review and approval of the alteration or waiver of authorization may be carried out by the chair of the privacy board, or by one or more members of the privacy board as designated by the chair; and

(v) *Required signature.* The documentation of the alteration or waiver of authorization must be signed by the chair or other member, as designated by the chair, of the IRB or the privacy board, as applicable.

(j) *Standard: Uses and disclosures to avert a serious threat to health or safety* —

(1) *Permitted disclosures.* A covered entity may, consistent with applicable law and standards of ethical conduct, use or disclose protected health information, if the covered entity, in good faith, believes the use or disclosure:

(i)

(A) Is necessary to prevent or lessen a serious and imminent threat to the health or safety of a person or the public; and

(B) Is to a person or persons reasonably able to prevent or lessen the threat, including the target of the threat; or

(ii) Is necessary for law enforcement authorities to identify or apprehend an individual:

(A) Because of a statement by an individual admitting participation in a violent crime that the covered entity reasonably believes may have caused serious physical harm to the victim; or

(B) Where it appears from all the circumstances that the individual has escaped from a correctional institution or from lawful custody, as those terms are defined in § 164.501.

(2) **Use or disclosure not permitted.** A use or disclosure pursuant to paragraph (j)(1)(ii)(A) of this section may not be made if the information described in paragraph (j)(1)(ii)(A) of this section is learned by the covered entity:

(i) In the course of treatment to affect the propensity to commit the criminal conduct that is the basis for the disclosure under paragraph (j)(1)(ii)(A) of this section, or counseling or therapy; or

(ii) Through a request by the individual to initiate or to be referred for the treatment, counseling, or therapy described in paragraph (j)(2)(i) of this section.

(3) **Limit on information that may be disclosed.** A disclosure made pursuant to paragraph (j)(1)(ii)(A) of this section shall contain only the statement described in paragraph (j)(1)(ii)(A) of this section and the protected health information described in paragraph (f)(2)(i) of this section.

(4) **Presumption of good faith belief.** A covered entity that uses or discloses protected health information pursuant to paragraph (j)(1) of this section is presumed to have acted in good faith with regard to a belief described in paragraph (j)(1)(i) or (ii) of this section, if the belief is based upon the covered entity's actual knowledge or in reliance on a credible representation by a person with apparent knowledge or authority.

(k) **Standard: Uses and disclosures for specialized government functions —**

(1) **Military and veterans activities —**

(i) **Armed Forces personnel.** A covered entity may use and disclose the protected health information of individuals who are Armed Forces personnel for activities deemed necessary by appropriate military command authorities to assure the proper execution of the military mission, if the appropriate military authority has published by notice in the Federal Register the following information:

(A) Appropriate military command authorities; and

(B) The purposes for which the protected health information may be used or disclosed.

(ii) *Separation or discharge from military service.* A covered entity that is a component of the Departments of Defense or Homeland Security may disclose to the Department of Veterans Affairs (DVA) the protected health information of an individual who is a member of the Armed Forces upon the separation or discharge of the individual from military service for the purpose of a determination by DVA of the individual's eligibility for or entitlement to benefits under laws administered by the Secretary of Veterans Affairs.

(iii) *Veterans.* A covered entity that is a component of the Department of Veterans Affairs may use and disclose protected health information to components of the Department that determine eligibility for or entitlement to, or that provide, benefits under the laws administered by the Secretary of Veterans Affairs.

(iv) *Foreign military personnel.* A covered entity may use and disclose the protected health information of individuals who are foreign military personnel to their appropriate foreign military authority for the same purposes for which uses and disclosures are permitted for Armed Forces personnel under the notice published in the Federal Register pursuant to paragraph (k)(1)(i) of this section.

(2) *National security and intelligence activities.* A covered entity may disclose protected health information to authorized federal officials for the conduct of lawful intelligence, counter-intelligence, and other national security activities authorized by the National Security Act (50 U.S.C. 401, *et seq.*) and implementing authority (*e.g.,* Executive Order 12333).

(3) *Protective services for the President and others.* A covered entity may disclose protected health information to authorized Federal officials for the provision of protective services to the President or other persons authorized by 18 U.S.C. 3056 or to foreign heads of state or other persons authorized by 22 U.S.C. 2709(a)(3), or for the conduct of investigations authorized by 18 U.S.C. 871 and 879.

(4) *Medical suitability determinations.* A covered entity that is a component of the Department of State may use protected health information to make medical suitability determinations and may disclose whether or not the individual was determined to be medically suitable to the officials in the Department of State who need access to such information for the following purposes:

(i) For the purpose of a required security clearance conducted pursuant to Executive Orders 10450 and 12968;

(ii) As necessary to determine worldwide availability or availability for mandatory service abroad under sections 101(a)(4) and 504 of the Foreign Service Act; or

(iii) For a family to accompany a Foreign Service member abroad, consistent with section 101(b)(5) and 904 of the Foreign Service Act.

(5) *Correctional institutions and other law enforcement custodial situations —*

(i) *Permitted disclosures.* A covered entity may disclose to a correctional institution or a law enforcement official having lawful custody of an inmate or other individual protected health information about such inmate or individual, if the correctional institution or such law enforcement official represents that such protected health information is necessary for:

(A) The provision of health care to such individuals;

(B) The health and safety of such individual or other inmates;

(C) The health and safety of the officers or employees of or others at the correctional institution;

(D) The health and safety of such individuals and officers or other persons responsible for the transporting of inmates or their transfer from one institution, facility, or setting to another;

(E) Law enforcement on the premises of the correctional institution; or

(F) The administration and maintenance of the safety, security, and good order of the correctional institution.

(ii) *Permitted uses.* A covered entity that is a correctional institution may use protected health information of individuals who are inmates for any purpose for which such protected health information may be disclosed.

(iii) *No application after release.* For the purposes of this provision, an individual is no longer an inmate when released on parole, probation, supervised release, or otherwise is no longer in lawful custody.

(6) *Covered entities that are government programs providing public benefits.*

(i) A health plan that is a government program providing public benefits may disclose protected health information relating to eligibility for or enrollment in the health plan to another agency administering a government program providing public benefits if the sharing of eligibility or enrollment information among such government agencies or the maintenance of such information in a single or combined data system accessible to all such government agencies is required or expressly authorized by statute or regulation.

(ii) A covered entity that is a government agency administering a government program providing public benefits may disclose protected health information relating to the program to another covered entity that is a government agency administering a government program providing public benefits if the programs serve the same or similar populations and the disclosure of protected health information is necessary to coordinate the covered functions of such programs or to improve administration and management relating to the covered functions of such programs.

(7) *National Instant Criminal Background Check System.* A covered entity may use or disclose protected health information for purposes of reporting to the National Instant Criminal Background Check System the identity of an individual who is prohibited from possessing a firearm under 18 U.S.C. 922(g)(4), provided the covered entity:

(i) Is a State agency or other entity that is, or contains an entity that is:

(A) An entity designated by the State to report, or which collects information for purposes of reporting, on behalf of the State, to the National Instant Criminal Background Check System; or

(B) A court, board, commission, or other lawful authority that makes the commitment or adjudication that causes an individual to become subject to 18 U.S.C. 922(g)(4); and

(ii) Discloses the information only to:

(A) The National Instant Criminal Background Check System; or

(B) An entity designated by the State to report, or which collects information for purposes of reporting, on behalf of the State, to the National Instant Criminal Background Check System; and

(iii)

(A) Discloses only the limited demographic and certain other information needed for purposes of reporting to the National Instant Criminal Background Check System; and

(B) Does not disclose diagnostic or clinical information for such purposes.

(l) *Standard: Disclosures for workers' compensation.* A covered entity may disclose protected health information as authorized by and to the extent necessary to comply with laws relating to workers' compensation or other similar programs, established by law, that provide benefits for work-related injuries or illness without regard to fault.

[65 FR 82802, Dec. 28, 2000, as amended at 67 FR 53270, Aug. 14, 2002; 78 FR 5699, Jan. 25, 2013; 78 FR 34266, June 7, 2013; 81 FR 395, Jan. 6, 2016]

§ 164.514 Other requirements relating to uses and disclosures of protected health information.

(a) *Standard: De-identification of protected health information.* Health information that does not identify an individual and with respect to which there is no reasonable basis to believe that the information can be used to identify an individual is not individually identifiable health information.

(b) *Implementation specifications: Requirements for de-identification of protected health information.* A covered entity may determine that health information is not individually identifiable health information only if:

(1) A person with appropriate knowledge of and experience with generally accepted statistical and scientific principles and methods for rendering information not individually identifiable:

(i) Applying such principles and methods, determines that the risk is very small that the information could be used, alone or in combination with other reasonably available information, by an anticipated recipient to identify an individual who is a subject of the information; and

(ii) Documents the methods and results of the analysis that justify such determination; or

(2)

(i) The following identifiers of the individual or of relatives, employers, or household members of the individual, are removed:

(A) Names;

(B) All geographic subdivisions smaller than a State, including street address, city, county, precinct, zip code, and their equivalent geocodes, except for the initial three digits of a zip code if, according to the current publicly available data from the Bureau of the Census:

(1) The geographic unit formed by combining all zip codes with the same three initial digits contains more than 20,000 people; and

(2) The initial three digits of a zip code for all such geographic units containing 20,000 or fewer people is changed to 000.

(C) All elements of dates (except year) for dates directly related to an individual, including birth date, admission date, discharge date, date of death; and all ages over 89 and all elements of dates (including year) indicative of such age, except that such ages and elements may be aggregated into a single category of age 90 or older;

(D) Telephone numbers;

(E) Fax numbers;

(F) Electronic mail addresses;

(G) Social security numbers;

(H) Medical record numbers;

(I) Health plan beneficiary numbers;

(J) Account numbers;

(K) Certificate/license numbers;

(L) Vehicle identifiers and serial numbers, including license plate numbers;

(M) Device identifiers and serial numbers;

(N) Web Universal Resource Locators (URLs);

(O) Internet Protocol (IP) address numbers;

(P) Biometric identifiers, including finger and voice prints;

(Q) Full face photographic images and any comparable images; and

(R) Any other unique identifying number, characteristic, or code, except as permitted by paragraph (c) of this section; and

(ii) The covered entity does not have actual knowledge that the information could be used alone or in combination with other information to identify an individual who is a subject of the information.

(c) **Implementation specifications: Re-identification.** A covered entity may assign a code or other means of record identification to allow information de-identified under this section to be re-identified by the covered entity, provided that:

(1) **Derivation.** The code or other means of record identification is not derived from or related to information about the individual and is not otherwise capable of being translated so as to identify the individual; and

(2) **Security.** The covered entity does not use or disclose the code or other means of record identification for any other purpose, and does not disclose the mechanism for re-identification.

(d)

(1) **Standard: minimum necessary requirements.** In order to comply with § 164.502(b) and this section, a covered entity must meet the requirements of paragraphs (d)(2) through (d)(5) of this section with respect to a request for, or the use and disclosure of, protected health information.

(2) **Implementation specifications: Minimum necessary uses of protected health information.**

(i) A covered entity must identify:

(A) Those persons or classes of persons, as appropriate, in its workforce who need access to protected health information to carry out their duties; and

(B) For each such person or class of persons, the category or categories of protected health information to which access is needed and any conditions appropriate to such access.

(ii) A covered entity must make reasonable efforts to limit the access of such persons or classes identified in paragraph (d)(2)(i)(A) of this section to protected health information consistent with paragraph (d)(2)(i)(B) of this section.

(3) **Implementation specification: Minimum necessary disclosures of protected health information.**

(i) For any type of disclosure that it makes on a routine and recurring basis, a covered entity must implement policies and procedures (which may be standard protocols) that limit the protected health information disclosed to the amount reasonably necessary to achieve the purpose of the disclosure.

(ii) For all other disclosures, a covered entity must:

(A) Develop criteria designed to limit the protected health information disclosed to the information reasonably necessary to accomplish the purpose for which disclosure is sought; and

(B) Review requests for disclosure on an individual basis in accordance with such criteria.

(iii) A covered entity may rely, if such reliance is reasonable under the circumstances, on a requested disclosure as the minimum necessary for the stated purpose when:

(A) Making disclosures to public officials that are permitted under § 164.512, if the public official represents that the information requested is the minimum necessary for the stated purpose(s);

(B) The information is requested by another covered entity;

(C) The information is requested by a professional who is a member of its workforce or is a business associate of the covered entity for the purpose of providing professional services to the covered entity, if the professional represents that the information requested is the minimum necessary for the stated purpose(s); or

(D) Documentation or representations that comply with the applicable requirements of § 164.512(i) have been provided by a person requesting the information for research purposes.

(4) *Implementation specifications: Minimum necessary requests for protected health information.*

(i) A covered entity must limit any request for protected health information to that which is reasonably necessary to accomplish the purpose for which the request is made, when requesting such information from other covered entities.

(ii) For a request that is made on a routine and recurring basis, a covered entity must implement policies and procedures (which may be standard protocols) that limit the protected health information requested to the amount reasonably necessary to accomplish the purpose for which the request is made.

(iii) For all other requests, a covered entity must:

(A) Develop criteria designed to limit the request for protected health information to the information reasonably necessary to accomplish the purpose for which the request is made; and

(B) Review requests for disclosure on an individual basis in accordance with such criteria.

(5) *Implementation specification: Other content requirement.* For all uses, disclosures, or requests to which the requirements in paragraph (d) of this section apply, a covered entity may not use, disclose or request an entire medical record, except when the entire medical record is

specifically justified as the amount that is reasonably necessary to accomplish the purpose of the use, disclosure, or request.

(e)

(1) **Standard: Limited data set.** A covered entity may use or disclose a limited data set that meets the requirements of paragraphs (e)(2) and (e)(3) of this section, if the covered entity enters into a data use agreement with the limited data set recipient, in accordance with paragraph (e)(4) of this section.

(2) *Implementation specification: Limited data set:* A limited data set is protected health information that excludes the following direct identifiers of the individual or of relatives, employers, or household members of the individual:

(i) Names;

(ii) Postal address information, other than town or city, State, and zip code;

(iii) Telephone numbers;

(iv) Fax numbers;

(v) Electronic mail addresses;

(vi) Social security numbers;

(vii) Medical record numbers;

(viii) Health plan beneficiary numbers;

(ix) Account numbers;

(x) Certificate/license numbers;

(xi) Vehicle identifiers and serial numbers, including license plate numbers;

(xii) Device identifiers and serial numbers;

(xiii) Web Universal Resource Locators (URLs);

(xiv) Internet Protocol (IP) address numbers;

(xv) Biometric identifiers, including finger and voice prints; and

(xvi) Full face photographic images and any comparable images.

(3) *Implementation specification: Permitted purposes for uses and disclosures.*

(i) A covered entity may use or disclose a limited data set under paragraph (e)(1) of this section only for the purposes of research, public health, or health care operations.

(ii) A covered entity may use protected health information to create a limited data set that meets the requirements of paragraph (e)(2) of this section, or disclose protected health information only to a business associate for such purpose, whether or not the limited data set is to be used by the covered entity.

(4) *Implementation specifications: Data use agreement —*

(i) *Agreement required.* A covered entity may use or disclose a limited data set under paragraph (e)(1) of this section only if the covered entity obtains satisfactory assurance, in the form of a data use agreement that meets the requirements of this section, that the limited data set recipient will only use or disclose the protected health information for limited purposes.

(ii) *Contents.* A data use agreement between the covered entity and the limited data set recipient must:

(A) Establish the permitted uses and disclosures of such information by the limited data set recipient, consistent with paragraph (e)(3) of this section. The data use agreement may not authorize the limited data set recipient to use or further disclose the information in a manner that would violate the requirements of this subpart, if done by the covered entity;

(B) Establish who is permitted to use or receive the limited data set; and

(C) Provide that the limited data set recipient will:

(*1*) Not use or further disclose the information other than as permitted by the data use agreement or as otherwise required by law;

(*2*) Use appropriate safeguards to prevent use or disclosure of the information other than as provided for by the data use agreement;

(*3*) Report to the covered entity any use or disclosure of the information not provided for by its data use agreement of which it becomes aware;

(*4*) Ensure that any agents to whom it provides the limited data set agree to the same restrictions and conditions that apply to the limited data set recipient with respect to such information; and

(*5*) Not identify the information or contact the individuals.

(iii) *Compliance.*

(A) A covered entity is not in compliance with the standards in paragraph (e) of this section if the covered entity knew of a pattern of activity or practice of the limited data set recipient that constituted a material breach or violation of the data use agreement, unless the covered entity took reasonable steps to cure the breach or end the violation, as applicable, and, if such steps were unsuccessful:

(1) Discontinued disclosure of protected health information to the recipient; and

(2) Reported the problem to the Secretary.

(B) A covered entity that is a limited data set recipient and violates a data use agreement will be in noncompliance with the standards, implementation specifications, and requirements of paragraph (e) of this section.

(f) *Fundraising communications —*

(1) **Standard: Uses and disclosures for fundraising.** Subject to the conditions of paragraph (f)(2) of this section, a covered entity may use, or disclose to a business associate or to an institutionally related foundation, the following protected health information for the purpose of raising funds for its own benefit, without an authorization meeting the requirements of § 164.508:

(i) Demographic information relating to an individual, including name, address, other contact information, age, gender, and date of birth;

(ii) Dates of health care provided to an individual;

(iii) Department of service information;

(iv) Treating physician;

(v) Outcome information; and

(vi) Health insurance status.

(2) **Implementation specifications: Fundraising requirements.**

(i) A covered entity may not use or disclose protected health information for fundraising purposes as otherwise permitted by paragraph (f)(1) of this section unless a statement required by § 164.520(b)(1)(iii)(A) is included in the covered entity's notice of privacy practices.

(ii) With each fundraising communication made to an individual under this paragraph, a covered entity must provide the individual with a clear and conspicuous opportunity to elect not to receive any further fundraising communications. The method for an individual to elect not to receive further fundraising communications may not cause the individual to incur an undue burden or more than a nominal cost.

(iii) A covered entity may not condition treatment or payment on the individual's choice with respect to the receipt of fundraising communications.

(iv) A covered entity may not make fundraising communications to an individual under this paragraph where the individual has elected not to receive such communications under paragraph (f)(2)(ii) of this section.

(v) A covered entity may provide an individual who has elected not to receive further fundraising communications with a method to opt back in to receive such communications.

(g) **Standard: Uses and disclosures for underwriting and related purposes.** If a health plan receives protected health information for the purpose of underwriting, premium rating, or other activities relating to the creation, renewal, or replacement of a contract of health insurance or health benefits, and if such health insurance or health benefits are not placed with the health plan, such health plan may only use or disclose such protected health information for such purpose or as may be required by law, subject to the prohibition at § 164.502(a)(5)(i) with respect to genetic information included in the protected health information.

(h)

    (1) **Standard: Verification requirements.** Prior to any disclosure permitted by this subpart, a covered entity must:

        (i) Except with respect to disclosures under § 164.510, verify the identity of a person requesting protected health information and the authority of any such person to have access to protected health information under this subpart, if the identity or any such authority of such person is not known to the covered entity; and

        (ii) Obtain any documentation, statements, or representations, whether oral or written, from the person requesting the protected health information when such documentation, statement, or representation is a condition of the disclosure under this subpart.

    (2) **Implementation specifications: Verification —**

        (i) **Conditions on disclosures.** If a disclosure is conditioned by this subpart on particular documentation, statements, or representations from the person requesting the protected health information, a covered entity may rely, if such reliance is reasonable under the circumstances, on documentation, statements, or representations that, on their face, meet the applicable requirements.

            (A) The conditions in § 164.512(f)(1)(ii)(C) may be satisfied by the administrative subpoena or similar process or by a separate written statement that, on its face, demonstrates that the applicable requirements have been met.

            (B) The documentation required by § 164.512(i)(2) may be satisfied by one or more written statements, provided that each is appropriately dated and signed in accordance with § 164.512(i)(2)(i) and (v).

        (ii) **Identity of public officials.** A covered entity may rely, if such reliance is reasonable under the circumstances, on any of the following to verify identity when the disclosure of protected health information is to a public official or a person acting on behalf of the public official:

            (A) If the request is made in person, presentation of an agency identification badge, other official credentials, or other proof of government status;

            (B) If the request is in writing, the request is on the appropriate government letterhead; or

            (C) If the disclosure is to a person acting on behalf of a public official, a written statement on appropriate government letterhead that the person is acting under the government's authority or other evidence or documentation of agency, such as a contract for services, memorandum of understanding, or purchase order, that establishes that the person is acting on behalf of the public official.

(iii) *Authority of public officials.* A covered entity may rely, if such reliance is reasonable under the circumstances, on any of the following to verify authority when the disclosure of protected health information is to a public official or a person acting on behalf of the public official:

(A) A written statement of the legal authority under which the information is requested, or, if a written statement would be impracticable, an oral statement of such legal authority;

(B) If a request is made pursuant to legal process, warrant, subpoena, order, or other legal process issued by a grand jury or a judicial or administrative tribunal is presumed to constitute legal authority.

(iv) *Exercise of professional judgment.* The verification requirements of this paragraph are met if the covered entity relies on the exercise of professional judgment in making a use or disclosure in accordance with § 164.510 or acts on a good faith belief in making a disclosure in accordance with § 164.512(j).

[65 FR 82802, Dec. 28, 2000, as amended at 67 FR 53270, Aug. 14, 2002; 78 FR 5700, Jan. 25, 2013; 78 FR 34266, June 7, 2013]

§ 164.520 Notice of privacy practices for protected health information.

(a) *Standard: Notice of privacy practices —*

(1) *Right to notice.* Except as provided by paragraph (a)(2) or (3) of this section, an individual has a right to adequate notice of the uses and disclosures of protected health information that may be made by the covered entity, and of the individual's rights and the covered entity's legal duties with respect to protected health information.

(2) *Exception for group health plans.*

(i) An individual enrolled in a group health plan has a right to notice:

(A) From the group health plan, if, and to the extent that, such an individual does not receive health benefits under the group health plan through an insurance contract with a health insurance issuer or HMO; or

(B) From the health insurance issuer or HMO with respect to the group health plan through which such individuals receive their health benefits under the group health plan.

(ii) A group health plan that provides health benefits solely through an insurance contract with a health insurance issuer or HMO, and that creates or receives protected health information in addition to summary health information as defined in § 164.504(a) or information on whether the individual is participating in the group health plan, or is enrolled in or has disenrolled from a health insurance issuer or HMO offered by the plan, must:

(A) Maintain a notice under this section; and

(B) Provide such notice upon request to any person. The provisions of paragraph (c)(1) of this section do not apply to such group health plan.

(iii) A group health plan that provides health benefits solely through an insurance contract with a health insurance issuer or HMO, and does not create or receive protected health information other than summary health information as defined in § 164.504(a) or information on whether an individual is participating in the group health plan, or is enrolled in or has disenrolled from a health insurance issuer or HMO offered by the plan, is not required to maintain or provide a notice under this section.

(3) **Exception for inmates.** An inmate does not have a right to notice under this section, and the requirements of this section do not apply to a correctional institution that is a covered entity.

(b) **Implementation specifications: Content of notice —**

(1) **Required elements.** The covered entity must provide a notice that is written in plain language and that contains the elements required by this paragraph.

(i) **Header.** The notice must contain the following statement as a header or otherwise prominently displayed:

"THIS NOTICE DESCRIBES HOW MEDICAL INFORMATION ABOUT YOU MAY BE USED AND DISCLOSED AND HOW YOU CAN GET ACCESS TO THIS INFORMATION. PLEASE REVIEW IT CAREFULLY."

(ii) **Uses and disclosures.** The notice must contain:

(A) A description, including at least one example, of the types of uses and disclosures that the covered entity is permitted by this subpart to make for each of the following purposes: treatment, payment, and health care operations.

(B) A description of each of the other purposes for which the covered entity is permitted or required by this subpart to use or disclose protected health information without the individual's written authorization.

(C) If a use or disclosure for any purpose described in paragraphs (b)(1)(ii)(A) or (B) of this section is prohibited or materially limited by other applicable law, the description of such use or disclosure must reflect the more stringent law as defined in § 160.202 of this subchapter.

(D) For each purpose described in paragraph (b)(1)(ii)(A) or (B) of this section, the description must include sufficient detail to place the individual on notice of the uses and disclosures that are permitted or required by this subpart and other applicable law.

(E) A description of the types of uses and disclosures that require an authorization under § 164.508(a)(2)–(a)(4), a statement that other uses and disclosures not described in the notice will be made only with the individual's written authorization, and a statement that the individual may revoke an authorization as provided by § 164.508(b)(5).

(iii) **Separate statements for certain uses or disclosures.** If the covered entity intends to engage in any of the following activities, the description required by paragraph (b)(1)(ii)(A) of this section must include a separate statement informing the individual of such activities, as applicable:

(A) In accordance with § 164.514(f)(1), the covered entity may contact the individual to raise funds for the covered entity and the individual has a right to opt out of receiving such communications;

(B) In accordance with § 164.504(f), the group health plan, or a health insurance issuer or HMO with respect to a group health plan, may disclose protected health information to the sponsor of the plan; or

(C) If a covered entity that is a health plan, excluding an issuer of a long-term care policy falling within paragraph (1)(viii) of the definition of *health plan,* intends to use or disclose protected health information for underwriting purposes, a statement that the covered entity is prohibited from using or disclosing protected health information that is genetic information of an individual for such purposes.

(iv) **Individual rights.** The notice must contain a statement of the individual's rights with respect to protected health information and a brief description of how the individual may exercise these rights, as follows:

(A) The right to request restrictions on certain uses and disclosures of protected health information as provided by § 164.522(a), including a statement that the covered entity is not required to agree to a requested restriction, except in case of a disclosure restricted under § 164.522(a)(1)

(B) The right to receive confidential communications of protected health information as provided by § 164.522(b), as applicable;

(C) The right to inspect and copy protected health information as provided by § 164.524;

(D) The right to amend protected health information as provided by § 164.526;

(E) The right to receive an accounting of disclosures of protected health information as provided by § 164.528; and

(F) The right of an individual, including an individual who has agreed to receive the notice electronically in accordance with paragraph (c)(3) of this section, to obtain a paper copy of the notice from the covered entity upon request.

(v) **Covered entity's duties.** The notice must contain:

(A) A statement that the covered entity is required by law to maintain the privacy of protected health information, to provide individuals with notice of its legal duties and privacy practices with respect to protected health information, and to notify affected individuals following a breach of unsecured protected health information;

(B) A statement that the covered entity is required to abide by the terms of the notice currently in effect; and

(C) For the covered entity to apply a change in a privacy practice that is described in the notice to protected health information that the covered entity created or received prior to issuing a revised notice, in accordance with § 164.530(i)(2)(ii), a statement that it reserves the right to change the terms of its notice and to make the new notice provisions effective for all protected health information that it maintains. The statement must also describe how it will provide individuals with a revised notice.

(vi) *Complaints.* The notice must contain a statement that individuals may complain to the covered entity and to the Secretary if they believe their privacy rights have been violated, a brief description of how the individual may file a complaint with the covered entity, and a statement that the individual will not be retaliated against for filing a complaint.

(vii) *Contact.* The notice must contain the name, or title, and telephone number of a person or office to contact for further information as required by § 164.530(a)(1)(ii).

(viii) *Effective date.* The notice must contain the date on which the notice is first in effect, which may not be earlier than the date on which the notice is printed or otherwise published.

(2) *Optional elements.*

(i) In addition to the information required by paragraph (b)(1) of this section, if a covered entity elects to limit the uses or disclosures that it is permitted to make under this subpart, the covered entity may describe its more limited uses or disclosures in its notice, provided that the covered entity may not include in its notice a limitation affecting its right to make a use or disclosure that is required by law or permitted by § 164.512(j)(1)(i).

(ii) For the covered entity to apply a change in its more limited uses and disclosures to protected health information created or received prior to issuing a revised notice, in accordance with § 164.530(i)(2)(ii), the notice must include the statements required by paragraph (b)(1)(v)(C) of this section.

(3) *Revisions to the notice.* The covered entity must promptly revise and distribute its notice whenever there is a material change to the uses or disclosures, the individual's rights, the covered entity's legal duties, or other privacy practices stated in the notice. Except when required by law, a material change to any term of the notice may not be implemented prior to the effective date of the notice in which such material change is reflected.

(c) *Implementation specifications: Provision of notice.* A covered entity must make the notice required by this section available on request to any person and to individuals as specified in paragraphs (c)(1) through (c)(3) of this section, as applicable.

(1) *Specific requirements for health plans.*

(i) A health plan must provide the notice:

(A) No later than the compliance date for the health plan, to individuals then covered by the plan;

(B) Thereafter, at the time of enrollment, to individuals who are new enrollees.

(ii) No less frequently than once every three years, the health plan must notify individuals then covered by the plan of the availability of the notice and how to obtain the notice.

(iii) The health plan satisfies the requirements of paragraph (c)(1) of this section if notice is provided to the named insured of a policy under which coverage is provided to the named insured and one or more dependents.

(iv) If a health plan has more than one notice, it satisfies the requirements of paragraph (c)(1) of this section by providing the notice that is relevant to the individual or other person requesting the notice.

(v) If there is a material change to the notice:

(A) A health plan that posts its notice on its web site in accordance with paragraph (c)(3)(i) of this section must prominently post the change or its revised notice on its web site by the effective date of the material change to the notice, and provide the revised notice, or information about the material change and how to obtain the revised notice, in its next annual mailing to individuals then covered by the plan.

(B) A health plan that does not post its notice on a web site pursuant to paragraph (c)(3)(i) of this section must provide the revised notice, or information about the material change and how to obtain the revised notice, to individuals then covered by the plan within 60 days of the material revision to the notice.

(2) **Specific requirements for certain covered health care providers.** A covered health care provider that has a direct treatment relationship with an individual must:

(i) Provide the notice:

(A) No later than the date of the first service delivery, including service delivered electronically, to such individual after the compliance date for the covered health care provider; or

(B) In an emergency treatment situation, as soon as reasonably practicable after the emergency treatment situation.

(ii) Except in an emergency treatment situation, make a good faith effort to obtain a written acknowledgment of receipt of the notice provided in accordance with paragraph (c)(2)(i) of this section, and if not obtained, document its good faith efforts to obtain such acknowledgment and the reason why the acknowledgment was not obtained;

(iii) If the covered health care provider maintains a physical service delivery site:

(A) Have the notice available at the service delivery site for individuals to request to take with them; and

(B) Post the notice in a clear and prominent location where it is reasonable to expect individuals seeking service from the covered health care provider to be able to read the notice; and

(iv) Whenever the notice is revised, make the notice available upon request on or after the effective date of the revision and promptly comply with the requirements of paragraph (c)(2)(iii) of this section, if applicable.

(3) *Specific requirements for electronic notice.*

(i) A covered entity that maintains a web site that provides information about the covered entity's customer services or benefits must prominently post its notice on the web site and make the notice available electronically through the web site.

(ii) A covered entity may provide the notice required by this section to an individual by e-mail, if the individual agrees to electronic notice and such agreement has not been withdrawn. If the covered entity knows that the e-mail transmission has failed, a paper copy of the notice must be provided to the individual. Provision of electronic notice by the covered entity will satisfy the provision requirements of paragraph (c) of this section when timely made in accordance with paragraph (c)(1) or (2) of this section.

(iii) For purposes of paragraph (c)(2)(i) of this section, if the first service delivery to an individual is delivered electronically, the covered health care provider must provide electronic notice automatically and contemporaneously in response to the individual's first request for service. The requirements in paragraph (c)(2)(ii) of this section apply to electronic notice.

(iv) The individual who is the recipient of electronic notice retains the right to obtain a paper copy of the notice from a covered entity upon request.

(d) *Implementation specifications: Joint notice by separate covered entities.* Covered entities that participate in organized health care arrangements may comply with this section by a joint notice, provided that:

(1) The covered entities participating in the organized health care arrangement agree to abide by the terms of the notice with respect to protected health information created or received by the covered entity as part of its participation in the organized health care arrangement;

(2) The joint notice meets the implementation specifications in paragraph (b) of this section, except that the statements required by this section may be altered to reflect the fact that the notice covers more than one covered entity; and

(i) Describes with reasonable specificity the covered entities, or class of entities, to which the joint notice applies;

(ii) Describes with reasonable specificity the service delivery sites, or classes of service delivery sites, to which the joint notice applies; and

(iii) If applicable, states that the covered entities participating in the organized health care arrangement will share protected health information with each other, as necessary to carry out treatment, payment, or health care operations relating to the organized health care arrangement.

(3) The covered entities included in the joint notice must provide the notice to individuals in accordance with the applicable implementation specifications of paragraph (c) of this section. Provision of the joint notice to an individual by any one of the covered entities included in the joint notice will satisfy the provision requirement of paragraph (c) of this section with respect to all others covered by the joint notice.

(e) *Implementation specifications: Documentation.* A covered entity must document compliance with the notice requirements, as required by § 164.530(j), by retaining copies of the notices issued by the covered entity and, if applicable, any written acknowledgments of receipt of the notice or documentation of good faith efforts to obtain such written acknowledgment, in accordance with paragraph (c)(2)(ii) of this section.

[65 FR 82802, Dec. 28, 2000, as amended at 67 FR 53271, Aug. 14, 2002; 78 FR 5701, Jan. 25, 2013]

§ 164.522 Rights to request privacy protection for protected health information.

(a)

(1) *Standard: Right of an individual to request restriction of uses and disclosures.*

(i) A covered entity must permit an individual to request that the covered entity restrict:

(A) Uses or disclosures of protected health information about the individual to carry out treatment, payment, or health care operations; and

(B) Disclosures permitted under § 164.510(b).

(ii) Except as provided in paragraph (a)(1)(vi) of this section, a covered entity is not required to agree to a restriction.

(iii) A covered entity that agrees to a restriction under paragraph (a)(1)(i) of this section may not use or disclose protected health information in violation of such restriction, except that, if the individual who requested the restriction is in need of emergency treatment and the restricted protected health information is needed to provide the emergency treatment, the covered entity may use the restricted protected health information, or may disclose such information to a health care provider, to provide such treatment to the individual.

(iv) If restricted protected health information is disclosed to a health care provider for emergency treatment under paragraph (a)(1)(iii) of this section, the covered entity must request that such health care provider not further use or disclose the information.

(v) A restriction agreed to by a covered entity under paragraph (a) of this section, is not effective under this subpart to prevent uses or disclosures permitted or required under § 164.502(a)(2)(ii), § 164.510(a) or § 164.512.

(vi) A covered entity must agree to the request of an individual to restrict disclosure of protected health information about the individual to a health plan if:

(A) The disclosure is for the purpose of carrying out payment or health care operations and is not otherwise required by law; and

(B) The protected health information pertains solely to a health care item or service for which the individual, or person other than the health plan on behalf of the individual, has paid the covered entity in full.

(2) *Implementation specifications: Terminating a restriction.* A covered entity may terminate a restriction, if:

(i) The individual agrees to or requests the termination in writing;

(ii) The individual orally agrees to the termination and the oral agreement is documented; or

(iii) The covered entity informs the individual that it is terminating its agreement to a restriction, except that such termination is:

(A) Not effective for protected health information restricted under paragraph (a)(1)(vi) of this section; and

(B) Only effective with respect to protected health information created or received after it has so informed the individual.

(3) *Implementation specification: Documentation.* A covered entity must document a restriction in accordance with § 160.530(j) of this subchapter.

(b)

(1) *Standard: Confidential communications requirements.*

(i) A covered health care provider must permit individuals to request and must accommodate reasonable requests by individuals to receive communications of protected health information from the covered health care provider by alternative means or at alternative locations.

(ii) A health plan must permit individuals to request and must accommodate reasonable requests by individuals to receive communications of protected health information from the health plan by alternative means or at alternative locations, if the individual clearly states that the disclosure of all or part of that information could endanger the individual.

(2) *Implementation specifications: Conditions on providing confidential communications.*

(i) A covered entity may require the individual to make a request for a confidential communication described in paragraph (b)(1) of this section in writing.

(ii) A covered entity may condition the provision of a reasonable accommodation on:

(A) When appropriate, information as to how payment, if any, will be handled; and

(B) Specification of an alternative address or other method of contact.

(iii) A covered health care provider may not require an explanation from the individual as to the basis for the request as a condition of providing communications on a confidential basis.

(iv) A health plan may require that a request contain a statement that disclosure of all or part of the information to which the request pertains could endanger the individual.

[65 FR 82802, Dec. 28, 2000, as amended at 67 FR 53271, Aug. 14, 2002; 78 FR 5701, Jan. 25, 2013]

§ 164.524 Access of individuals to protected health information.

(a) *Standard: Access to protected health information* —

(1) *Right of access.* Except as otherwise provided in paragraph (a)(2) or (a)(3) of this section, an individual has a right of access to inspect and obtain a copy of protected health information about the individual in a designated record set, for as long as the protected health information is maintained in the designated record set, except for:

(i) Psychotherapy notes; and

(ii) Information compiled in reasonable anticipation of, or for use in, a civil, criminal, or administrative action or proceeding.

(2) *Unreviewable grounds for denial.* A covered entity may deny an individual access without providing the individual an opportunity for review, in the following circumstances.

(i) The protected health information is excepted from the right of access by paragraph (a)(1) of this section.

(ii) A covered entity that is a correctional institution or a covered health care provider acting under the direction of the correctional institution may deny, in whole or in part, an inmate's request to obtain a copy of protected health information, if obtaining such copy would jeopardize the health, safety, security, custody, or rehabilitation of the individual or of other inmates, or the safety of any officer, employee, or other person at the correctional institution or responsible for the transporting of the inmate.

(iii) An individual's access to protected health information created or obtained by a covered health care provider in the course of research that includes treatment may be temporarily suspended for as long as the research is in progress, provided that the individual has agreed to the denial of access when consenting to participate in the research that includes treatment, and the covered health care provider has informed the individual that the right of access will be reinstated upon completion of the research.

(iv) An individual's access to protected health information that is contained in records that are subject to the Privacy Act, 5 U.S.C. 552a, may be denied, if the denial of access under the Privacy Act would meet the requirements of that law.

(v) An individual's access may be denied if the protected health information was obtained from someone other than a health care provider under a promise of confidentiality and the access requested would be reasonably likely to reveal the source of the information.

(3) **Reviewable grounds for denial.** A covered entity may deny an individual access, provided that the individual is given a right to have such denials reviewed, as required by paragraph (a)(4) of this section, in the following circumstances:

(i) A licensed health care professional has determined, in the exercise of professional judgment, that the access requested is reasonably likely to endanger the life or physical safety of the individual or another person;

(ii) The protected health information makes reference to another person (unless such other person is a health care provider) and a licensed health care professional has determined, in the exercise of professional judgment, that the access requested is reasonably likely to cause substantial harm to such other person; or

(iii) The request for access is made by the individual's personal representative and a licensed health care professional has determined, in the exercise of professional judgment, that the provision of access to such personal representative is reasonably likely to cause substantial harm to the individual or another person.

(4) **Review of a denial of access.** If access is denied on a ground permitted under paragraph (a)(3) of this section, the individual has the right to have the denial reviewed by a licensed health care professional who is designated by the covered entity to act as a reviewing official and who did not participate in the original decision to deny. The covered entity must provide or deny access in accordance with the determination of the reviewing official under paragraph (d)(4) of this section.

(b) **Implementation specifications: Requests for access and timely action —**

(1) **Individual's request for access.** The covered entity must permit an individual to request access to inspect or to obtain a copy of the protected health information about the individual that is maintained in a designated record set. The covered entity may require individuals to make requests for access in writing, provided that it informs individuals of such a requirement.

(2) **Timely action by the covered entity.**

(i) Except as provided in paragraph (b)(2)(ii) of this section, the covered entity must act on a request for access no later than 30 days after receipt of the request as follows.

(A) If the covered entity grants the request, in whole or in part, it must inform the individual of the acceptance of the request and provide the access requested, in accordance with paragraph (c) of this section.

(B) If the covered entity denies the request, in whole or in part, it must provide the individual with a written denial, in accordance with paragraph (d) of this section.

(ii) If the covered entity is unable to take an action required by paragraph (b)(2)(i)(A) or (B) of this section within the time required by paragraph (b)(2)(i) of this section, as applicable, the covered entity may extend the time for such actions by no more than 30 days, provided that:

(A) The covered entity, within the time limit set by paragraph (b)(2)(i) of this section, as applicable, provides the individual with a written statement of the reasons for the delay and the date by which the covered entity will complete its action on the request; and

(B) The covered entity may have only one such extension of time for action on a request for access.

(c) *Implementation specifications: Provision of access.* If the covered entity provides an individual with access, in whole or in part, to protected health information, the covered entity must comply with the following requirements.

(1) *Providing the access requested.* The covered entity must provide the access requested by individuals, including inspection or obtaining a copy, or both, of the protected health information about them in designated record sets. If the same protected health information that is the subject of a request for access is maintained in more than one designated record set or at more than one location, the covered entity need only produce the protected health information once in response to a request for access.

(2) *Form of access requested.*

(i) The covered entity must provide the individual with access to the protected health information in the form and format requested by the individual, if it is readily producible in such form and format; or, if not, in a readable hard copy form or such other form and format as agreed to by the covered entity and the individual.

(ii) Notwithstanding paragraph (c)(2)(i) of this section, if the protected health information that is the subject of a request for access is maintained in one or more designated record sets electronically and if the individual requests an electronic copy of such information, the covered entity must provide the individual with access to the protected health information in the electronic form and format requested by the individual, if it is readily producible in such form and format; or, if not, in a readable electronic form and format as agreed to by the covered entity and the individual.

(iii) The covered entity may provide the individual with a summary of the protected health information requested, in lieu of providing access to the protected health information or may provide an explanation of the protected health information to which access has been provided, if:

(A) The individual agrees in advance to such a summary or explanation; and

(B) The individual agrees in advance to the fees imposed, if any, by the covered entity for such summary or explanation.

(3) *Time and manner of access.*

(i) The covered entity must provide the access as requested by the individual in a timely manner as required by paragraph (b)(2) of this section, including arranging with the individual for a convenient time and place to inspect or obtain a copy of the protected health information, or mailing the copy of the protected health information at the individual's request. The covered entity may discuss the scope, format, and other aspects of the request for access with the individual as necessary to facilitate the timely provision of access.

(ii) If an individual's request for access directs the covered entity to transmit the copy of protected health information directly to another person designated by the individual, the covered entity must provide the copy to the person designated by the individual. The individual's request must be in writing, signed by the individual, and clearly identify the designated person and where to send the copy of protected health information.

(4) **Fees.** If the individual requests a copy of the protected health information or agrees to a summary or explanation of such information, the covered entity may impose a reasonable, cost-based fee, provided that the fee includes only the cost of:

(i) Labor for copying the protected health information requested by the individual, whether in paper or electronic form;

(ii) Supplies for creating the paper copy or electronic media if the individual requests that the electronic copy be provided on portable media;

(iii) Postage, when the individual has requested the copy, or the summary or explanation, be mailed; and

(iv) Preparing an explanation or summary of the protected health information, if agreed to by the individual as required by paragraph (c)(2)(iii) of this section.

(d) **Implementation specifications: Denial of access.** If the covered entity denies access, in whole or in part, to protected health information, the covered entity must comply with the following requirements.

(1) **Making other information accessible.** The covered entity must, to the extent possible, give the individual access to any other protected health information requested, after excluding the protected health information as to which the covered entity has a ground to deny access.

(2) **Denial.** The covered entity must provide a timely, written denial to the individual, in accordance with paragraph (b)(2) of this section. The denial must be in plain language and contain:

(i) The basis for the denial;

(ii) If applicable, a statement of the individual's review rights under paragraph (a)(4) of this section, including a description of how the individual may exercise such review rights; and

(iii) A description of how the individual may complain to the covered entity pursuant to the complaint procedures in § 164.530(d) or to the Secretary pursuant to the procedures in § 160.306. The description must include the name, or title, and telephone number of the contact person or office designated in § 164.530(a)(1)(ii).

(3) **Other responsibility.** If the covered entity does not maintain the protected health information that is the subject of the individual's request for access, and the covered entity knows where the requested information is maintained, the covered entity must inform the individual where to direct the request for access.

(4) **Review of denial requested.** If the individual has requested a review of a denial under paragraph (a)(4) of this section, the covered entity must designate a licensed health care professional, who was not directly involved in the denial to review the decision to deny access. The covered entity must promptly refer a request for review to such designated reviewing official. The designated reviewing official must determine, within a reasonable period of time, whether or not to deny the access requested based on the standards in paragraph (a)(3) of this section. The covered entity must promptly provide written notice to the individual of the determination of the designated reviewing official and take other action as required by this section to carry out the designated reviewing official's determination.

(e) **Implementation specification: Documentation.** A covered entity must document the following and retain the documentation as required by § 164.530(j):

(1) The designated record sets that are subject to access by individuals; and

(2) The titles of the persons or offices responsible for receiving and processing requests for access by individuals.

[65 FR 82802, Dec. 28, 2000, as amended at 78 FR 5701, Jan. 25, 2013; 78 FR 34266, June 7, 2013; 79 FR 7316, Feb. 6, 2014]

§ 164.526 Amendment of protected health information.

(a) **Standard: Right to amend.**

(1) **Right to amend.** An individual has the right to have a covered entity amend protected health information or a record about the individual in a designated record set for as long as the protected health information is maintained in the designated record set.

(2) **Denial of amendment.** A covered entity may deny an individual's request for amendment, if it determines that the protected health information or record that is the subject of the request:

(i) Was not created by the covered entity, unless the individual provides a reasonable basis to believe that the originator of protected health information is no longer available to act on the requested amendment;

(ii) Is not part of the designated record set;

(iii) Would not be available for inspection under § 164.524; or

(iv) Is accurate and complete.

(b) **Implementation specifications: Requests for amendment and timely action —**

(1) *Individual's request for amendment.* The covered entity must permit an individual to request that the covered entity amend the protected health information maintained in the designated record set. The covered entity may require individuals to make requests for amendment in writing and to provide a reason to support a requested amendment, provided that it informs individuals in advance of such requirements.

(2) *Timely action by the covered entity.*

(i) The covered entity must act on the individual's request for an amendment no later than 60 days after receipt of such a request, as follows.

(A) If the covered entity grants the requested amendment, in whole or in part, it must take the actions required by paragraphs (c)(1) and (2) of this section.

(B) If the covered entity denies the requested amendment, in whole or in part, it must provide the individual with a written denial, in accordance with paragraph (d)(1) of this section.

(ii) If the covered entity is unable to act on the amendment within the time required by paragraph (b)(2)(i) of this section, the covered entity may extend the time for such action by no more than 30 days, provided that:

(A) The covered entity, within the time limit set by paragraph (b)(2)(i) of this section, provides the individual with a written statement of the reasons for the delay and the date by which the covered entity will complete its action on the request; and

(B) The covered entity may have only one such extension of time for action on a request for an amendment.

(c) *Implementation specifications: Accepting the amendment.* If the covered entity accepts the requested amendment, in whole or in part, the covered entity must comply with the following requirements.

(1) *Making the amendment.* The covered entity must make the appropriate amendment to the protected health information or record that is the subject of the request for amendment by, at a minimum, identifying the records in the designated record set that are affected by the amendment and appending or otherwise providing a link to the location of the amendment.

(2) *Informing the individual.* In accordance with paragraph (b) of this section, the covered entity must timely inform the individual that the amendment is accepted and obtain the individual's identification of and agreement to have the covered entity notify the relevant persons with which the amendment needs to be shared in accordance with paragraph (c)(3) of this section.

(3) *Informing others.* The covered entity must make reasonable efforts to inform and provide the amendment within a reasonable time to:

(i) Persons identified by the individual as having received protected health information about the individual and needing the amendment; and

(ii) Persons, including business associates, that the covered entity knows have the protected health information that is the subject of the amendment and that may have relied, or could foreseeably rely, on such information to the detriment of the individual.

(d) ***Implementation specifications: Denying the amendment.*** If the covered entity denies the requested amendment, in whole or in part, the covered entity must comply with the following requirements.

(1) ***Denial.*** The covered entity must provide the individual with a timely, written denial, in accordance with paragraph (b)(2) of this section. The denial must use plain language and contain:

(i) The basis for the denial, in accordance with paragraph (a)(2) of this section;

(ii) The individual's right to submit a written statement disagreeing with the denial and how the individual may file such a statement;

(iii) A statement that, if the individual does not submit a statement of disagreement, the individual may request that the covered entity provide the individual's request for amendment and the denial with any future disclosures of the protected health information that is the subject of the amendment; and

(iv) A description of how the individual may complain to the covered entity pursuant to the complaint procedures established in § 164.530(d) or to the Secretary pursuant to the procedures established in § 160.306. The description must include the name, or title, and telephone number of the contact person or office designated in § 164.530(a)(1)(ii).

(2) ***Statement of disagreement.*** The covered entity must permit the individual to submit to the covered entity a written statement disagreeing with the denial of all or part of a requested amendment and the basis of such disagreement. The covered entity may reasonably limit the length of a statement of disagreement.

(3) ***Rebuttal statement.*** The covered entity may prepare a written rebuttal to the individual's statement of disagreement. Whenever such a rebuttal is prepared, the covered entity must provide a copy to the individual who submitted the statement of disagreement.

(4) ***Recordkeeping.*** The covered entity must, as appropriate, identify the record or protected health information in the designated record set that is the subject of the disputed amendment and append or otherwise link the individual's request for an amendment, the covered entity's denial of the request, the individual's statement of disagreement, if any, and the covered entity's rebuttal, if any, to the designated record set.

(5) ***Future disclosures.***

(i) If a statement of disagreement has been submitted by the individual, the covered entity must include the material appended in accordance with paragraph (d)(4) of this section, or, at the election of the covered entity, an accurate summary of any such information, with any subsequent disclosure of the protected health information to which the disagreement relates.

(ii) If the individual has not submitted a written statement of disagreement, the covered entity must include the individual's request for amendment and its denial, or an accurate summary of such information, with any subsequent disclosure of the protected health information only if the individual has requested such action in accordance with paragraph (d)(1)(iii) of this section.

(iii) When a subsequent disclosure described in paragraph (d)(5)(i) or (ii) of this section is made using a standard transaction under part 162 of this subchapter that does not permit the additional material to be included with the disclosure, the covered entity may separately transmit the material required by paragraph (d)(5)(i) or (ii) of this section, as applicable, to the recipient of the standard transaction.

(e) *Implementation specification: Actions on notices of amendment.* A covered entity that is informed by another covered entity of an amendment to an individual's protected health information, in accordance with paragraph (c)(3) of this section, must amend the protected health information in designated record sets as provided by paragraph (c)(1) of this section.

(f) *Implementation specification: Documentation.* A covered entity must document the titles of the persons or offices responsible for receiving and processing requests for amendments by individuals and retain the documentation as required by § 164.530(j).

§ 164.528 Accounting of disclosures of protected health information.

(a) *Standard: Right to an accounting of disclosures of protected health information.*

(1) An individual has a right to receive an accounting of disclosures of protected health information made by a covered entity in the six years prior to the date on which the accounting is requested, except for disclosures:

(i) To carry out treatment, payment and health care operations as provided in § 164.506;

(ii) To individuals of protected health information about them as provided in § 164.502;

(iii) Incident to a use or disclosure otherwise permitted or required by this subpart, as provided in § 164.502;

(iv) Pursuant to an authorization as provided in § 164.508;

(v) For the facility's directory or to persons involved in the individual's care or other notification purposes as provided in § 164.510;

(vi) For national security or intelligence purposes as provided in § 164.512(k)(2);

(vii) To correctional institutions or law enforcement officials as provided in § 164.512(k)(5);

(viii) As part of a limited data set in accordance with § 164.514(e); or

(ix) That occurred prior to the compliance date for the covered entity.

(2)

(i) The covered entity must temporarily suspend an individual's right to receive an accounting of disclosures to a health oversight agency or law enforcement official, as provided in § 164.512(d) or (f), respectively, for the time specified by such agency or official, if such agency or official provides the covered entity with a written statement that such an accounting to the individual would be reasonably likely to impede the agency's activities and specifying the time for which such a suspension is required.

(ii) If the agency or official statement in paragraph (a)(2)(i) of this section is made orally, the covered entity must:

(A) Document the statement, including the identity of the agency or official making the statement;

(B) Temporarily suspend the individual's right to an accounting of disclosures subject to the statement; and

(C) Limit the temporary suspension to no longer than 30 days from the date of the oral statement, unless a written statement pursuant to paragraph (a)(2)(i) of this section is submitted during that time.

(3) An individual may request an accounting of disclosures for a period of time less than six years from the date of the request.

(b) *Implementation specifications: Content of the accounting.* The covered entity must provide the individual with a written accounting that meets the following requirements.

(1) Except as otherwise provided by paragraph (a) of this section, the accounting must include disclosures of protected health information that occurred during the six years (or such shorter time period at the request of the individual as provided in paragraph (a)(3) of this section) prior to the date of the request for an accounting, including disclosures to or by business associates of the covered entity.

(2) Except as otherwise provided by paragraphs (b)(3) or (b)(4) of this section, the accounting must include for each disclosure:

(i) The date of the disclosure;

(ii) The name of the entity or person who received the protected health information and, if known, the address of such entity or person;

(iii) A brief description of the protected health information disclosed; and

(iv) A brief statement of the purpose of the disclosure that reasonably informs the individual of the basis for the disclosure or, in lieu of such statement, a copy of a written request for a disclosure under § 164.502(a)(2)(ii) or § 164.512, if any.

(3) If, during the period covered by the accounting, the covered entity has made multiple disclosures of protected health information to the same person or entity for a single purpose under § 164.502(a)(2)(ii) or § 164.512, the accounting may, with respect to such multiple disclosures, provide:

(i) The information required by paragraph (b)(2) of this section for the first disclosure during the accounting period;

(ii) The frequency, periodicity, or number of the disclosures made during the accounting period; and

(iii) The date of the last such disclosure during the accounting period.

(4)

(i) If, during the period covered by the accounting, the covered entity has made disclosures of protected health information for a particular research purpose in accordance with § 164.512(i) for 50 or more individuals, the accounting may, with respect to such disclosures for which the protected health information about the individual may have been included, provide:

(A) The name of the protocol or other research activity;

(B) A description, in plain language, of the research protocol or other research activity, including the purpose of the research and the criteria for selecting particular records;

(C) A brief description of the type of protected health information that was disclosed;

(D) The date or period of time during which such disclosures occurred, or may have occurred, including the date of the last such disclosure during the accounting period;

(E) The name, address, and telephone number of the entity that sponsored the research and of the researcher to whom the information was disclosed; and

(F) A statement that the protected health information of the individual may or may not have been disclosed for a particular protocol or other research activity.

(ii) If the covered entity provides an accounting for research disclosures, in accordance with paragraph (b)(4) of this section, and if it is reasonably likely that the protected health information of the individual was disclosed for such research protocol or activity, the covered entity shall, at the request of the individual, assist in contacting the entity that sponsored the research and the researcher.

(c) *Implementation specifications: Provision of the accounting.*

(1) The covered entity must act on the individual's request for an accounting, no later than 60 days after receipt of such a request, as follows.

(i) The covered entity must provide the individual with the accounting requested; or

(ii) If the covered entity is unable to provide the accounting within the time required by paragraph (c)(1) of this section, the covered entity may extend the time to provide the accounting by no more than 30 days, provided that:

(A) The covered entity, within the time limit set by paragraph (c)(1) of this section, provides the individual with a written statement of the reasons for the delay and the date by which the covered entity will provide the accounting; and

(B) The covered entity may have only one such extension of time for action on a request for an accounting.

(2) The covered entity must provide the first accounting to an individual in any 12 month period without charge. The covered entity may impose a reasonable, cost-based fee for each subsequent request for an accounting by the same individual within the 12 month period, provided that the covered entity informs the individual in advance of the fee and provides the individual with an opportunity to withdraw or modify the request for a subsequent accounting in order to avoid or reduce the fee.

(d) **Implementation specification: Documentation.** A covered entity must document the following and retain the documentation as required by § 164.530(j):

(1) The information required to be included in an accounting under paragraph (b) of this section for disclosures of protected health information that are subject to an accounting under paragraph (a) of this section;

(2) The written accounting that is provided to the individual under this section; and

(3) The titles of the persons or offices responsible for receiving and processing requests for an accounting by individuals.

[65 FR 82802, Dec. 28, 2000, as amended at 67 FR 53271, Aug. 14, 2002]

§ 164.530 Administrative requirements.

(a)

(1) **Standard: Personnel designations.**

(i) A covered entity must designate a privacy official who is responsible for the development and implementation of the policies and procedures of the entity.

(ii) A covered entity must designate a contact person or office who is responsible for receiving complaints under this section and who is able to provide further information about matters covered by the notice required by § 164.520.

(2) **Implementation specification: Personnel designations.** A covered entity must document the personnel designations in paragraph (a)(1) of this section as required by paragraph (j) of this section.

(b)

(1) **Standard: Training.** A covered entity must train all members of its workforce on the policies and procedures with respect to protected health information required by this subpart

and subpart D of this part, as necessary and appropriate for the members of the workforce to carry out their functions within the covered entity.

(2) *Implementation specifications: Training.*

    (i) A covered entity must provide training that meets the requirements of paragraph (b)(1) of this section, as follows:

        (A) To each member of the covered entity's workforce by no later than the compliance date for the covered entity;

        (B) Thereafter, to each new member of the workforce within a reasonable period of time after the person joins the covered entity's workforce; and

        (C) To each member of the covered entity's workforce whose functions are affected by a material change in the policies or procedures required by this subpart or subpart D of this part, within a reasonable period of time after the material change becomes effective in accordance with paragraph (i) of this section.

    (ii) A covered entity must document that the training as described in paragraph (b)(2)(i) of this section has been provided, as required by paragraph (j) of this section.

(c)

(1) *Standard: Safeguards.* A covered entity must have in place appropriate administrative, technical, and physical safeguards to protect the privacy of protected health information.

(2)

    (i) *Implementation specification: Safeguards.* A covered entity must reasonably safeguard protected health information from any intentional or unintentional use or disclosure that is in violation of the standards, implementation specifications or other requirements of this subpart.

    (ii) A covered entity must reasonably safeguard protected health information to limit incidental uses or disclosures made pursuant to an otherwise permitted or required use or disclosure.

(d)

(1) *Standard: Complaints to the covered entity.* A covered entity must provide a process for individuals to make complaints concerning the covered entity's policies and procedures required by this subpart and subpart D of this part or its compliance with such policies and procedures or the requirements of this subpart or subpart D of this part.

(2) *Implementation specification: Documentation of complaints.* As required by paragraph (j) of this section, a covered entity must document all complaints received, and their disposition, if any.

(e)

(1) **Standard: Sanctions.** A covered entity must have and apply appropriate sanctions against members of its workforce who fail to comply with the privacy policies and procedures of the covered entity or the requirements of this subpart or subpart D of this part. This standard does not apply to a member of the covered entity's workforce with respect to actions that are covered by and that meet the conditions of § 164.502(j) or paragraph (g)(2) of this section.

(2) **Implementation specification: Documentation.** As required by paragraph (j) of this section, a covered entity must document the sanctions that are applied, if any.

(f) **Standard: Mitigation.** A covered entity must mitigate, to the extent practicable, any harmful effect that is known to the covered entity of a use or disclosure of protected health information in violation of its policies and procedures or the requirements of this subpart by the covered entity or its business associate.

(g) **Standard: Refraining from intimidating or retaliatory acts.** A covered entity—

(1) May not intimidate, threaten, coerce, discriminate against, or take other retaliatory action against any individual for the exercise by the individual of any right established, or for participation in any process provided for, by this subpart or subpart D of this part, including the filing of a complaint under this section; and

(2) Must refrain from intimidation and retaliation as provided in § 160.316 of this subchapter.

(h) **Standard: Waiver of rights.** A covered entity may not require individuals to waive their rights under § 160.306 of this subchapter, this subpart, or subpart D of this part, as a condition of the provision of treatment, payment, enrollment in a health plan, or eligibility for benefits.

(i)

(1) **Standard: Policies and procedures.** A covered entity must implement policies and procedures with respect to protected health information that are designed to comply with the standards, implementation specifications, or other requirements of this subpart and subpart D of this part. The policies and procedures must be reasonably designed, taking into account the size and the type of activities that relate to protected health information undertaken by a covered entity, to ensure such compliance. This standard is not to be construed to permit or excuse an action that violates any other standard, implementation specification, or other requirement of this subpart.

(2) **Standard: Changes to policies and procedures.**

(i) A covered entity must change its policies and procedures as necessary and appropriate to comply with changes in the law, including the standards, requirements, and implementation specifications of this subpart or subpart D of this part.

(ii) When a covered entity changes a privacy practice that is stated in the notice described in § 164.520, and makes corresponding changes to its policies and procedures, it may make the changes effective for protected health information that it created or received prior to the effective date of the notice revision, if the covered entity has, in accordance with § 164.520(b)(1)(v)(C), included in the notice a statement reserving its right to make such a change in its privacy practices; or

(iii) A covered entity may make any other changes to policies and procedures at any time, provided that the changes are documented and implemented in accordance with paragraph (i)(5) of this section.

(3) **Implementation specification: Changes in law.** Whenever there is a change in law that necessitates a change to the covered entity's policies or procedures, the covered entity must promptly document and implement the revised policy or procedure. If the change in law materially affects the content of the notice required by § 164.520, the covered entity must promptly make the appropriate revisions to the notice in accordance with § 164.520(b)(3). Nothing in this paragraph may be used by a covered entity to excuse a failure to comply with the law.

(4) **Implementation specifications: Changes to privacy practices stated in the notice.**

(i) To implement a change as provided by paragraph (i)(2)(ii) of this section, a covered entity must:

(A) Ensure that the policy or procedure, as revised to reflect a change in the covered entity's privacy practice as stated in its notice, complies with the standards, requirements, and implementation specifications of this subpart;

(B) Document the policy or procedure, as revised, as required by paragraph (j) of this section; and

(C) Revise the notice as required by § 164.520(b)(3) to state the changed practice and make the revised notice available as required by § 164.520(c). The covered entity may not implement a change to a policy or procedure prior to the effective date of the revised notice.

(ii) If a covered entity has not reserved its right under § 164.520(b)(1)(v)(C) to change a privacy practice that is stated in the notice, the covered entity is bound by the privacy practices as stated in the notice with respect to protected health information created or received while such notice is in effect. A covered entity may change a privacy practice that is stated in the notice, and the related policies and procedures, without having reserved the right to do so, provided that:

(A) Such change meets the implementation specifications in paragraphs (i)(4)(i)(A)–(C) of this section; and

(B) Such change is effective only with respect to protected health information created or received after the effective date of the notice.

(5) **Implementation specification: Changes to other policies or procedures.** A covered entity may change, at any time, a policy or procedure that does not materially affect the content of the notice required by § 164.520, provided that:

(i) The policy or procedure, as revised, complies with the standards, requirements, and implementation specifications of this subpart; and

(ii) Prior to the effective date of the change, the policy or procedure, as revised, is documented as required by paragraph (j) of this section.

(j)

(1) *Standard: Documentation.* A covered entity must:

(i) Maintain the policies and procedures provided for in paragraph (i) of this section in written or electronic form;

(ii) If a communication is required by this subpart to be in writing, maintain such writing, or an electronic copy, as documentation; and

(iii) If an action, activity, or designation is required by this subpart to be documented, maintain a written or electronic record of such action, activity, or designation.

(iv) Maintain documentation sufficient to meet its burden of proof under § 164.414(b).

(2) *Implementation specification: Retention period.* A covered entity must retain the documentation required by paragraph (j)(1) of this section for six years from the date of its creation or the date when it last was in effect, whichever is later.

(k) *Standard: Group health plans.*

(1) A group health plan is not subject to the standards or implementation specifications in paragraphs (a) through (f) and (i) of this section, to the extent that:

(i) The group health plan provides health benefits solely through an insurance contract with a health insurance issuer or an HMO; and

(ii) The group health plan does not create or receive protected health information, except for:

(A) Summary health information as defined in § 164.504(a); or

(B) Information on whether the individual is participating in the group health plan, or is enrolled in or has disenrolled from a health insurance issuer or HMO offered by the plan.

(2) A group health plan described in paragraph (k)(1) of this section is subject to the standard and implementation specification in paragraph (j) of this section only with respect to plan documents amended in accordance with § 164.504(f).

[65 FR 82802, Dec. 28, 2000, as amended at 67 FR 53272, Aug. 14, 2002; 71 FR 8433, Feb. 16, 2006; 74 FR 42769, Aug. 24, 2009]

§ 164.532 Transition provisions.

(a) *Standard: Effect of prior authorizations.* Notwithstanding §§ 164.508 and 164.512(i), a covered entity may use or disclose protected health information, consistent with paragraphs (b) and (c) of this section, pursuant to an authorization or other express legal permission obtained from an individual permitting the use or disclosure of protected health information, informed consent of the individual to participate in research, a waiver of informed consent by an IRB, or a waiver of authorization in accordance with § 164.512(i)(1)(i).

(b) *Implementation specification: Effect of prior authorization for purposes other than research.* Notwithstanding any provisions in § 164.508, a covered entity may use or disclose protected health information that it created or received prior to the applicable compliance date of this subpart pursuant to an authorization or other express legal permission obtained from an individual prior to the applicable compliance date of this subpart, provided that the authorization or other express legal permission specifically permits such use or disclosure and there is no agreed-to restriction in accordance with § 164.522(a).

(c) *Implementation specification: Effect of prior permission for research.* Notwithstanding any provisions in §§ 164.508 and 164.512(i), a covered entity may, to the extent allowed by one of the following permissions, use or disclose, for research, protected health information that it created or received either before or after the applicable compliance date of this subpart, provided that there is no agreed-to restriction in accordance with § 164.522(a), and the covered entity has obtained, prior to the applicable compliance date, either:

(1) An authorization or other express legal permission from an individual to use or disclose protected health information for the research;

(2) The informed consent of the individual to participate in the research;

(3) A waiver, by an IRB, of informed consent for the research, in accordance with 7 CFR 1c.116(d), 10 CFR 745.116(d), 14 CFR 1230.116(d), 15 CFR 27.116(d), 16 CFR 1028.116(d), 21 CFR 50.24, 22 CFR 225.116(d), 24 CFR 60.116(d), 28 CFR 46.116(d), 32 CFR 219.116(d), 34 CFR 97.116(d), 38 CFR 16.116(d), 40 CFR 26.116(d), 45 CFR 46.116(d), 45 CFR 690.116(d), or 49 CFR 11.116(d), provided that a covered entity must obtain authorization in accordance with § 164.508 if, after the compliance date, informed consent is sought from an individual participating in the research; or

(4) A waiver of authorization in accordance with § 164.512(i)(1)(i).

(d) *Standard: Effect of prior contracts or other arrangements with business associates.* Notwithstanding any other provisions of this part, a covered entity, or business associate with respect to a subcontractor, may disclose protected health information to a business associate and may allow a business associate to create, receive, maintain, or transmit protected health information on its behalf pursuant to a written contract or other written arrangement with such business associate that does not comply with §§ 164.308(b), 164.314(a), 164.502(e), and 164.504(e), only in accordance with paragraph (e) of this section.

(e) *Implementation specification: Deemed compliance —*

(1) *Qualification.* Notwithstanding other sections of this part, a covered entity, or business associate with respect to a subcontractor, is deemed to be in compliance with the documentation and contract requirements of §§ 164.308(b), 164.314(a), 164.502(e), and 164.504(e), with respect to a particular business associate relationship, for the time period set forth in paragraph (e)(2) of this section, if:

(i) Prior to January 25, 2013, such covered entity, or business associate with respect to a subcontractor, has entered into and is operating pursuant to a written contract or other written arrangement with the business associate that complies with the applicable provisions of § 164.314(a) or § 164.504(e) that were in effect on such date; and

(ii) The contract or other arrangement is not renewed or modified from March 26, 2013, until September 23, 2013.

(2) *Limited deemed compliance period.* A prior contract or other arrangement that meets the qualification requirements in paragraph (e) of this section shall be deemed compliant until the earlier of:

(i) The date such contract or other arrangement is renewed or modified on or after September 23, 2013; or

(ii) September 22, 2014.

(3) *Covered entity responsibilities.* Nothing in this section shall alter the requirements of a covered entity to comply with part 160, subpart C of this subchapter and §§ 164.524, 164.526, 164.528, and 164.530(f) with respect to protected health information held by a business associate.

(f) *Effect of prior data use agreements.* If, prior to January 25, 2013, a covered entity has entered into and is operating pursuant to a data use agreement with a recipient of a limited data set that complies with § 164.514(e), notwithstanding § 164.502(a)(5)(ii), the covered entity may continue to disclose a limited data set pursuant to such agreement in exchange for remuneration from or on behalf of the recipient of the protected health information until the earlier of:

(1) The date such agreement is renewed or modified on or after September 23, 2013; or

(2) September 22, 2014.

[65 FR 82802, Dec. 28, 2000, as amended at 67 FR 53272, Aug. 14, 2002; 78 FR 5702, Jan. 25, 2013; 78 FR 34266, June 7, 2013]

§ 164.534 Compliance dates for initial implementation of the privacy standards.

(a) *Health care providers.* A covered health care provider must comply with the applicable requirements of this subpart no later than April 14, 2003.

(b) *Health plans.* A health plan must comply with the applicable requirements of this subpart no later than the following as applicable:

(1) *Health plans other than small health plans.* April 14, 2003.

(2) *Small health plans.* April 14, 2004.

(c) **Health clearinghouses.** A health care clearinghouse must comply with the applicable requirements of this subpart no later than April 14, 2003.

[66 FR 12434, Feb. 26, 2001]

Intentionally Blank

45 CFR PART 102—ADJUSTMENT OF CIVIL MONETARY PENALTIES FOR INFLATION

Authority: Pub. L. 101–410, Sec. 701 of Pub. L. 114–74, 31 U.S.C. 3801–3812.
Source:81 FR 61565, Sept. 6, 2016, unless otherwise noted.

§ 102.1 Applicability.

This part applies to each statutory provision under the laws administered by the Department of Health and Human Services concerning the civil monetary penalties which may be assessed or enforced by an agency pursuant to Federal law or is assessed or enforced pursuant to civil judicial actions in the Federal courts or administrative proceedings. The regulations cited in this part supersede existing HHS regulations setting forth civil monetary penalty amounts. If applicable, the HHS agencies responsible for specific civil monetary penalties will amend their regulations to reflect the adjusted amounts and/or a cross-reference to 45 CFR part 102 in separate actions as soon as practicable.

§ 102.2 Applicability date.

The increased penalty amounts set forth in the right-most column of the table in Section 102.3, "Maximum Adjusted Penalty ($)", apply to all civil monetary penalties which are assessed after August 1, 2016, including those penalties whose associated violations occurred after November 2, 2015.

§ 102.3 Penalty adjustment and table.

The adjusted statutory penalty provisions and their applicable amounts are set out in the following table. The right-most column in the table, "Maximum Adjusted Penalty ($)", provides the maximum adjusted civil penalty amounts. The civil monetary penalty amounts are adjusted annually.

Table 1 to § 102.3—Civil Monetary Penalty Authorities Administered by HHS

U.S.C. section(s)	CFR[1]	HHS agency	Description[2]	Date of last penalty figure or adjustment[3]	2022 Maximum adjusted penalty ($)	2023 Maximum adjusted penalty ($)[4]
21 U.S.C.:						
333(b)(2)(A)		FDA	Penalty for violations related to drug samples resulting in a conviction of any representative of manufacturer or distributor in any 10-year period	2022	115,054	123,965
333(b)(2)(B)		FDA	Penalty for violation related to drug samples resulting in a	2022	2,301,065	2,479,282

U.S.C. section(s)	CFR[1]	HHS agency	Description[2]	Date of last penalty figure or adjustment[3]	2022 Maximum adjusted penalty ($)	2023 Maximum adjusted penalty ($)[4]
			conviction of any representative of manufacturer or distributor after the second conviction in any 10-yr period			
333(b)(3)		FDA	Penalty for failure to make a report required by 21 U.S.C. 353(d)(3)(E) relating to drug samples	2022	230,107	247,929
333(f)(1)(A)		FDA	Penalty for any person who violates a requirement related to devices for each such violation	2022	31,076	33,483
		FDA	Penalty for aggregate of all violations related to devices in a single proceeding	2022	2,071,819	2,232,281
333(f)(2)(A)		FDA	Penalty for any individual who introduces or delivers for introduction into interstate commerce food that is adulterated per 21 U.S.C. 342(a)(2)(B) or any individual who does not comply with a recall order under 21 U.S.C. 350l	2022	87,362	94,128
		FDA	Penalty in the case of any other person (other than an individual) for such introduction or delivery of adulterated food	2022	436,809	470,640
		FDA	Penalty for aggregate of all such violations related to adulterated food	2022	873,618	941,280

U.S.C. section(s)	CFR[1]	HHS agency	Description[2]	Date of last penalty figure or adjustment[3]	2022 Maximum adjusted penalty ($)	2023 Maximum adjusted penalty ($)[4]
			adjudicated in a single proceeding			
333(f)(3)(A)		FDA	Penalty for all violations adjudicated in a single proceeding for any person who violates 21 U.S.C. 331(jj) by failing to submit the certification required by 42 U.S.C. 282(j)(5)(B) or knowingly submitting a false certification; by failing to submit clinical trial information under 42 U.S.C. 282(j); or by submitting clinical trial information under 42 U.S.C. 282(j) that is false or misleading in any particular under 42 U.S.C. 282(j)(5)(D)	2022	13,237	14,262
333(f)(3)(B)		FDA	Penalty for each day any above violation is not corrected after a 30-day period following notification until the violation is corrected	2022	13,237	14,262
333(f)(4)(A)(i)		FDA	Penalty for any responsible person that violates a requirement of 21 U.S.C. 355(o) (post-marketing studies, clinical trials, labeling), 21 U.S.C. 355(p) (risk evaluation and mitigation (REMS)), or 21 U.S.C. 355–1 (REMS)	2022	330,948	356,580

U.S.C. section(s)	CFR[1]	HHS agency	Description[2]	Date of last penalty figure or adjustment[3]	2022 Maximum adjusted penalty ($)	2023 Maximum adjusted penalty ($)[4]
		FDA	Penalty for aggregate of all such above violations in a single proceeding	2022	1,323,791	1,426,319
333(f)(4)(A)(ii)		FDA	Penalty for REMS violation that continues after written notice to the responsible person for the first 30-day period (or any portion thereof) the responsible person continues to be in violation	2022	330,948	356,580
		FDA	Penalty for REMS violation that continues after written notice to responsible person doubles for every 30-day period thereafter the violation continues, but may not exceed penalty amount for any 30-day period	2022	1,323,791	1,426,319
		FDA	Penalty for aggregate of all such above violations adjudicated in a single proceeding	2022	13,237,910	14,263,186
333(f)(9)(A)		FDA	Penalty for any person who violates a requirement which relates to tobacco products for each such violation	2022	19,192	20,678
		FDA	Penalty for aggregate of all such violations of tobacco product requirement adjudicated in a single proceeding	2022	1,279,448	1,378,541

U.S.C. section(s)	CFR[1]	HHS agency	Description[2]	Date of last penalty figure or adjustment[3]	2022 Maximum adjusted penalty ($)	2023 Maximum adjusted penalty ($)[4]
333(f)(9)(B)(i)(I)		FDA	Penalty per violation related to violations of tobacco requirements	2022	319,863	344,636
		FDA	Penalty for aggregate of all such violations of tobacco product requirements adjudicated in a single proceeding	2022	1,279,448	1,378,541
333(f)(9)(B)(i)(II)		FDA	Penalty in the case of a violation of tobacco product requirements that continues after written notice to such person, for the first 30-day period (or any portion thereof) the person continues to be in violation	2022	319,863	344,636
		FDA	Penalty for violation of tobacco product requirements that continues after written notice to such person shall double for every 30-day period thereafter the violation continues, but may not exceed penalty amount for any 30-day period	2022	1,279,448	1,378,541
		FDA	Penalty for aggregate of all such violations related to tobacco product requirements adjudicated in a single proceeding	2022	12,794,487	13,785,420
333(f)(9)(B)(ii)(I)		FDA	Penalty for any person who either does not conduct post-market surveillance and	2022	319,863	344,636

U.S.C. section(s)	CFR[1]	HHS agency	Description[2]	Date of last penalty figure or adjustment[3]	2022 Maximum adjusted penalty ($)	2023 Maximum adjusted penalty ($)[4]
			studies to determine impact of a modified risk tobacco product for which the HHS Secretary has provided them an order to sell, or who does not submit a protocol to the HHS Secretary after being notified of a requirement to conduct post-market surveillance of such tobacco products			
		FDA	Penalty for aggregate of for all such above violations adjudicated in a single proceeding	2022	1,279,448	1,378,541
333(f)(9)(B)(ii)(II)		FDA	Penalty for violation of modified risk tobacco product post-market surveillance that continues after written notice to such person for the first 30-day period (or any portion thereof) that the person continues to be in violation	2022	319,863	344,636
		FDA	Penalty for post-notice violation of modified risk tobacco product post-market surveillance shall double for every 30-day period thereafter that the tobacco product requirement violation continues for any 30-day	2022	1,279,448	1,378,541

U.S.C. section(s)	CFR[1]	HHS agency	Description[2]	Date of last penalty figure or adjustment[3]	2022 Maximum adjusted penalty ($)	2023 Maximum adjusted penalty ($)[4]
			period, but may not exceed penalty amount for any 30-day period			
			Penalty for aggregate above tobacco product requirement violations adjudicated in a single proceeding	2022	12,794,487	13,785,420
333(g)(1)		FDA	Penalty for any person who disseminates or causes another party to disseminate a direct-to-consumer advertisement that is false or misleading for the first such violation in any 3-year period	2022	330,948	356,580
			Penalty for each subsequent above violation in any 3-year period	2022	661,896	713,160
333 note		FDA	Penalty to be applied for violations of 21 U.S.C. 387f(d)(5) or of violations of restrictions on the sale or distribution of tobacco products promulgated under 21 U.S.C. 387f(d) (*e.g.,* violations of regulations in 21 CFR part 1140) with respect to a retailer with an approved training program in the case of a second regulation violation within a 12-month period	2022	320	345
		FDA	Penalty in the case of a third violation	2022	638	687

U.S.C. section(s)	CFR[1]	HHS agency	Description[2]	Date of last penalty figure or adjustment[3]	2022 Maximum adjusted penalty ($)	2023 Maximum adjusted penalty ($)[4]
			of 21 U.S.C. 387f(d)(5) or of the tobacco product regulations within a 24-month period			
		FDA	Penalty in the case of a fourth violation of 21 U.S.C. 387f(d)(5) or of the tobacco product regulations within a 24-month period	2022	2,559	2,757
		FDA	Penalty in the case of a fifth violation of 21 U.S.C. 387f(d)(5) or of the tobacco product regulations within a 36-month period	2022	6,397	6,892
		FDA	Penalty in the case of a sixth or subsequent violation of 21 U.S.C. 387f(d)(5) or of the tobacco product regulations within a 48-month period as determined on a case-by-case basis	2022	12,794	13,785
		FDA	Penalty to be applied for violations of 21 U.S.C. 387f(d)(5) or of violations of restrictions on the sale or distribution of tobacco products promulgated under 21 U.S.C. 387f(d) (e.g., violations of regulations in 21 CFR part 1140) with respect to a retailer that does not have an approved training program in the case	2022	320	345

U.S.C. section(s)	CFR[1]	HHS agency	Description[2]	Date of last penalty figure or adjustment[3]	2022 Maximum adjusted penalty ($)	2023 Maximum adjusted penalty ($)[4]
			of the first regulation violation			
		FDA	Penalty in the case of a second violation of 21 U.S.C. 387f(d)(5) or of the tobacco product regulations within a 12-month period	2022	638	687
		FDA	Penalty in the case of a third violation of 21 U.S.C. 387f(d)(5) or of the tobacco product regulations within a 24-month period	2022	1,280	1,379
		FDA	Penalty in the case of a fourth violation of 21 U.S.C. 387f(d)(5) or of the tobacco product regulations within a 24-month period	2022	2,559	2,757
		FDA	Penalty in the case of a fifth violation of 21 U.S.C. 387f(d)(5) or of the tobacco product regulations within a 36-month period	2022	6,397	6,892
		FDA	Penalty in the case of a sixth or subsequent violation of 21 U.S.C. 387f(d)(5) or of the tobacco product regulations within a 48-month period as determined on a case-by-case basis	2022	12,794	13,785
335b(a)		FDA	Penalty for each violation for any individual who made a false statement or misrepresentation of a material fact,	2022	487,638	525,406

U.S.C. section(s)	CFR[1]	HHS agency	Description[2]	Date of last penalty figure or adjustment[3]	2022 Maximum adjusted penalty ($)	2023 Maximum adjusted penalty ($)[4]
			bribed, destroyed, altered, removed, or secreted, or procured the destruction, alteration, removal, or secretion of, any material document, failed to disclose a material fact, obstructed an investigation, employed a consultant who was debarred, debarred individual provided consultant services			
		FDA	Penalty in the case of any other person (other than an individual) per above violation	2022	1,950,548	2,101,618
360pp(b)(1)		FDA	Penalty for any person who violates any such requirements for electronic products, with each unlawful act or omission constituting a separate violation	2022	3,198	3,446
		FDA	Penalty imposed for any related series of violations of requirements relating to electronic products	2022	1,090,241	1,174,680
42 U.S.C.				2022	0	
262(d)		FDA	Penalty per day for violation of order of recall of biological product presenting imminent or substantial hazard	2022	250,759	270,180
263b(h)(3)		FDA	Penalty for failure to obtain a mammography certificate as required	2022	19,507	21,018

U.S.C. section(s)	CFR[1]	HHS agency	Description[2]	Date of last penalty figure or adjustment[3]	2022 Maximum adjusted penalty ($)	2023 Maximum adjusted penalty ($)[4]
300aa–28(b)(1)		FDA	Penalty per occurrence for any vaccine manufacturer that intentionally destroys, alters, falsifies, or conceals any record or report required	2022	250,759	270,180
256b(d)(1)(B)(vi)		HRSA	Penalty for each instance of overcharging a 340B covered entity	2022	6,323	6,813
299c–3(d)		AHRQ	Penalty for using or disclosing identifiable information obtained in the course of activities undertaken pursuant to Title IX of the Public Health Service Act, for a purpose other than that for which the information was supplied, without consent to do so	2022	16,443	17,717
653(l)(2)	45 CFR 303.21(f)	ACF	Penalty for Misuse of Information in the National Directory of New Hires	2022	1,687	1,818
262a(i)(1)	42 CFR 1003.910	OIG	Penalty for each individual who violates safety and security procedures related to handling dangerous biological agents and toxins	2022	381,393	410,932
		OIG	Penalty for any other person who violates safety and security procedures related to handling dangerous biological agents and toxins	2022	762,790	821,868

U.S.C. section(s)	CFR[1]	HHS agency	Description[2]	Date of last penalty figure or adjustment[3]	2022 Maximum adjusted penalty ($)	2023 Maximum adjusted penalty ($)[4]
300jj–51		OIG	Penalty per violation for committing information blocking	2022	1,162,924	1,252,992
1320a–7a(a)	42 CFR 1003.210(a)(1)	OIG	Penalty for knowingly presenting or causing to be presented to an officer, employee, or agent of the United States a false claim	2022	22,427	24,164
		OIG	Penalty for knowingly presenting or causing to be presented a request for payment which violates the terms of an assignment, agreement, or PPS agreement	2022	22,427	24,164
	42 CFR 1003.210(a)(2)	OIG	Penalty for knowingly giving or causing to be presented to a participating provider or supplier false or misleading information that could reasonably be expected to influence a discharge decision	2022	33,641	36,246
	42 CFR 1003.210(a)(3)	OIG	Penalty for an excluded party retaining ownership or control interest in a participating entity	2022	22,427	24,164
	42 CFR 1003.1010	OIG	Penalty for remuneration offered to induce program beneficiaries to use particular providers, practitioners, or suppliers	2022	22,427	24,164

U.S.C. section(s)	CFR[1]	HHS agency	Description[2]	Date of last penalty figure or adjustment[3]	2022 Maximum adjusted penalty ($)	2023 Maximum adjusted penalty ($)[4]
	42 CFR 1003.210(a)(4)	OIG	Penalty for employing or contracting with an excluded individual	2022	22,427	24,164
	42 CFR 1003.310(a)(3)	OIG	Penalty for knowing and willful solicitation, receipt, offer, or payment of remuneration for referring an individual for a service or for purchasing, leasing, or ordering an item to be paid for by a Federal health care program	2022	112,131	120,816
	42 CFR 1003.210(a)(1)	OIG	Penalty for ordering or prescribing medical or other item or service during a period in which the person was excluded	2022	22,427	24,164
	42 CFR 1003.210(a)(6)	OIG	Penalty for knowingly making or causing to be made a false statement, omission or misrepresentation of a material fact in any application, bid, or contract to participate or enroll as a provider or supplier	2022	112,131	120,816
	42 CFR 1003.210(a)(8)	OIG	Penalty for knowing of an overpayment and failing to report and return	2022	22,427	24,164
	42 CFR 1003.210(a)(7)	OIG	Penalty for making or using a false record or statement that is material to a false or fraudulent claim	2022	63,231	68,128
	42 CFR 1003.210(a)(9)	OIG	Penalty for failure to grant timely	2022	33,641	36,246

U.S.C. section(s)	CFR[1]	HHS agency	Description[2]	Date of last penalty figure or adjustment[3]	2022 Maximum adjusted penalty ($)	2023 Maximum adjusted penalty ($)[4]
			access to HHS OIG for audits, investigations, evaluations, and other statutory functions of HHS OIG			
1320a–7a(b)		OIG	Penalty for payments by a hospital or critical access hospital to induce a physician to reduce or limit services to individuals under direct care of physician or who are entitled to certain medical assistance benefits	2022	5,606	6,040
		OIG	Penalty for physicians who knowingly receive payments from a hospital or critical access hospital to induce such physician to reduce or limit services to individuals under direct care of physician or who are entitled to certain medical assistance benefits	2022	5,606	6,040
	42 CFR 1003.210(a)(10)	OIG	Penalty for a physician who executes a document that falsely certifies home health needs for Medicare beneficiaries	2022	11,213	12,081
1320a–7a(o)		OIG	Penalty for knowingly presenting or causing to be presented a false or fraudulent specified claim under a grant, contract, or other	2022	10,937	11,784

U.S.C. section(s)	CFR[1]	HHS agency	Description[2]	Date of last penalty figure or adjustment[3]	2022 Maximum adjusted penalty ($)	2023 Maximum adjusted penalty ($)[4]
			agreement for which the Secretary provides funding			
		OIG	Penalty for knowingly making, using, or causing to be made or used any false statement, omission, or misrepresentation of a material fact in any application, proposal, bid, progress report, or other document required to directly or indirectly receive or retain funds provided pursuant to grant, contract, or other agreement	2022	54,686	58,921
		OIG	Penalty for Knowingly making, using, or causing to be made or used, a false record or statement material to a false or fraudulent specified claim under grant, contract, or other agreement	2022	54,686	58,921
		OIG	Penalty for knowingly making, using, or causing to be made or used, a false record or statement material to an obligation to pay or transmit funds or property with respect to grant, contract, or other agreement, or knowingly conceals or improperly avoids or decreases any such obligation	2022	53,772 each false record or statement, 10,754 per day	61,458 each false record or statement, 12,308 per day
		OIG	Penalty for failure to grant timely access, upon	2022	16,406	17,677

U.S.C. section(s)	CFR[1]	HHS agency	Description[2]	Date of last penalty figure or adjustment[3]	2022 Maximum adjusted penalty ($)	2023 Maximum adjusted penalty ($)[4]
			reasonable request, to the I.G. for purposes of audits, investigations, evaluations, or other statutory functions of I.G. in matters involving grants, contracts, or other agreements			
1320a–7e(b)(6)(A)	42 CFR 1003.810	OIG	Penalty for failure to report any final adverse action taken against a health care provider, supplier, or practitioner	2022	42,788	46,102
1320b–10(b)(1)	42 CFR 1003.610(a)	OIG	Penalty for the misuse of words, symbols, or emblems in communications in a manner in which a person could falsely construe that such item is approved, endorsed, or authorized by HHS	2022	11,506	12,397
1320b–10(b)(2)	42 CFR 1003.610(a)	OIG	Penalty for the misuse of words, symbols, or emblems in a broadcast or telecast in a manner in which a person could falsely construe that such item is approved, endorsed, or authorized by HHS	2022	57,527	61,982
1395i–3(b)(3)(B)(ii)(1)	42 CFR 1003.210(a)(11)	OIG	Penalty for certification of a false statement in assessment of functional capacity of a Skilled Nursing Facility resident assessment	2022	2,400	2,586
1395i–3(b)(3)(B)(ii)(2)	42 CFR 1003.210(a)(11)	OIG	Penalty for causing another to certify	2022	11,995	12,924

U.S.C. section(s)	CFR[1]	HHS agency	Description[2]	Date of last penalty figure or adjustment[3]	2022 Maximum adjusted penalty ($)	2023 Maximum adjusted penalty ($)[4]
			or make a false statement in assessment of functional capacity of a Skilled Nursing Facility resident assessment			
1395i–3(g)(2)(A)	42 CFR 1003.1310	OIG	Penalty for any individual who notifies or causes to be notified a Skilled Nursing Facility of the time or date on which a survey is to be conducted	2022	4,799	5,171
1395w–27(g)(2)(A)	42 CFR 1003.410	OIG	Penalty for a Medicare Advantage organization that substantially fails to provide medically necessary, required items and services	2022	43,678	47,061
		OIG	Penalty for a Medicare Advantage organization that charges excessive premiums	2022	42,788	46,102
		OIG	Penalty for a Medicare Advantage organization that improperly expels or refuses to reenroll a beneficiary	2022	42,788	46,102
		OIG	Penalty for a Medicare Advantage organization that engages in practice that would reasonably be expected to have the effect of denying or discouraging enrollment	2022	171,156	184,412

U.S.C. section(s)	CFR[1]	HHS agency	Description[2]	Date of last penalty figure or adjustment[3]	2022 Maximum adjusted penalty ($)	2023 Maximum adjusted penalty ($)[4]
		OIG	Penalty per individual who does not enroll as a result of a Medicare Advantage organization's practice that would reasonably be expected to have the effect of denying or discouraging enrollment	2022	25,673	27,661
		OIG	Penalty for a Medicare Advantage organization misrepresenting or falsifying information to Secretary	2022	171,156	184,412
		OIG	Penalty for a Medicare Advantage organization misrepresenting or falsifying information to individual or other entity	2022	42,788	46,102
		OIG	Penalty for Medicare Advantage organization interfering with provider's advice to enrollee and non-MCO affiliated providers that balance bill enrollees	2022	42,788	46,102
		OIG	Penalty for a Medicare Advantage organization that employs or contracts with excluded individual or entity	2022	42,788	46,102
		OIG	Penalty for a Medicare	2022	42,788	46,102

U.S.C. section(s)	CFR[1]	HHS agency	Description[2]	Date of last penalty figure or adjustment[3]	2022 Maximum adjusted penalty ($)	2023 Maximum adjusted penalty ($)[4]
			Advantage organization enrolling an individual in without prior written consent			
		OIG	Penalty for a Medicare Advantage organization transferring an enrollee to another plan without consent or solely for the purpose of earning a commission	2022	42,788	46,102
		OIG	Penalty for a Medicare Advantage organization failing to comply with marketing restrictions or applicable implementing regulations or guidance	2022	42,788	46,102
		OIG	Penalty for a Medicare Advantage organization employing or contracting with an individual or entity who violates 1395w–27(g)(1)(A)–(J)	2022	42,788	46,102
1395w–141(i)(3)		OIG	Penalty for a prescription drug card sponsor that falsifies or misrepresents marketing materials, overcharges program enrollees, or misuse transitional assistance funds	2022	14,950	16,108
1395cc(g)	42 CFR 1003.210(a)(5)	OIG	Penalty for improper billing by	2022	5,816	6,266

U.S.C. section(s)	CFR[1]	HHS agency	Description[2]	Date of last penalty figure or adjustment[3]	2022 Maximum adjusted penalty ($)	2023 Maximum adjusted penalty ($)[4]
			Hospitals, Critical Access Hospitals, or Skilled Nursing Facilities			
1395dd(d)(1)	42 CFR 1003.510	OIG	Penalty for a hospital with 100 beds or more or responsible physician dumping patients needing emergency medical care	2022	119,942	129,232
			Penalty for a hospital with less than 100 beds dumping patients needing emergency medical care	2022	59,973	64,618
1395mm(i)(6)(B)(i)	42 CFR 1003.410	OIG	Penalty for a HMO or competitive medical plan if such plan substantially fails to provide medically necessary, required items or services	2022	59,973	64,618
		OIG	Penalty for HMOs/competitive medical plans that charge premiums in excess of permitted amounts	2022	59,973	64,618
		OIG	Penalty for a HMO or competitive medical plan that expels or refuses to reenroll an individual per prescribed conditions	2022	59,973	64,618
		OIG	Penalty for a HMO or competitive medical plan that implements practices to discourage enrollment of individuals needing services in future	2022	239,885	258,464

U.S.C. section(s)	CFR[1]	HHS agency	Description[2]	Date of last penalty figure or adjustment[3]	2022 Maximum adjusted penalty ($)	2023 Maximum adjusted penalty ($)[4]
		OIG	Penalty per individual not enrolled in a plan as a result of a HMO or competitive medical plan that implements practices to discourage enrollment of individuals needing services in the future	2022	34,517	37,190
		OIG	Penalty for a HMO or competitive medical plan that misrepresents or falsifies information to the Secretary	2022	239,885	258,464
		OIG	Penalty for a HMO or competitive medical plan that misrepresents or falsifies information to an individual or any other entity	2022	59,973	64,618
		OIG	Penalty for failure by HMO or competitive medical plan to assure prompt payment of Medicare risk sharing contracts or incentive plan provisions	2022	59,973	64,618
		OIG	Penalty for HMO that employs or contracts with excluded individual or entity	2022	55,052	59,316
1395nn(g)(3)	42 CFR 1003.310	OIG	Penalty for submitting or causing to be submitted claims in violation of the Stark Law's restrictions on physician self-referrals	2022	27,750	29,899

U.S.C. section(s)	CFR[1]	HHS agency	Description[2]	Date of last penalty figure or adjustment[3]	2022 Maximum adjusted penalty ($)	2023 Maximum adjusted penalty ($)[4]
1395nn(g)(4)	42 CFR 1003.310	OIG	Penalty for circumvention schemes in violation of the Stark Law's restrictions on physician self-referrals	2022	185,009	199,338
1395ss(d)(1)	42 CFR 1003.1110	OIG	Penalty for a material misrepresentation regarding Medigap compliance policies	2022	11,506	12,397
1395ss(d)(2)	42 CFR 1003.1110	OIG	Penalty for selling Medigap policy under false pretense	2022	11,506	12,397
1395ss(d)(3)(A)(ii)	42 CFR 1003.1110	OIG	Penalty for an issuer that sells health insurance policy that duplicates benefits	2022	51,796	55,808
		OIG	Penalty for someone other than issuer that sells health insurance that duplicates benefits	2022	31,076	33,483
1395ss(d)(4)(A)	42 CFR 1003.1110	OIG	Penalty for using mail to sell a non-approved Medigap insurance policy	2022	11,506	12,397
1396b(m)(5)(B)(i)	42 CFR 1003.410	OIG	Penalty for a Medicaid MCO that substantially fails to provide medically necessary, required items or services	2022	57,527	61,982
		OIG	Penalty for a Medicaid MCO that charges excessive premiums	2022	57,527	61,982
		OIG	Penalty for a Medicaid MCO that improperly expels or refuses to reenroll a beneficiary	2022	230,107	247,929
		OIG	Penalty per individual who does not enroll as a	2022	34,517	37,190

U.S.C. section(s)	CFR[1]	HHS agency	Description[2]	Date of last penalty figure or adjustment[3]	2022 Maximum adjusted penalty ($)	2023 Maximum adjusted penalty ($)[4]
			result of a Medicaid MCO's practice that would reasonably be expected to have the effect of denying or discouraging enrollment			
		OIG	Penalty for a Medicaid MCO misrepresenting or falsifying information to the Secretary	2022	230,107	247,929
		OIG	Penalty for a Medicaid MCO misrepresenting or falsifying information to an individual or another entity	2022	57,527	61,982
		OIG	Penalty for a Medicaid MCO that fails to comply with contract requirements with respect to physician incentive plans	2022	51,796	55,808
1396r(b)(3)(B)(ii)(I)	42 CFR 1003.210(a)(11)	OIG	Penalty for willfully and knowingly certifying a material and false statement in a Skilled Nursing Facility resident assessment	2022	2,400	2,586
1396r(b)(3)(B)(ii)(II)	42 CFR 1003.210(a)(11)	OIG	Penalty for willfully and knowingly causing another individual to certify a material and false statement in a Skilled Nursing Facility resident assessment	2022	11,995	12,924
1396r(g)(2)(A)(i)	42 CFR 1003.1310	OIG	Penalty for notifying or causing to be notified a Skilled Nursing Facility of the time	2022	4,799	5,171

U.S.C. section(s)	CFR[1]	HHS agency	Description[2]	Date of last penalty figure or adjustment[3]	2022 Maximum adjusted penalty ($)	2023 Maximum adjusted penalty ($)[4]
			or date on which a survey is to be conducted			
1396r–8(b)(3)(B)	42 CFR 1003.1210	OIG	Penalty for the knowing provision of false information or refusing to provide information about charges or prices of a covered outpatient drug	2022	207,183	223,229
1396r–8(b)(3)(C)(i)	42 CFR 1003.1210	OIG	Penalty per day for failure to timely provide information by drug manufacturer with rebate agreement	2022	20,719	22,324
1396r–8(b)(3)(C)(ii)	42 CFR 1003.1210	OIG	Penalty for knowing provision of false information by drug manufacturer with rebate agreement	2022	207,183	223,229
1396t(i)(3)(A)	42 CFR 1003.1310	OIG	Penalty for notifying home and community-based providers or settings of survey	2022	4,144	4,465
11131(c)	42 CFR 1003.810	OIG	Penalty for failing to report a medical malpractice claim to National Practitioner Data Bank	2022	25,076	27,018
11137(b)(2)	42 CFR 1003.810	OIG	Penalty for breaching confidentiality of information reported to National Practitioner Data Bank	2022	25,076	27,018
299b–22(f)(1)	42 CFR 3.404	OCR	Penalty for violation of confidentiality provision of the Patient Safety and	2022	13,885	14,960

U.S.C. section(s)	CFR[1]	HHS agency	Description[2]	Date of last penalty figure or adjustment[3]	2022 Maximum adjusted penalty ($)	2023 Maximum adjusted penalty ($)[4]
			Quality Improvement Act			
	45 CFR 160.404(b)(1)(i), (ii)	OCR	Penalty for each pre-February 18, 2009 violation of the HIPAA administrative simplification provisions	2022	174	187
			Calendar Year Cap	2022	43,678	47,061
1320(d)–5(a)	45 CFR 160.404(b)(2)(i)(A), (B)	OCR	Penalty for each February 18, 2009 or later violation of a HIPAA administrative simplification provision in which it is established that the covered entity or business associate did not know and, by exercising reasonable diligence, would not have known that the covered entity or business associate violated such a provision:	2022		
			Minimum	2022	127	137
			Maximum	2022	63,973	68,928
			Calendar Year Cap	2022	1,919,173	2,067,813
	45 CFR 160.404(b)(2)(ii)(A), (B)	OCR	Penalty for each February 18, 2009 or later violation of a HIPAA administrative simplification provision in which it is established that the violation was due to reasonable cause and not to willful neglect:	2022		
			Minimum	2022	1,280	1,379
			Maximum	2022	63,973	68,928
			Calendar Year Cap	2022	1,919,173	2,067,813

U.S.C. section(s)	CFR[1]	HHS agency	Description[2]	Date of last penalty figure or adjustment[3]	2022 Maximum adjusted penalty ($)	2023 Maximum adjusted penalty ($)[4]
	45 CFR 160.404(b)(2)(iii)(A),(B)	OCR	Penalty for each February 18, 2009 or later violation of a HIPAA administrative simplification provision in which it is established that the violation was due to willful neglect and was corrected during the 30-day period beginning on the first date the covered entity or business associate knew, or, by exercising reasonable diligence, would have known that the violation occurred:	2022		
			Minimum	2022	12,794	13,785
			Maximum	2022	63,973	68,928
			Calendar Year Cap	2022	1,919,173	2,067,813
	45 CFR 160.404(b)(2)(iv)(A),(B)	OCR	Penalty for each February 18, 2009 or later violation of a HIPAA administrative simplification provision in which it is established that the violation was due to willful neglect and was not corrected during the 30-day period beginning on the first date the covered entity or business associate knew, or, by exercising reasonable diligence, would have known that the violation occurred:	2022		

U.S.C. section(s)	CFR[1]	HHS agency	Description[2]	Date of last penalty figure or adjustment[3]	2022 Maximum adjusted penalty ($)	2023 Maximum adjusted penalty ($)[4]
			Minimum	2022	63,973	68,928
			Maximum	2022	1,919,173	2,067,813
			Calendar Year Cap	2022	1,919,173	2,067,813
42 U.S.C. 300gg–18, 42 U.S.C. 1302	45 CFR 180.90	CMS	Penalty for a hospital's non-compliance with making public standard charges for hospital items and services	2022	300	323
			Per Day (Maximum)	2022	5,500	5,926
	45 CFR 180.90(c)(2)(i)	CMS	Per day penalty for a hospital's noncompliance with making public standard charges for hospital items and services	2022	304	328
	45 CFR 180.90(c)(2)(ii)(A)	CMS	Per day penalty for hospitals with equal to or less than 30 beds	2022	300	323
	45 CFR 180.90(c)(2)(ii)(B)	CMS	Per day, per bed penalty for hospitals having at least 31 and up to and including 550 beds	2022	10	11
	45 CFR 180.90(c)(2)(ii)(C)	CMS	Per day penalty for hospitals having greater than 550 beds	2022	5,500	5,926
CARES Act, Public Law 116–136, section 3202(b)(2)	45 CFR 182.70	CMS	Penalty for a provider's non-compliance with price transparency requirements regarding diagnostic tests for COVID–19	2022		
			Per Day (Maximum)	2022	300	323
263a(h)(2)(B) & 1395w–2(b)(2)(A)(ii)	42 CFR 493.1834(d)(2)(i).	CMS	Penalty for a clinical laboratory's failure to meet participation and certification requirements and	2022		

U.S.C. section(s)	CFR[1]	HHS agency	Description[2]	Date of last penalty figure or adjustment[3]	2022 Maximum adjusted penalty ($)	2023 Maximum adjusted penalty ($)[4]
			poses immediate jeopardy:			
			Minimum	2022	7,018	7,562
			Maximum	2022	23,011	24,793
	42 CFR 493.1834(d)(2)(ii)	CMS	Penalty for a clinical laboratory's failure to meet participation and certification requirements and the failure does not pose immediate jeopardy:	2022		
			Minimum	2022	116	125
			Maximum	2022	6,902	7,437
	42 CFR 493.1834(d)(2)(iii)	CMS	Penalty for a clinical laboratory's failure to meet SARS–CoV–2 test reporting requirements:	2022		
			First day of noncompliance	2022		
			Each additional day of noncompliance	2022		
300gg–15(f)	45 CFR 147.200(e)	CMS	Failure to provide the Summary of Benefits and Coverage	2022	1,264	1,362
300gg–18	45 CFR 158.606	CMS	Penalty for violations of regulations related to the medical loss ratio reporting and rebating	2022	126	136
	45 CFR 180.90	CMS	Price against hospital identified by CMS as noncompliant according to § 182.50 with respect to price transparency requirements regarding diagnostic tests for COVID–19	2022		
42 U.S.C. 300gg–118 note, 300gg–134		CMS	Penalties for failure to comply with No	2022	10,622	11,445

U.S.C. section(s)	CFR[1]	HHS agency	Description[2]	Date of last penalty figure or adjustment[3]	2022 Maximum adjusted penalty ($)	2023 Maximum adjusted penalty ($)[4]
			Surprises Act requirements on providers, facilities, providers of air ambulance services			
1320a–7h(b)(1)	42 CFR 402.105(d)(5), 42 CFR 403.912(a) & (c)	CMS	Penalty for manufacturer or group purchasing organization failing to report information required under 42 U.S.C. 1320a–7h(a), relating to physician ownership or investment interests:	2022		
			Minimum	2022	1,264	1,362
			Maximum	2022	12,646	13,625
			Calendar Year Cap	2022	189,692	204,384
1320a–7h(b)(2)	42 CFR 402.105(h), 42 CFR 403.912(b) & (c)	CMS	Penalty for manufacturer or group purchasing organization knowingly failing to report information required under 42 U.S.C. 1320a–7h(a), relating to physician ownership or investment interests:	2022		
			Minimum	2022	12,646	13,625
			Maximum	2022	126,463	136,258
			Calendar Year Cap	2022	1,264,622	1,362,567
		CMS	Penalty for an administrator of a facility that fails to comply with notice requirements for the closure of a facility	2022	126,463	136,258
1320a–7j(h)(3)(A)	42 CFR 488.446(a)(1), (2), & (3)	CMS	Minimum penalty for the first offense of an administrator who fails to provide notice of facility closure	2022	632	681

U.S.C. section(s)	CFR[1]	HHS agency	Description[2]	Date of last penalty figure or adjustment[3]	2022 Maximum adjusted penalty ($)	2023 Maximum adjusted penalty ($)[4]
			Minimum penalty for the second offense of an administrator who fails to provide notice of facility closure	2022	1,898	2,045
			Minimum penalty for the third and subsequent offenses of an administrator who fails to provide notice of facility closure	2022	3,793	4,087
1320a–8(a)(1)		CMS	Penalty for an entity knowingly making a false statement or representation of material fact in the determination of the amount of benefits or payments related to old-age, survivors, and disability insurance benefits, special benefits for certain World War II veterans, or supplemental security income for the aged, blind, and disabled	2022	9,250	9,966
			Penalty for violation of 42 U.S.C. 1320a–8(a)(1) if the violator is a person who receives a fee or other income for services performed in connection with determination of the benefit amount or the person is a physician or other health care provider who submits evidence in	2022	8,723	9,399

U.S.C. section(s)	CFR[1]	HHS agency	Description[2]	Date of last penalty figure or adjustment[3]	2022 Maximum adjusted penalty ($)	2023 Maximum adjusted penalty ($)[4]
			connection with such a determination			
1320a–8(a)(3)		CMS	Penalty for a representative payee (under 42 U.S.C. 405(j), 1007, or 1383(a)(2)) converting any part of a received payment from the benefit programs described in the previous civil monetary penalty to a use other than for the benefit of the beneficiary	2022	7,244	7,805
1320b–25(c)(1)(A)		CMS	Penalty for failure of covered individuals to report to the Secretary and 1 or more law enforcement officials any reasonable suspicion of a crime against a resident, or individual receiving care, from a long-term care facility	2022	252,925	272,514
1320b–25(c)(2)(A)		CMS	Penalty for failure of covered individuals to report to the Secretary and 1 or more law enforcement officials any reasonable suspicion of a crime against a resident, or individual receiving care, from a long-term care facility if such failure exacerbates the harm to the victim of the crime	2022	379,386	408,769

U.S.C. section(s)	CFR[1]	HHS agency	Description[2]	Date of last penalty figure or adjustment[3]	2022 Maximum adjusted penalty ($)	2023 Maximum adjusted penalty ($)[4]
			or results in the harm to another individual			
1320b–25(d)(2)		CMS	Penalty for a long-term care facility that retaliates against any employee because of lawful acts done by the employee, or files a complaint or report with the State professional disciplinary agency against an employee or nurse for lawful acts done by the employee or nurse	2022	252,925	272,514
1395b–7(b)(2)(B)	42 CFR 402.105(g)	CMS	Penalty for any person who knowingly and willfully fails to furnish a beneficiary with an itemized statement of items or services within 30 days of the beneficiary's request	2022	171	184
1395i–3(h)(2)(B)(ii)(I)	42 CFR 488.408(d)(1)(iii)	CMS	Penalty per day for a Skilled Nursing Facility that has a Category 2 violation of certification requirements:	2022		
			Minimum	2022	120	129
			Maximum	2022	7,195	7,752
	42 CFR 488.408(d)(1)(iv)	CMS	Penalty per instance of Category 2 noncompliance by a Skilled Nursing Facility:	2022		
			Minimum	2022	2,400	2,586
			Maximum	2022	23,989	25,847
	42 CFR 488.408(e)(1)(iii)	CMS	Penalty per day for a Skilled Nursing Facility that has a Category 3 violation of	2022		

U.S.C. section(s)	CFR[1]	HHS agency	Description[2]	Date of last penalty figure or adjustment[3]	2022 Maximum adjusted penalty ($)	2023 Maximum adjusted penalty ($)[4]
			certification requirements:			
			Minimum	2022	7,317	7,884
			Maximum	2022	23,989	25,847
	42 CFR 488.408(e)(1)(iv)	CMS	Penalty per instance of Category 3 noncompliance by a Skilled Nursing Facility:	2022		
			Minimum	2022	2,400	2,586
			Maximum	2022	23,989	25,847
	42 CFR 488.408(e)(2)(ii)	CMS	Penalty per day and per instance for a Skilled Nursing Facility that has Category 3 noncompliance with Immediate Jeopardy:	2022		
			Per Day (Minimum)	2022	7,317	7,884
			Per Day (Maximum)	2022	23,989	25,847
			Per Instance (Minimum)	2022	2,400	2,586
			Per Instance (Maximum)	2022	23,989	25,847
	42 CFR 488.438(a)(1)(i)	CMS	Penalty per day of a Skilled Nursing Facility that fails to meet certification requirements. These amounts represent the upper range per day:	2022		
			Minimum	2022	7,317	7,884
			Maximum	2022	23,989	25,847
	42 CFR 488.438(a)(1)(ii)	CMS	Penalty per day of a Skilled Nursing Facility that fails to meet certification requirements. These amounts represent the lower range per day:	2022		
			Minimum	2022	120	129
			Maximum	2022	7,195	7,752

U.S.C. section(s)	CFR[1]	HHS agency	Description[2]	Date of last penalty figure or adjustment[3]	2022 Maximum adjusted penalty ($)	2023 Maximum adjusted penalty ($)[4]
	42 CFR 488.438(a)(2)	CMS	Penalty per instance of a Skilled Nursing Facility that fails to meet certification requirements:	2022		
			Minimum	2022	2,400	2,586
			Maximum	2022	23,989	25,847
	42 CFR 488.447	CMS	Penalty imposed for failure to comply with infection control weekly reporting requirements at 42 CFR 483.80(g)(1) and (2)	2022		
			First occurrence	2022	1,075	1,158
			Incremental increases for each subsequent occurrence	2022	537	579
1395i–6(c)(5)(B)(i)	42 CFR 488.1245	CMS	Penalty for noncompliance by hospice program with requirements specified in section 1395x(dd) of 42 USC	2022	10,000	10,775
	42 CFR 488.1245(b)(2)(iii)	CMS	Adjustment to penalties. Maximum penalty assessment for each day a hospice is not in substantial compliance with one or more conditions of participation	2022	10,000	10,775
	42 CFR 488.1245(b)(3)	CMS	Penalty imposed for hospice condition-level deficiency that is immediate jeopardy. These amounts represent the upper range of penalty			
		CMS	Minimum	2022	8,500	9,158
			Maximum	2022	10,000	10,775

U.S.C. section(s)	CFR[1]	HHS agency	Description[2]	Date of last penalty figure or adjustment[3]	2022 Maximum adjusted penalty ($)	2023 Maximum adjusted penalty ($)[4]
	42 CFR 488.1245(b)(3)(i)	CMS	Penalty imposed for hospice condition-level deficiency that is immediate jeopardy. These amounts represent the upper range of penalty	2022	10,000	10,775
	42 CFR 488.1245(b)(3)(ii)	CMS	Penalty imposed for hospice condition-level deficiency that is immediate jeopardy. These amounts represent the upper range of penalty	2022	9,000	9,697
	42 CFR 488.1245(b)(3)(iii)	CMS	Penalty imposed for hospice condition-level deficiency that is immediate jeopardy. These amounts represent the upper range of penalty	2022	8,500	9,158
	42 CFR 488.1245(b)(4)	CMS	Penalty imposed for hospice repeat or condition-level deficiency or both that does not constitute immediate jeopardy but is directly related to poor quality patient care outcomes. These amounts represent the middle range of penalty	2022		
			Minimum	2022	1,500	1,616
			Maximum	2022	8,500	9,158
	42 CFR 488.1245(b)(5)	CMS	Penalty imposed for hospice repeat or condition-level deficiency or both that does not constitute immediate jeopardy	2022		

U.S.C. section(s)	CFR[1]	HHS agency	Description[2]	Date of last penalty figure or adjustment[3]	2022 Maximum adjusted penalty ($)	2023 Maximum adjusted penalty ($)[4]
			and are related predominantly to structure or process-oriented conditions rather than directly related to patient outcomes. These amounts represent the lower range of penalty			
			Minimum	2022	500	539
			Maximum	2022	4,000	4,310
	42 CFR 488.1245(b)(6)	CMS	Penalty range imposed for per instance of hospice noncompliance	2022		
		CMS	Minimum	2022	1,000	1,077
			Maximum	2022	10,000	10,775
	42 CFR 488.1245(d)(1)(ii)	CMS	Penalty for each per instance of hospice noncompliance, maximum per day per hospice program	2022	10,000	10,775
1395l(h)(5)(D)	42 CFR 402.105(d)(2)(i)	CMS	Penalty for knowingly, willfully, and repeatedly billing for a clinical diagnostic laboratory test other than on an assignment-related basis. (Penalties are assessed in the same manner as 42 U.S.C. 1395u(j)(2)(B), which is assessed according to 1320a–7a(a))	2022	17,472	18,825
1395l(i)(6)		CMS	Penalty for knowingly and willfully presenting or causing to be presented a bill or request for payment for an intraocular lens inserted during or after cataract	2022	4,603	4,960

U.S.C. section(s)	CFR[1]	HHS agency	Description[2]	Date of last penalty figure or adjustment[3]	2022 Maximum adjusted penalty ($)	2023 Maximum adjusted penalty ($)[4]
			surgery for which the Medicare payment rate includes the cost of acquiring the class of lens involved			
1395l(q)(2)(B)(i)	42 CFR 402.105(a)	CMS	Penalty for knowingly and willfully failing to provide information about a referring physician when seeking payment on an unassigned basis	2022	4,404	4,745
1395m(a)(11)(A)	42 CFR 402.1(c)(4), 402.105(d)(2)(ii)	CMS	Penalty for any durable medical equipment supplier that knowingly and willfully charges for a covered service that is furnished on a rental basis after the rental payments may no longer be made. (Penalties are assessed in the same manner as 42 U.S.C. 1395u(j)(2)(B), which is assessed according to 1320a–7a(a))	2022	17,472	18,825
1395m(a)(18)(B)	42 CFR 402.1(c)(5), 402.105(d)(2)(iii)	CMS	Penalty for any nonparticipating durable medical equipment supplier that knowingly and willfully fails to make a refund to Medicare beneficiaries for a covered service for which payment is precluded due to an unsolicited telephone contact from the supplier. (Penalties are assessed in the same manner as 42	2022	17,472	18,825

U.S.C. section(s)	CFR[1]	HHS agency	Description[2]	Date of last penalty figure or adjustment[3]	2022 Maximum adjusted penalty ($)	2023 Maximum adjusted penalty ($)[4]
			U.S.C. 1395u(j)(2)(B), which is assessed according to 1320a–7a(a))			
1395m(b)(5)(C)	42 CFR 402.1(c)(6), 402.105(d)(2)(iv)	CMS	Penalty for any nonparticipating physician or supplier that knowingly and willfully charges a Medicare beneficiary more than the limiting charge for radiologist services. (Penalties are assessed in the same manner as 42 U.S.C. 1395u(j)(2)(B), which is assessed according to 1320a–7a(a))	2022	17,472	18,825
1395m(h)(3)	42 CFR 402.1(c)(8), 402.105(d)(2)(vi)	CMS	Penalty for any supplier of prosthetic devices, orthotics, and prosthetics that knowing and willfully charges for a covered prosthetic device, orthotic, or prosthetic that is furnished on a rental basis after the rental payment may no longer be made. (Penalties are assessed in the same manner as 42 U.S.C. 1395m(a)(11)(A), that is in the same manner as 1395u(j)(2)(B), which is assessed according to 1320a–7a(a))	2022	17,472	18,825

U.S.C. section(s)	CFR[1]	HHS agency	Description[2]	Date of last penalty figure or adjustment[3]	2022 Maximum adjusted penalty ($)	2023 Maximum adjusted penalty ($)[4]
1395m(j)(2)(A)(iii)		CMS	Penalty for any supplier of durable medical equipment including a supplier of prosthetic devices, prosthetics, orthotics, or supplies that knowingly and willfully distributes a certificate of medical necessity in violation of Section 1834(j)(2)(A)(i) of the Act or fails to provide the information required under Section 1834(j)(2)(A)(ii) of the Act	2022	1,850	1,993
1395m(j)(4)	42 CFR 402.1(c)(10), 402.105(d)(2)(vii)	CMS	Penalty for any supplier of durable medical equipment, including a supplier of prosthetic devices, prosthetics, orthotics, or supplies that knowingly and willfully fails to make refunds in a timely manner to Medicare beneficiaries for series billed other than on as assignment-related basis under certain conditions. (Penalties are assessed in the same manner as 42 U.S.C. 1395m(j)(4) and 1395u(j)(2)(B), which is assessed according to 1320a–7a(a))	2022	17,472	18,825
1395m–1(a)	42 CFR 414.504(e)	CMS	Penalty for an applicable entity that has failed to	2022	11,649	12,551

U.S.C. section(s)	CFR[1]	HHS agency	Description[2]	Date of last penalty figure or adjustment[3]	2022 Maximum adjusted penalty ($)	2023 Maximum adjusted penalty ($)[4]
			report or made a misrepresentation or omission in reporting applicable information with respect to a clinical diagnostic laboratory test			
	42 CFR 402.1(c)(31), 402.105(d)(3)	CMS	Penalty for any person or entity who knowingly and willfully bills or collects for any outpatient therapy services or comprehensive outpatient rehabilitation services on other than an assignment-related basis. (Penalties are assessed in the same manner as 42 U.S.C. 1395m(k)(6) and 1395u(j)(2)(B), which is assessed according to 1320a–7a(a))	2022	17,472	18,825
1395m(l)(6)	42 CFR 402.1(c)(32), 402.105(d)(4)	CMS	Penalty for any supplier of ambulance services who knowingly and willfully fills or collects for any services on other than an assignment-related basis. (Penalties are assessed in the same manner as 42 U.S.C. 1395u(b)(18)(B), which is assessed according to 1320a–7a(a))	2022	17,472	18,825
1395u(b)(18)(B)	42 CFR 402.1(c)(11), 402.105(d)(2)(viii)	CMS	Penalty for any practitioner specified in Section 1842(b)(18)(C) of the Act or other	2022	17,472	18,825

U.S.C. section(s)	CFR[1]	HHS agency	Description[2]	Date of last penalty figure or adjustment[3]	2022 Maximum adjusted penalty ($)	2023 Maximum adjusted penalty ($)[4]
			person that knowingly and willfully bills or collects for any services by the practitioners on other than an assignment-related basis. (Penalties are assessed in the same manner as 42 U.S.C. 1395u(j)(2)(B), which is assessed according to 1320a–7a(a))			
1395u(j)(2)(B)	42 CFR 402.1(c)	CMS	Penalty for any physician who charges more than 125% for a non-participating referral. (Penalties are assessed in the same manner as 42 U.S.C. 1320a–7a(a))	2022	17,472	18,825
1395u(k)	42 CFR 402.1(c)(12), 402.105(d)(2)(ix) 1834A(a)(9) and 42 CFR 414.504(e)	CMS	Penalty for any physician who knowingly and willfully presents or causes to be presented a claim for bill for an assistant at a cataract surgery performed on or after March 1, 1987, for which payment may not be made because of section 1862(a)(15). (Penalties are assessed in the same manner as 42 U.S.C. 1395u(j)(2)(B), which is assessed according to 1320a–7a(a))	2022	17,472	18,825
1395u(l)(3)	42 CFR 402.1(c)(13), 402.105(d)(2)(x)	CMS	Penalty for any nonparticipating physician who does	2022	17,472	18,825

U.S.C. section(s)	CFR[1]	HHS agency	Description[2]	Date of last penalty figure or adjustment[3]	2022 Maximum adjusted penalty ($)	2023 Maximum adjusted penalty ($)[4]
			not accept payment on an assignment-related basis and who knowingly and willfully fails to refund on a timely basis any amounts collected for services that are not reasonable or medically necessary or are of poor quality under 1842(l)(1)(A). (Penalties are assessed in the same manner as 42 U.S.C. 1395u(j)(2)(B), which is assessed according to 1320a–7a(a))			
1395u(m)(3)	42 CFR 402.1(c)(14), 402.105(d)(2)(xi)	CMS	Penalty for any nonparticipating physician charging more than $500 who does not accept payment for an elective surgical procedure on an assignment related basis and who knowingly and willfully fails to disclose the required information regarding charges and coinsurance amounts and fails to refund on a timely basis any amount collected for the procedure in excess of the charges recognized and approved by the Medicare program. (Penalties are assessed in the same manner as 42	2022	17,472	18,825

U.S.C. section(s)	CFR[1]	HHS agency	Description[2]	Date of last penalty figure or adjustment[3]	2022 Maximum adjusted penalty ($)	2023 Maximum adjusted penalty ($)[4]
			U.S.C. 1395u(j)(2)(B), which is assessed according to 1320a–7a(a))			
1395u(n)(3)	42 CFR 402.1(c)(15), 402.105(d)(2)(xii)	CMS	Penalty for any physician who knowingly, willfully, and repeatedly bills one or more beneficiaries for purchased diagnostic tests any amount other than the payment amount specified by the Act. (Penalties are assessed in the same manner as 42 U.S.C. 1395u(j)(2)(B), which is assessed according to 1320a–7a(a))	2022	17,472	18,825
1395u(o)(3)(B)	42 CFR 414.707(b)	CMS	Penalty for any practitioner specified in Section 1842(b)(18)(C) of the Act or other person that knowingly and willfully bills or collects for any services pertaining to drugs or biologics by the practitioners on other than an assignment-related basis. (Penalties are assessed in the same manner as 42 U.S.C. 1395u(b)(18)(B) and 1395u(j)(2)(B), which is assessed according to 1320a–7a(a))	2022	17,472	18,825
1395u(p)(3)(A)		CMS	Penalty for any physician or	2022	4,603	4,960

U.S.C. section(s)	CFR[1]	HHS agency	Description[2]	Date of last penalty figure or adjustment[3]	2022 Maximum adjusted penalty ($)	2023 Maximum adjusted penalty ($)[4]
			practitioner who knowingly and willfully fails promptly to provide the appropriate diagnosis codes upon CMS or Medicare administrative contractor request for payment or bill not submitted on an assignment-related basis			
1395w–3a(d)(4)(A)	42 CFR 414.806	CMS	Penalty for a pharmaceutical manufacturer's misrepresentation of average sales price of a drug, or biologic	2022	14,950	16,108
1395w–4(g)(1)(B)	42 CFR 402.1(c)(17), 402.105(d)(2)(xiii)	CMS	Penalty for any nonparticipating physician, supplier, or other person that furnishes physician services not on an assignment-related basis who either knowingly and willfully bills or collects in excess of the statutorily-defined limiting charge or fails to make a timely refund or adjustment. (Penalties are assessed in the same manner as 42 U.S.C. 1395u(j)(2)(B), which is assessed according to 1320a–7a(a))	2022	17,472	18,825
1395w–4(g)(3)(B)	42 CFR 402.1(c)(18), 402.105(d)(2)(xiv)	CMS	Penalty for any person that knowingly and	2022	17,472	18,825

U.S.C. section(s)	CFR[1]	HHS agency	Description[2]	Date of last penalty figure or adjustment[3]	2022 Maximum adjusted penalty ($)	2023 Maximum adjusted penalty ($)[4]
			willfully bills for statutorily defined State-plan approved physicians' services on any other basis than an assignment-related basis for a Medicare/Medicaid dual eligible beneficiary. (Penalties are assessed in the same manner as 42 U.S.C. 1395u(j)(2)(B), which is assessed according to 1320a–7a(a))			
1395w–27(g)(3)(A); 1857(g)(3); 1860D–12(b)(3)(E)	42 CFR 422.760(b); 42 CFR 423.760(b)	CMS	Penalty for each termination determination the Secretary makes that is the result of actions by a Medicare Advantage organization or Part D sponsor that has adversely affected (or has the substantial likelihood of adversely affecting) an individual covered under the organization's contract	2022	42,788	46,102
1395w–27(g)(3)(B); 1857(g)(3); 1860D–12(b)(3)(E)		CMS	Penalty for each week beginning after the initiation of civil money penalty procedures by the Secretary because a Medicare Advantage organization or Part D sponsor has failed to carry out a contract, or has carried out a contract	2022	17,116	18,442

U.S.C. section(s)	CFR[1]	HHS agency	Description[2]	Date of last penalty figure or adjustment[3]	2022 Maximum adjusted penalty ($)	2023 Maximum adjusted penalty ($)[4]
			inconsistently with regulations			
1395w–27(g)(3)(D); 1857(g)(3): 1860D–12(b)(3)(E)		CMS	Penalty for a Medicare Advantage organization's or Part D sponsor's early termination of its contract	2022	158,947	171,257
1395y(b)(3)(C)	42 CFR 411.103(b)	CMS	Penalty for an employer or other entity to offer any financial or other incentive for an individual entitled to benefits not to enroll under a group health plan or large group health plan which would be a primary plan	2022	10,360	11,162
1395y(b)(5)(C)(ii)	42 CFR 402.1(c)(20), 42 CFR 402.105(b)(2)	CMS	Penalty for any non-governmental employer that, before October 1, 1998, willfully or repeatedly failed to provide timely and accurate information requested relating to an employee's group health insurance coverage	2022	1,687	1,818
1395y(b)(6)(B)	42 CFR 402.1(c)(20), 402.105(a)	CMS	Penalty for any entity that knowingly, willfully, and repeatedly fails to complete a claim form relating to the availability of other health benefits in accordance with statute or provides inaccurate information relating to such on the claim form	2022	3,701	3,988

U.S.C. section(s)	CFR[1]	HHS agency	Description[2]	Date of last penalty figure or adjustment[3]	2022 Maximum adjusted penalty ($)	2023 Maximum adjusted penalty ($)[4]
1395y(b)(7)(B)(i)	42 CFR 402.1(c)(21), 402.105(a)	CMS	Penalty for any entity serving as insurer, third party administrator, or fiduciary for a group health plan that fails to provide information that identifies situations where the group health plan is or was a primary plan to Medicare to the HHS Secretary	2022	1,325	1,428
1395y(b)(8)(E)		CMS	Penalty for any non-group health plan that fails to identify claimants who are Medicare beneficiaries and provide information to the HHS Secretary to coordinate benefits and pursue any applicable recovery claim	2022	1,325	1,428
1395y(b)(8)(E)(i)	42 CFR 402.1(c)(22), 402.105(b)(2)	CMS	Penalty for any entity serving as insurer, third party administrator, or fiduciary for a non-group health plan that fails to provide information that identifies situations where the group health plan is or was a primary plan to Medicare to the HHS Secretary	2022	1,325	1,428
1395nn(g)(5)	42 CFR 411.361	CMS	Penalty for any person that fails to report information required by HHS under Section 1877(f) concerning ownership, investment, and compensation arrangements	2022	22,021	23,727

U.S.C. section(s)	CFR[1]	HHS agency	Description[2]	Date of last penalty figure or adjustment[3]	2022 Maximum adjusted penalty ($)	2023 Maximum adjusted penalty ($)[4]
1395pp(h)	42 CFR 402.1(c)(23), 402.105(d)(2)(xv)	CMS	Penalty for any durable medical equipment supplier, including a supplier of prosthetic devices, prosthetics, orthotics, or supplies, that knowingly and willfully fails to make refunds in a timely manner to Medicare beneficiaries under certain conditions. (42 U.S.C. 1395(m)(18) sanctions apply here in the same manner, which is under 1395u(j)(2) and 1320a–7a(a))	2022	17,472	18,825
1395ss(a)(2)	402.102(f)(1)	CMS	Penalty for any person that issues a Medicare supplemental policy that has not been approved by the State regulatory program or does not meet Federal standards after a statutorily defined effective date	2022	59,972	64,617
1395ss(d)(3)(A)(vi)(II)	42 CFR 402.1(c)(25), 402.105(e), 402.105(f)(2)	CMS	Penalty for someone other than issuer that sells or issues a Medicare supplemental policy to beneficiary without a disclosure statement	2022	31,076	33,483
		CMS	Penalty for an issuer that sells or issues a Medicare supplemental policy without disclosure statement	2022	51,796	55,808
1395ss(d)(3)(B)(iv)		CMS	Penalty for someone other than issuer that sells or	2022	31,076	33,483

U.S.C. section(s)	CFR[1]	HHS agency	Description[2]	Date of last penalty figure or adjustment[3]	2022 Maximum adjusted penalty ($)	2023 Maximum adjusted penalty ($)[4]
			issues a Medicare supplemental policy without acknowledgement form			
		CMS	Penalty for issuer that sells or issues a Medicare supplemental policy without an acknowledgement form	2022	51,796	55,808
1395ss(p)(8)	42 CFR 402.1(c)(25), 402.105(e)	CMS	Penalty for someone other than issuer that sells or issues Medicare supplemental polices after a given date that fail to conform to the NAIC or Federal standards established by statute	2022	31,076	33,483
	42 CFR 402.1(c)(25), 405402.105(f)(2)	CMS	Penalty for an issuer that sells or issues Medicare supplemental polices after a given date that fail to conform to the NAIC or Federal standards established by statute	2022	51,796	55,808
1395ss(p)(9)(C)	42 CFR 402.1(c)(26), 402.105(e), 402.105(f)(3), (4)	CMS	Penalty for someone other than issuer that sells a Medicare supplemental policy and fails to make available for sale the core group of basic benefits when selling other Medicare supplemental policies with additional benefits or fails to provide the individual,	2022	31,076	33,483

U.S.C. section(s)	CFR[1]	HHS agency	Description[2]	Date of last penalty figure or adjustment[3]	2022 Maximum adjusted penalty ($)	2023 Maximum adjusted penalty ($)[4]
			before selling the policy, an outline of coverage describing benefits			
	402.105(f)(3), (4)	CMS	Penalty for an issuer that sells a Medicare supplemental policy and fails to make available for sale the core group of basic benefits when selling other Medicare supplemental policies with additional benefits or fails to provide the individual, before selling the policy, an outline of coverage describing benefits	2022	51,796	55,808
1395ss(q)(5)(C)	402.105(f)(5)	CMS	Penalty for any person that fails to suspend the policy of a policyholder made eligible for medical assistance or automatically reinstates the policy of a policyholder who has lost eligibility for medical assistance, under certain circumstances	2022	51,796	55,808
1395ss(r)(6)(A)	402.105(f)(6)	CMS	Penalty for any person that fails to provide refunds or credits as required by section 1882(r)(1)(B)	2022	51,796	55,808
1395ss(s)(4)	42 CFR 402.1(c)(29), 402.105(c)	CMS	Penalty for any issuer of a Medicare supplemental policy that does not waive listed time periods if they were already satisfied under a proceeding	2022	21,989	23,692

U.S.C. section(s)	CFR[1]	HHS agency	Description[2]	Date of last penalty figure or adjustment[3]	2022 Maximum adjusted penalty ($)	2023 Maximum adjusted penalty ($)[4]
			Medicare supplemental policy, or denies a policy, or conditions the issuances or effectiveness of the policy, or discriminates in the pricing of the policy base on health status or other specified criteria			
1395ss(t)(2)	42 CFR 402.1(c)(30), 402.105(f)(7)	CMS	Penalty for any issuer of a Medicare supplemental policy that fails to fulfill listed responsibilities	2022	51,796	55,808
1395ss(v)(4)(A)		CMS	Penalty someone other than issuer who sells, issues, or renews a medigap Rx policy to an individual who is a Part D enrollee	2022	22,426	24,163
		CMS	Penalty for an issuer who sells, issues, or renews a Medigap Rx policy who is a Part D enrollee	2022	37,377	40,272
1395bbb(c)(1)	42 CFR 488.725(c)	CMS	Penalty for any individual who notifies or causes to be notified a home health agency of the time or date on which a survey of such agency is to be conducted	2022	4,799	5,171
1395bbb(f)(2)(A)(i)	42 CFR 488.845(b)(2)(iii), 42 CFR 488.845(b)(3)–(6); and 42 CFR 488.845(d)(1)(ii)	CMS	Maximum daily penalty amount for each day a home health agency is not in compliance with statutory requirements	2022	23,011	24,793
	42 CFR 488.845(b)(3)	CMS	Penalty per day for home health	2022		

U.S.C. section(s)	CFR[1]	HHS agency	Description[2]	Date of last penalty figure or adjustment[3]	2022 Maximum adjusted penalty ($)	2023 Maximum adjusted penalty ($)[4]
			agency's noncompliance (Upper Range):			
			Minimum	2022	19,559	21,074
			Maximum	2022	23,011	24,793
	42 CFR 488.845(b)(3)(i)	CMS	Penalty for a home health agency's deficiency or deficiencies that cause immediate jeopardy and result in actual harm	2022	23,011	24,793
	42 CFR 488.845(b)(3)(ii)	CMS	Penalty for a home health agency's deficiency or deficiencies that cause immediate jeopardy and result in potential for harm	2022	20,709	22,313
	42 CFR 488.845(b)(3)(iii)	CMS	Penalty for an isolated incident of noncompliance in violation of established HHA policy	2022	19,559	21,074
	42 CFR 488.845(b)(4)	CMS	Penalty for a repeat and/or condition-level deficiency that does not constitute immediate jeopardy, but is directly related to poor quality patient care outcomes (Lower Range):	2022		
			Minimum	2022	3,453	3,720
			Maximum	2022	19,559	21,074
	42 CFR 488.845(b)(5)	CMS	Penalty for a repeat and/or condition-level deficiency that does not constitute immediate jeopardy and that is related predominately to structure or process-oriented conditions (Lower Range):	2022		
			Minimum	2022	1,151	1,240

U.S.C. section(s)	CFR[1]	HHS agency	Description[2]	Date of last penalty figure or adjustment[3]	2022 Maximum adjusted penalty ($)	2023 Maximum adjusted penalty ($)[4]
			Maximum	2022	2,301	2,479
	42 CFR 488.845(b)(6)	CMS	Penalty imposed for instance of noncompliance that may be assessed for one or more singular events of condition-level noncompliance that are identified and where the noncompliance was corrected during the onsite survey:	2022		
			Penalty for each day of noncompliance (Minimum)	2022	2,301	2,479
			Penalty for each day of noncompliance (Maximum)	2022	23,011	24,793
	42 CFR 488.845(d)(1)(ii)	CMS	Penalty for each day of noncompliance (Maximum)	2022	23,011	24,793
1395eee(e)(6)(B); 1396u–4(e)(6)(B)	42 CFR 460.46	CMS	Penalty for PACE organization that discriminates in enrollment or disenrollment, or engages in any practice that would reasonably be expected to have the effect of denying or discouraging enrollment, on the basis of health status or the need for services:	2022	42,788	46,102
		CMS	For each individual not enrolled as a result of the PACE organization's discrimination in enrollment or disenrollment or practice that would	2022		

U.S.C. section(s)	CFR[1]	HHS agency	Description[2]	Date of last penalty figure or adjustment[3]	2022 Maximum adjusted penalty ($)	2023 Maximum adjusted penalty ($)[4]
			deny or discourage enrollment			
			Minimum	2022	16,121	17,370
			Maximum	2022	107,478	115,802
		CMS	Penalty for a PACE organization that charges excessive premiums	2022	42,788	46,102
		CMS	Penalty for a PACE organization misrepresenting or falsifying information to CMS or the State	2022	171,156	184,412
		CMS	Penalty for any other violation specified in 42 C.F.R. 460.40	2022	42,788	46,102
1396r(h)(3)(C)(ii)(I)	42 CFR 488.408(d)(1)(iii)	CMS	Penalty per day for a nursing facility's failure to meet a Category 2 Certification:	2022		
			Minimum	2022	120	129
			Maximum	2022	7,195	7,752
	42 CFR 488.408(d)(1)(iv)	CMS	Penalty per instance for a nursing facility's failure to meet Category 2 certification:	2022		
			Minimum	2022	2,400	2,586
			Maximum	2022	23,989	25,847
	42 CFR 488.408(e)(1)(iii)	CMS	Penalty per day for a nursing facility's failure to meet Category 3 certification:	2022		
			Minimum	2022	7,317	7,884
			Maximum	2022	23,989	25,847
	42 CFR 488.408(e)(1)(iv)	CMS	Penalty per instance for a nursing facility's failure to meet Category 3 certification:	2022		
			Minimum	2022	2,400	2,586
			Maximum	2022	23,989	25,847
	42 CFR 488.408(e)(2)(ii)	CMS	Penalty per instance for a nursing	2022		

U.S.C. section(s)	CFR[1]	HHS agency	Description[2]	Date of last penalty figure or adjustment[3]	2022 Maximum adjusted penalty ($)	2023 Maximum adjusted penalty ($)[4]
			facility's failure to meet Category 3 certification, which results in immediate jeopardy:			
			Minimum	2022	2,400	2,586
			Maximum	2022	23,989	25,847
	42 CFR 488.438(a)(1)(i)	CMS	Penalty per day for nursing facility's failure to meet certification (Upper Range):	2022		
			Minimum	2022	7,317	7,884
			Maximum	2022	23,989	25,847
	42 CFR 488.438(a)(1)(ii)	CMS	Penalty per day for nursing facility's failure to meet certification (Lower Range):	2022		
			Minimum	2022	120	129
			Maximum	2022	7,195	7,752
	42 CFR 488.438(a)(2)	CMS	Penalty per instance for nursing facility's failure to meet certification:	2022		
			Minimum	2022	2,400	2,586
			Maximum	2022	23,989	25,847
	42 CFR 488.447	CMS	Penalty imposed for failure to comply with infection control weekly reporting requirements at 42 CFR 483.80(g)(1) and (2)	2022		
			First occurrence (Minimum)	2022	1,075	1,158
			Incremental increases for each subsequent occurrence	2022	537	579
1396r(f)(2)(B)(iii)(I)(c)	42 CFR 483.151(b)(2)(iv) and (b)(3)(iii)	CMS	Grounds to prohibit approval of Nurse Aide Training Program—if assessed a penalty in 1819(h)(2)(B)(i) or 1919(h)(2)(A)(ii)	2022	11,995	12,924

U.S.C. section(s)	CFR[1]	HHS agency	Description[2]	Date of last penalty figure or adjustment[3]	2022 Maximum adjusted penalty ($)	2023 Maximum adjusted penalty ($)[4]
			of "not less than $5,000" [Not CMP authority, but a specific CMP amount (CMP at this level) that is the triggering condition for disapproval]			
1396r(h)(3)(C)(ii)(I)	42 CFR 483.151(c)(2)	CMS	Grounds to waive disapproval of nurse aide training program—reference to disapproval based on imposition of CMP "not less than $5,000" [Not CMP authority but CMP imposition at this level determines eligibility to seek waiver of disapproval of nurse aide training program]	2022	11,995	12,924
1396t(j)(2)(C)		CMS	Penalty for each day of noncompliance for a home or community care provider that no longer meets the minimum requirements for home and community care:	2022		
			Minimum	2022	2	2
			Maximum	2022	20,719	22,324
1396u–2(e)(2)(A)(i)	42 CFR 438.704	CMS	Penalty for a Medicaid managed care organization that fails substantially to provide medically necessary items and services	2022	42,788	46,102
		CMS	Penalty for Medicaid managed care organization that imposes	2022	42,788	46,102

U.S.C. section(s)	CFR[1]	HHS agency	Description[2]	Date of last penalty figure or adjustment[3]	2022 Maximum adjusted penalty ($)	2023 Maximum adjusted penalty ($)[4]
			premiums or charges on enrollees in excess of the premiums or charges permitted			
		CMS	Penalty for a Medicaid managed care organization that misrepresents or falsifies information to another individual or entity	2022	42,788	46,102
		CMS	Penalty for a Medicaid managed care organization that fails to comply with the applicable statutory requirements for such organizations	2022	42,788	46,102
1396u–2(e)(2)(A)(ii)	42 CFR 438.704	CMS	Penalty for a Medicaid managed care organization that misrepresents or falsifies information to the HHS Secretary	2022	171,156	184,412
		CMS	Penalty for Medicaid managed care organization that acts to discriminate among enrollees on the basis of their health status	2022	171,156	184,412
1396u–2(e)(2)(A)(iv)	42 CFR 438.704	CMS	Penalty for each individual that does not enroll as a result of a Medicaid managed care organization that acts to discriminate among enrollees on the basis of their health status	2022	25,673	27,661
1396u(h)(2)	42 CFR Part 441, Subpart I	CMS	Penalty for a provider not meeting one of the requirements	2022	23,989	25,847

U.S.C. section(s)	CFR[1]	HHS agency	Description[2]	Date of last penalty figure or adjustment[3]	2022 Maximum adjusted penalty ($)	2023 Maximum adjusted penalty ($)[4]
			relating to the protection of the health, safety, and welfare of individuals receiving community supported living arrangements services			
1396w–2(c)(1)	42 U.S.C. 300gg–22(b)(2)(C)(i) 45 CFR 150.315	CMS	Penalty for each day, for each individual affected by the failure of a health insurance issuer or non-Federal governmental group health plan to comply with federal market reform provisions in part A or D of title XXVII of the PHS Act | 2022 | 174 | 177	2022	12,794	13,785
42 U.S.C. 300gg–22(b)(2)(C)(i)	45 CFR 150.315	CMS	Penalty for each day, for each individual affected by the failure of a health insurance issuer or non-Federal governmental group health plan to comply with federal market reform provisions in part A or D of title XXVII of the PHS Act	2022	174	177
18041(c)(2)	45 CFR 156.805(c)	CMS	Failure to comply with ACA requirements related to risk adjustment, reinsurance, risk corridors, Exchanges (including QHP standards) and	2022	174	187

U.S.C. section(s)	CFR[1]	HHS agency	Description[2]	Date of last penalty figure or adjustment[3]	2022 Maximum adjusted penalty ($)	2023 Maximum adjusted penalty ($)[4]
			other ACA Subtitle D standards; Penalty for violations of rules or standards of behavior associated with issuer compliance with risk adjustment, reinsurance, risk corridors, Exchanges (including QHP standards) and other ACA Subtitle D standards			
18081(h)(1)(A)(i)(II)	45 CFR 155.285	CMS	Penalty for providing false information on Exchange application	2022	31,616	34,065
18081(h)(1)(B)	45 CFR 155.285	CMS	Penalty for knowingly or willfully providing false information on Exchange application	2022	316,155	340,641
18081(h)(2)	45 CFR 155.260	CMS	Penalty for knowingly or willfully disclosing protected information from Exchange	2022		
		CMS	Minimum	2022	31,616	34,065
		CMS	Maximum	2022	323	348
18041(c)(2)	45 CFR 155.206(i)	CMS	Penalties for violation of applicable Exchange standards by consumer assistance entities in Federally-facilitated Exchanges	2022	38,771	41,774
			Maximum (Per Day)	2022	107	115
31 U.S.C.				2022	323	348
1352	45 CFR 93.400(e)	HHS	Penalty for the first time an individual makes an expenditure	2022	22,021	23,727

U.S.C. section(s)	CFR[1]	HHS agency	Description[2]	Date of last penalty figure or adjustment[3]	2022 Maximum adjusted penalty ($)	2023 Maximum adjusted penalty ($)[4]
			prohibited by regulations regarding lobbying disclosure, absent aggravating circumstances			
			Penalty for second and subsequent offenses by individuals who make an expenditure prohibited by regulations regarding lobbying disclosure:	2022		
			Minimum	2022	22,021	23,727
			Maximum	2022	220,213	237,268
		HHS	Penalty for the first time an individual fails to file or amend a lobbying disclosure form, absent aggravating circumstances	2022	22,021	23,727
			Penalty for second and subsequent offenses by individuals who fail to file or amend a lobbying disclosure form, absent aggravating circumstances:	2022		
			Minimum	2022	22,021	23,727
			Maximum	2022	220,213	237,268
	45 CFR Part 93, Appendix A	HHS	Penalty for failure to provide certification regarding lobbying in the award documents for all sub-awards of all tiers:	2022		
			Minimum	2022	22,021	23,727
			Maximum	2022	220,213	237,268
		HHS	Penalty for failure to provide statement regarding	2022		

U.S.C. section(s)	CFR[1]	HHS agency	Description[2]	Date of last penalty figure or adjustment[3]	2022 Maximum adjusted penalty ($)	2023 Maximum adjusted penalty ($)[4]
			lobbying for loan guarantee and loan insurance transactions:			
			Minimum	2022	22,021	23,727
			Maximum	2022	220,213	237,268
3801–3812	45 CFR 79.3(a)(1)(iv)	HHS	Penalty against any individual who— with knowledge or reason to know— makes, presents or submits a false, fictitious or fraudulent claim to the Department	2022	11,507	12,398
	45 CFR 79.3(b)(1)(ii)	HHS	Penalty against any individual who— with knowledge or reason to know— makes, presents or submits a false, fictitious or fraudulent claim to the Department	2022	11,507	12,398

[1] Some HHS components have not promulgated regulations regarding their civil monetary penalty-specific statutory authorities.

[2] The description is not intended to be a comprehensive explanation of the underlying violation; the statute and corresponding regulation, if applicable, should be consulted.

[3] Statutory or Inflation Act Adjustment.

[4] OMB Memorandum *M–16–06,* Implementation of the Federal Civil Penalties Inflation Adjustment Act Improvements Act of 2015, published February 24, 2016, guided agencies on initial "catch-up" adjustment requirements, and *M–17–11,* Implementation of the 2017 annual adjustment pursuant to the Federal Civil Penalties Inflation Adjustment Act Improvements Act of 2015, published December 16, 2016; followed by *M–18–03, M–19–04, M–20–05, M–21–10, M–22–07,* and *M–23–05* guided agencies on annual adjustment requirements

[5] *OMB Circular A–136,* Financial Reporting Requirements, Section II.4.9, directs that agencies must make annual inflation adjustments to civil monetary penalties and report on the adjustments in the Agency Financial Report (AFR) or Performance and Accountability Report (PAR).

[6] Federal Civil Penalties Inflation Adjustment Act Improvements Act of 2015, § 701(b)(1)(A) (codified as amended at 28 U.S.C. 2461 note).

[7] Annual inflation adjustments are based on the percent change between each published October's CPI–U. In this case, October 2022 CPI–U (298.012) / October 2021 CPI–U (276.589) = 1.07745.

[81 FR 61565, Sept. 6, 2016, as amended at 87 FR 15101, Mar. 17, 2022; 88 FR 69532, Oct. 6, 2023; 88 FR 70373, Oct. 11, 2023; 88 FR 82787, Nov. 27, 2023]

42 USC CHAPTER 7, SUBCHAPTER XI, Part C: Administrative Simplification

From Title 42—THE PUBLIC HEALTH AND WELFARECHAPTER 7—SOCIAL SECURITYSUBCHAPTER XI—GENERAL PROVISIONS, PEER REVIEW, AND ADMINISTRATIVE SIMPLIFICATION

Part C—Administrative Simplification

§1320d. Definitions

For purposes of this part:

(1) Code set

The term "code set" means any set of codes used for encoding data elements, such as tables of terms, medical concepts, medical diagnostic codes, or medical procedure codes.

(2) Health care clearinghouse

The term "health care clearinghouse" means a public or private entity that processes or facilitates the processing of nonstandard data elements of health information into standard data elements.

(3) Health care provider

The term "health care provider" includes a provider of services (as defined in section 1395x(u) of this title), a provider of medical or other health services (as defined in section 1395x(s) of this title), and any other person furnishing health care services or supplies.

(4) Health information

The term "health information" means any information, whether oral or recorded in any form or medium, that—

(A) is created or received by a health care provider, health plan, public health authority, employer, life insurer, school or university, or health care clearinghouse; and

(B) relates to the past, present, or future physical or mental health or condition of an individual, the provision of health care to an individual, or the past, present, or future payment for the provision of health care to an individual.

(5) Health plan

The term "health plan" means an individual or group plan that provides, or pays the cost of, medical care (as such term is defined in section 300gg–91 of this title). Such term includes the following, and any combination thereof:

(A) A group health plan (as defined in section 300gg–91(a) of this title), but only if the plan—

(i) has 50 or more participants (as defined in section 1002(7) of title 29); or

(ii) is administered by an entity other than the employer who established and maintains the plan.

(B) A health insurance issuer (as defined in section 300gg–91(b) of this title).

(C) A health maintenance organization (as defined in section 300gg–91(b) of this title).

(D) Parts [1] A, B, C, or D of the Medicare program under subchapter XVIII.

(E) The medicaid program under subchapter XIX.

(F) A Medicare supplemental policy (as defined in section 1395ss(g)(1) of this title).

(G) A long-term care policy, including a nursing home fixed indemnity policy (unless the Secretary determines that such a policy does not provide sufficiently comprehensive coverage of a benefit so that the policy should be treated as a health plan).

(H) An employee welfare benefit plan or any other arrangement which is established or maintained for the purpose of offering or providing health benefits to the employees of 2 or more employers.

(I) The health care program for active military personnel under title 10.

(J) The veterans health care program under chapter 17 of title 38.

(K) The Civilian Health and Medical Program of the Uniformed Services (CHAMPUS), as defined in section 1072(4) of title 10.

(L) The Indian health service program under the Indian Health Care Improvement Act (25 U.S.C. 1601 et seq.).

(M) The Federal Employees Health Benefit Plan under chapter 89 of title 5.

(6) Individually identifiable health information

The term "individually identifiable health information" means any information, including demographic information collected from an individual, that—

(A) is created or received by a health care provider, health plan, employer, or health care clearinghouse; and

(B) relates to the past, present, or future physical or mental health or condition of an individual, the provision of health care to an individual, or the past, present, or future payment for the provision of health care to an individual, and—

(i) identifies the individual; or

(ii) with respect to which there is a reasonable basis to believe that the information can be used to identify the individual.

(7) Standard

The term "standard", when used with reference to a data element of health information or a transaction referred to in section 1320d–2(a)(1) of this title, means any such data element or transaction that meets each of the standards and implementation specifications adopted or established by the Secretary with respect to the data element or transaction under sections 1320d–1 through 1320d–3 of this title.

(8) Standard setting organization

The term "standard setting organization" means a standard setting organization accredited by the American National Standards Institute, including the National Council for Prescription Drug Programs, that develops standards for information transactions, data elements, or any other standard that is necessary to, or will facilitate, the implementation of this part.

(9) Operating rules

The term "operating rules" means the necessary business rules and guidelines for the electronic exchange of information that are not defined by a standard or its implementation specifications as adopted for purposes of this part.

(Aug. 14, 1935, ch. 531, title XI, §1171, as added Pub. L. 104–191, title II, §262(a), Aug. 21, 1996, 110 Stat. 2021; amended Pub. L. 107–105, §4, Dec. 27, 2001, 115 Stat. 1007; Pub. L. 111–5, div. A, title XIII, §13102, Feb. 17, 2009, 123 Stat. 242; Pub. L. 111–148, title I, §1104(b)(1), Mar. 23, 2010, 124 Stat. 146.)

§1320d–1. General requirements for adoption of standards

(a) Applicability

Any standard adopted under this part shall apply, in whole or in part, to the following persons:

(1) A health plan.

(2) A health care clearinghouse.

(3) A health care provider who transmits any health information in electronic form in connection with a transaction referred to in section 1320d–2(a)(1) of this title.

(b) Reduction of costs

Any standard adopted under this part shall be consistent with the objective of reducing the administrative costs of providing and paying for health care.

(c) Role of standard setting organizations
  (1) In general

Except as provided in paragraph (2), any standard adopted under this part shall be a standard that has been developed, adopted, or modified by a standard setting organization.

  (2) Special rules
    (A) Different standards

The Secretary may adopt a standard that is different from any standard developed, adopted, or modified by a standard setting organization, if—

(i) the different standard will substantially reduce administrative costs to health care providers and health plans compared to the alternatives; and

(ii) the standard is promulgated in accordance with the rulemaking procedures of subchapter III of chapter 5 of title 5.

    (B) No standard by standard setting organization

If no standard setting organization has developed, adopted, or modified any standard relating to a standard that the Secretary is authorized or required to adopt under this part—

(i) paragraph (1) shall not apply; and

(ii) subsection (f) shall apply.

  (3) Consultation requirement
    (A) In general

A standard may not be adopted under this part unless—

(i) in the case of a standard that has been developed, adopted, or modified by a standard setting organization, the organization consulted with each of the organizations described in subparagraph (B) in the course of such development, adoption, or modification; and

(ii) in the case of any other standard, the Secretary, in complying with the requirements of subsection (f), consulted with each of the organizations described in subparagraph (B) before adopting the standard.

(B) Organizations described

The organizations referred to in subparagraph (A) are the following:

(i) The National Uniform Billing Committee.

(ii) The National Uniform Claim Committee.

(iii) The Workgroup for Electronic Data Interchange.

(iv) The American Dental Association.

(d) Implementation specifications

The Secretary shall establish specifications for implementing each of the standards adopted under this part.

(e) Protection of trade secrets

Except as otherwise required by law, a standard adopted under this part shall not require disclosure of trade secrets or confidential commercial information by a person required to comply with this part.

(f) Assistance to Secretary

In complying with the requirements of this part, the Secretary shall rely on the recommendations of the National Committee on Vital and Health Statistics established under section 242k(k) of this title, and shall consult with appropriate Federal and State agencies and private organizations. The Secretary shall publish in the Federal Register any recommendation of the National Committee on Vital and Health Statistics regarding the adoption of a standard under this part.

(g) Application to modifications of standards

This section shall apply to a modification to a standard (including an addition to a standard) adopted under section 1320d–3(b) of this title in the same manner as it applies to an initial standard adopted under section 1320d–3(a) of this title.

(Aug. 14, 1935, ch. 531, title XI, §1172, as added <u>Pub. L. 104–191, title II, §262(a), Aug. 21, 1996, 110 Stat. 2023</u>.)

§1320d–2. Standards for information transactions and data elements

(a) Standards to enable electronic exchange

(1) In general

The Secretary shall adopt standards for transactions, and data elements for such transactions, to enable health information to be exchanged electronically, that are appropriate for—

(A) the financial and administrative transactions described in paragraph (2); and

(B) other financial and administrative transactions determined appropriate by the Secretary, consistent with the goals of improving the operation of the health care system and reducing administrative costs, and subject to the requirements under paragraph (5).

(2) Transactions

The transactions referred to in paragraph (1)(A) are transactions with respect to the following:

(A) Health claims or equivalent encounter information.

(B) Health claims attachments.

(C) Enrollment and disenrollment in a health plan.

(D) Eligibility for a health plan.

(E) Health care payment and remittance advice.

(F) Health plan premium payments.

(G) First report of injury.

(H) Health claim status.

(I) Referral certification and authorization.

(J) Electronic funds transfers.

(3) Accommodation of specific providers

The standards adopted by the Secretary under paragraph (1) shall accommodate the needs of different types of health care providers.

(4) Requirements for financial and administrative transactions
  (A) In general

The standards and associated operating rules adopted by the Secretary shall—

(i) to the extent feasible and appropriate, enable determination of an individual's eligibility and financial responsibility for specific services prior to or at the point of care;

(ii) be comprehensive, requiring minimal augmentation by paper or other communications;

(iii) provide for timely acknowledgment, response, and status reporting that supports a transparent claims and denial management process (including adjudication and appeals); and

(iv) describe all data elements (including reason and remark codes) in unambiguous terms, require that such data elements be required or conditioned upon set values in other fields, and prohibit additional conditions (except where necessary to implement State or Federal law, or to protect against fraud and abuse).

  (B) Reduction of clerical burden

In adopting standards and operating rules for the transactions referred to under paragraph (1), the Secretary shall seek to reduce the number and complexity of forms (including paper and electronic forms) and data entry required by patients and providers.

(5) Consideration of standardization of activities and items
  (A) In general

For purposes of carrying out paragraph (1)(B), the Secretary shall solicit, not later than January 1, 2012, and not less than every 3 years thereafter, input from entities described in subparagraph (B) on—

(i) whether there could be greater uniformity in financial and administrative activities and items, as determined appropriate by the Secretary; and

(ii) whether such activities should be considered financial and administrative transactions (as described in paragraph (1)(B)) for which the adoption of standards and operating rules would improve the operation of the health care system and reduce administrative costs.

  (B) Solicitation of input

For purposes of subparagraph (A), the Secretary shall seek input from—

(i) the National Committee on Vital and Health Statistics, the Health Information Technology Policy Committee, and the Health Information Technology Standards Committee; and

(ii) standard setting organizations and stakeholders, as determined appropriate by the Secretary.

(b) Unique health identifiers

(1) In general

The Secretary shall adopt standards providing for a standard unique health identifier for each individual, employer, health plan, and health care provider for use in the health care system. In carrying out the preceding sentence for each health plan and health care provider, the Secretary shall take into account multiple uses for identifiers and multiple locations and specialty classifications for health care providers.

(2) Use of identifiers

The standards adopted under paragraph (1) shall specify the purposes for which a unique health identifier may be used.

(c) Code sets

(1) In general

The Secretary shall adopt standards that—

(A) select code sets for appropriate data elements for the transactions referred to in subsection (a)(1) from among the code sets that have been developed by private and public entities; or

(B) establish code sets for such data elements if no code sets for the data elements have been developed.

(2) Distribution

The Secretary shall establish efficient and low-cost procedures for distribution (including electronic distribution) of code sets and modifications made to such code sets under section 1320d–3(b) of this title.

(d) Security standards for health information

(1) Security standards

The Secretary shall adopt security standards that—

(A) take into account—

(i) the technical capabilities of record systems used to maintain health information;

(ii) the costs of security measures;

(iii) the need for training persons who have access to health information;

(iv) the value of audit trails in computerized record systems; and

(v) the needs and capabilities of small health care providers and rural health care providers (as such providers are defined by the Secretary); and

(B) ensure that a health care clearinghouse, if it is part of a larger organization, has policies and security procedures which isolate the activities of the health care clearinghouse with respect to processing information in a manner that prevents unauthorized access to such information by such larger organization.

(2) Safeguards

Each person described in section 1320d–1(a) of this title who maintains or transmits health information shall maintain reasonable and appropriate administrative, technical, and physical safeguards—

(A) to ensure the integrity and confidentiality of the information;

(B) to protect against any reasonably anticipated—

(i) threats or hazards to the security or integrity of the information; and

(ii) unauthorized uses or disclosures of the information; and

(C) otherwise to ensure compliance with this part by the officers and employees of such person.

(e) Electronic signature
(1) Standards

The Secretary, in coordination with the Secretary of Commerce, shall adopt standards specifying procedures for the electronic transmission and authentication of signatures with respect to the transactions referred to in subsection (a)(1).

(2) Effect of compliance

Compliance with the standards adopted under paragraph (1) shall be deemed to satisfy Federal and State statutory requirements for written signatures with respect to the transactions referred to in subsection (a)(1).

(f) Transfer of information among health plans

The Secretary shall adopt standards for transferring among health plans appropriate standard data elements needed for the coordination of benefits, the sequential processing of claims, and other data elements for individuals who have more than one health plan.

(g) Operating rules
(1) In general

The Secretary shall adopt a single set of operating rules for each transaction referred to under subsection (a)(1) with the goal of creating as much uniformity in the implementation of the electronic standards as possible. Such operating rules shall be consensus-based and reflect the necessary business rules affecting health plans and health care providers and the manner in which they operate pursuant to standards issued under Health Insurance Portability and Accountability Act of 1996.

(2) Operating rules development

In adopting operating rules under this subsection, the Secretary shall consider recommendations for operating rules developed by a qualified nonprofit entity that meets the following requirements:

(A) The entity focuses its mission on administrative simplification.

(B) The entity demonstrates a multi-stakeholder and consensus-based process for development of operating rules, including representation by or participation from health plans, health care providers, vendors, relevant Federal agencies, and other standard development organizations.

(C) The entity has a public set of guiding principles that ensure the operating rules and process are open and transparent, and supports nondiscrimination and conflict of interest policies that demonstrate a commitment to open, fair, and nondiscriminatory practices.

(D) The entity builds on the transaction standards issued under Health Insurance Portability and Accountability Act of 1996.

(E) The entity allows for public review and updates of the operating rules.

(3) Review and recommendations

The National Committee on Vital and Health Statistics shall—

(A) advise the Secretary as to whether a nonprofit entity meets the requirements under paragraph (2);

(B) review the operating rules developed and recommended by such nonprofit entity;

(C) determine whether such operating rules represent a consensus view of the health care stakeholders and are consistent with and do not conflict with other existing standards;

(D) evaluate whether such operating rules are consistent with electronic standards adopted for health information technology; and

(E) submit to the Secretary a recommendation as to whether the Secretary should adopt such operating rules.

(4) Implementation
(A) In general

The Secretary shall adopt operating rules under this subsection, by regulation in accordance with subparagraph (C), following consideration of the operating rules developed by the non-profit entity described in paragraph (2) and the recommendation submitted by the National Committee on Vital and Health Statistics under paragraph (3)(E) and having ensured consultation with providers.

(B) Adoption requirements; effective dates
(i) Eligibility for a health plan and health claim status

The set of operating rules for eligibility for a health plan and health claim status transactions shall be adopted not later than July 1, 2011, in a manner ensuring that such operating rules are effective not later than January 1, 2013, and may allow for the use of a machine readable identification card.

(ii) Electronic funds transfers and health care payment and remittance advice

The set of operating rules for electronic funds transfers and health care payment and remittance advice transactions shall—

(I) allow for automated reconciliation of the electronic payment with the remittance advice; and

(II) be adopted not later than July 1, 2012, in a manner ensuring that such operating rules are effective not later than January 1, 2014.

(iii) Health claims or equivalent encounter information, enrollment and disenrollment in a health plan, health plan premium payments, referral certification and authorization

The set of operating rules for health claims or equivalent encounter information, enrollment and disenrollment in a health plan, health plan premium payments, and referral certification and authorization transactions shall be adopted not later than July 1, 2014, in a manner ensuring that such operating rules are effective not later than January 1, 2016.

(C) Expedited rulemaking

The Secretary shall promulgate an interim final rule applying any standard or operating rule recommended by the National Committee on Vital and Health Statistics pursuant to paragraph (3). The Secretary shall accept and consider public comments on any interim final rule published under this subparagraph for 60 days after the date of such publication.

(h) Compliance

(1) Health plan certification

(A) Eligibility for a health plan, health claim status, electronic funds transfers, health care payment and remittance advice

Not later than December 31, 2013, a health plan shall file a statement with the Secretary, in such form as the Secretary may require, certifying that the data and information systems for such plan are in compliance with any applicable standards (as described under paragraph (7) of section 1320d of this title) and associated operating rules (as described under paragraph (9) of such section) for electronic funds transfers, eligibility for a health plan, health claim status, and health care payment and remittance advice, respectively.

(B) Health claims or equivalent encounter information, enrollment and disenrollment in a health plan, health plan premium payments, health claims attachments, referral certification and authorization

Not later than December 31, 2015, a health plan shall file a statement with the Secretary, in such form as the Secretary may require, certifying that the data and information systems for such plan are in compliance with any applicable standards and associated operating rules for health claims or equivalent encounter information, enrollment and disenrollment in a health plan, health plan premium payments, health claims attachments, and referral certification and authorization, respectively. A health plan shall provide the same level of documentation to certify compliance with such transactions as is required to certify compliance with the transactions specified in subparagraph (A).

(2) Documentation of compliance

A health plan shall provide the Secretary, in such form as the Secretary may require, with adequate documentation of compliance with the standards and operating rules described under paragraph (1). A health plan shall not be considered to have provided adequate documentation and shall not be certified as being in compliance with such standards, unless the health plan—

(A) demonstrates to the Secretary that the plan conducts the electronic transactions specified in paragraph (1) in a manner that fully complies with the regulations of the Secretary; and

(B) provides documentation showing that the plan has completed end-to-end testing for such transactions with their partners, such as hospitals and physicians.

(3) Service contracts

A health plan shall be required to ensure that any entities that provide services pursuant to a contract with such health plan shall comply with any applicable certification and compliance requirements (and provide the Secretary with adequate documentation of such compliance) under this subsection.

(4) Certification by outside entity

The Secretary may designate independent, outside entities to certify that a health plan has complied with the requirements under this subsection, provided that the certification standards employed by such entities are in accordance with any standards or operating rules issued by the Secretary.

(5) Compliance with revised standards and operating rules
(A) In general

A health plan (including entities described under paragraph (3)) shall file a statement with the Secretary, in such form as the Secretary may require, certifying that the data and information systems for such plan are in compliance with any applicable revised standards and associated operating rules under this subsection for any interim final rule promulgated by the Secretary under subsection (i) that—

(i) amends any standard or operating rule described under paragraph (1) of this subsection; or

(ii) establishes a standard (as described under subsection (a)(1)(B)) or associated operating rules (as described under subsection (i)(5)) for any other financial and administrative transactions.

(B) Date of compliance

A health plan shall comply with such requirements not later than the effective date of the applicable standard or operating rule.

(6) Audits of health plans

The Secretary shall conduct periodic audits to ensure that health plans (including entities described under paragraph (3)) are in compliance with any standards and operating rules that are described under paragraph (1) or subsection (i)(5).

(i) Review and amendment of standards and operating rules
(1) Establishment

Not later than January 1, 2014, the Secretary shall establish a review committee (as described under paragraph (4)).

(2) Evaluations and reports
(A) Hearings

Not later than April 1, 2014, and not less than biennially thereafter, the Secretary, acting through the review committee, shall conduct hearings to evaluate and review the adopted standards and operating rules established under this section.

(B) Report

Not later than July 1, 2014, and not less than biennially thereafter, the review committee shall provide recommendations for updating and improving such standards and operating rules. The review committee shall recommend a single set of operating rules per transaction standard and maintain the goal of creating as much uniformity as possible in the implementation of the electronic standards.

(3) Interim final rulemaking

(A) In general

Any recommendations to amend adopted standards and operating rules that have been approved by the review committee and reported to the Secretary under paragraph (2)(B) shall be adopted by the Secretary through promulgation of an interim final rule not later than 90 days after receipt of the committee's report.

(B) Public comment

(i) Public comment period

The Secretary shall accept and consider public comments on any interim final rule published under this paragraph for 60 days after the date of such publication.

(ii) Effective date

The effective date of any amendment to existing standards or operating rules that is adopted through an interim final rule published under this paragraph shall be 25 months following the close of such public comment period.

(4) Review committee

(A) Definition

For the purposes of this subsection, the term "review committee' means a committee chartered by or within the Department of Health and Human services that has been designated by the Secretary to carry out this subsection, including—

(i) the National Committee on Vital and Health Statistics; or

(ii) any appropriate committee as determined by the Secretary.

(B) Coordination of HIT standards

In developing recommendations under this subsection, the review committee shall ensure coordination, as appropriate, with the standards that support the certified electronic health record technology approved by the Office of the National Coordinator for Health Information Technology.

(5) Operating rules for other standards adopted by the Secretary

The Secretary shall adopt a single set of operating rules (pursuant to the process described under subsection (g)) for any transaction for which a standard had been adopted pursuant to subsection (a)(1)(B).

(j) Penalties

(1) Penalty fee

(A) In general

Not later than April 1, 2014, and annually thereafter, the Secretary shall assess a penalty fee (as determined under subparagraph (B)) against a health plan that has failed to meet the requirements under subsection (h) with respect to certification and documentation of compliance with—

(i) the standards and associated operating rules described under paragraph (1) of such subsection; and

(ii) a standard (as described under subsection (a)(1)(B)) and associated operating rules (as described under subsection (i)(5)) for any other financial and administrative transactions.

(B) Fee amount

Subject to subparagraphs (C), (D), and (E), the Secretary shall assess a penalty fee against a health plan in the amount of $1 per covered life until certification is complete. The penalty shall be assessed per person covered by the plan for which its data systems for major medical policies are not in compliance and shall be imposed against the health plan for each day that the plan is not in compliance with the requirements under subsection (h).

(C) Additional penalty for misrepresentation

A health plan that knowingly provides inaccurate or incomplete information in a statement of certification or documentation of compliance under subsection (h) shall be subject to a penalty fee that is double the amount that would otherwise be imposed under this subsection.

(D) Annual fee increase

The amount of the penalty fee imposed under this subsection shall be increased on an annual basis by the annual percentage increase in total national health care expenditures, as determined by the Secretary.

(E) Penalty limit

A penalty fee assessed against a health plan under this subsection shall not exceed, on an annual basis—

(i) an amount equal to $20 per covered life under such plan; or

(ii) an amount equal to $40 per covered life under the plan if such plan has knowingly provided inaccurate or incomplete information (as described under subparagraph (C)).

(F) Determination of covered individuals

The Secretary shall determine the number of covered lives under a health plan based upon the most recent statements and filings that have been submitted by such plan to the Securities and Exchange Commission.

(2) Notice and dispute procedure

The Secretary shall establish a procedure for assessment of penalty fees under this subsection that provides a health plan with reasonable notice and a dispute resolution procedure prior to provision of a notice of assessment by the Secretary of the Treasury (as described under paragraph (4)(B)).

(3) Penalty fee report

Not later than May 1, 2014, and annually thereafter, the Secretary shall provide the Secretary of the Treasury with a report identifying those health plans that have been assessed a penalty fee under this subsection.

(4) Collection of penalty fee
(A) In general

The Secretary of the Treasury, acting through the Financial Management Service, shall administer the collection of penalty fees from health plans that have been identified by the Secretary in the penalty fee report provided under paragraph (3).

(B) Notice

Not later than August 1, 2014, and annually thereafter, the Secretary of the Treasury shall provide notice to each health plan that has been assessed a penalty fee by the Secretary under this subsection. Such notice shall include the amount of the penalty fee assessed by the Secretary and the due date for payment of such fee to the Secretary of the Treasury (as described in subparagraph (C)).

(C) Payment due date

Payment by a health plan for a penalty fee assessed under this subsection shall be made to the Secretary of the Treasury not later than November 1, 2014, and annually thereafter.

(D) Unpaid penalty fees

Any amount of a penalty fee assessed against a health plan under this subsection for which payment has not been made by the due date provided under subparagraph (C) shall be—

(i) increased by the interest accrued on such amount, as determined pursuant to the underpayment rate established under section 6621 of the Internal Revenue Code of 1986; and

(ii) treated as a past-due, legally enforceable debt owed to a Federal agency for purposes of section 6402(d) of the Internal Revenue Code of 1986.

(E) Administrative fees

Any fee charged or allocated for collection activities conducted by the Financial Management Service will be passed on to a health plan on a pro-rata basis and added to any penalty fee collected from the plan.

(Aug. 14, 1935, ch. 531, title XI, §1173, as added Pub. L. 104–191, title II, §262(a), Aug. 21, 1996, 110 Stat. 2024; amended Pub. L. 111–148, title I, §1104(b)(2), title X, §10109(a), Mar. 23, 2010, 124 Stat. 147, 915.)

§1320d–3. Timetables for adoption of standards

(a) Initial standards

The Secretary shall carry out section 1320d–2 of this title not later than 18 months after August 21, 1996, except that standards relating to claims attachments shall be adopted not later than 30 months after August 21, 1996.

(b) Additions and modifications to standards

(1) In general

Except as provided in paragraph (2), the Secretary shall review the standards adopted under section 1320d–2 of this title, and shall adopt modifications to the standards (including additions to the standards), as determined appropriate, but not more frequently than once every 12 months. Any addition or modification to a standard shall be completed in a manner which minimizes the disruption and cost of compliance.

(2) Special rules

(A) First 12-month period

Except with respect to additions and modifications to code sets under subparagraph (B), the Secretary may not adopt any modification to a standard adopted under this part during the 12-month period beginning on the date the standard is initially adopted, unless the Secretary determines that the modification is necessary in order to permit compliance with the standard.

(B) Additions and modifications to code sets

(i) In general

The Secretary shall ensure that procedures exist for the routine maintenance, testing, enhancement, and expansion of code sets.

(ii) Additional rules

If a code set is modified under this subsection, the modified code set shall include instructions on how data elements of health information that were encoded prior to the modification may be converted or translated so as to preserve the informational value of the data elements that existed before the modification. Any modification to a code set under this subsection shall be implemented in a manner that minimizes the disruption and cost of complying with such modification.

(Aug. 14, 1935, ch. 531, title XI, §1174, as added Pub. L. 104–191, title II, §262(a), Aug. 21, 1996, 110 Stat. 2026.)

§1320d–4. Requirements

(a) Conduct of transactions by plans

(1) In general

If a person desires to conduct a transaction referred to in section 1320d–2(a)(1) of this title with a health plan as a standard transaction—

(A) the health plan may not refuse to conduct such transaction as a standard transaction;

(B) the insurance plan may not delay such transaction, or otherwise adversely affect, or attempt to adversely affect, the person or the transaction on the ground that the transaction is a standard transaction; and

(C) the information transmitted and received in connection with the transaction shall be in the form of standard data elements of health information.

(2) Satisfaction of requirements

A health plan may satisfy the requirements under paragraph (1) by—

(A) directly transmitting and receiving standard data elements of health information; or

(B) submitting nonstandard data elements to a health care clearinghouse for processing into standard data elements and transmission by the health care clearinghouse, and receiving standard data elements through the health care clearinghouse.

(3) Timetable for compliance

Paragraph (1) shall not be construed to require a health plan to comply with any standard, implementation specification, or modification to a standard or specification adopted or established by the Secretary under sections 1320d–1 through 1320d–3 of this title at any time prior to the date on which the plan is required to comply with the standard or specification under subsection (b).

(b) Compliance with standards

  (1) Initial compliance

    (A) In general

Not later than 24 months after the date on which an initial standard or implementation specification is adopted or established under sections 1320d–1 and 1320d–2 of this title, each person to whom the standard or implementation specification applies shall comply with the standard or specification.

    (B) Special rule for small health plans

In the case of a small health plan, paragraph (1) shall be applied by substituting "36 months" for "24 months". For purposes of this subsection, the Secretary shall determine the plans that qualify as small health plans.

  (2) Compliance with modified standards

If the Secretary adopts a modification to a standard or implementation specification under this part, each person to whom the standard or implementation specification applies shall comply with the modified standard or implementation specification at such time as the Secretary determines appropriate, taking into account the time needed to comply due to the nature and extent of the modification. The time determined appropriate under the preceding sentence may not be earlier than the last day of the 180-day period beginning on the date such modification is adopted. The Secretary may extend the time for compliance for small health plans, if the Secretary determines that such extension is appropriate.

  (3) Construction

Nothing in this subsection shall be construed to prohibit any person from complying with a standard or specification by—

    (A) submitting nonstandard data elements to a health care clearinghouse for processing into standard data elements and transmission by the health care clearinghouse; or

    (B) receiving standard data elements through a health care clearinghouse.

(Aug. 14, 1935, ch. 531, title XI, §1175, as added Pub. L. 104–191, title II, §262(a), Aug. 21, 1996, 110 Stat. 2027.)

§1320d–5. General penalty for failure to comply with requirements and standards

(a) General penalty

  (1) In general

Except as provided in subsection (b), the Secretary shall impose on any person who violates a provision of this part—

(A) in the case of a violation of such provision in which it is established that the person did not know (and by exercising reasonable diligence would not have known) that such person violated such provision, a penalty for each such violation of an amount that is at least the amount described in paragraph (3)(A) but not to exceed the amount described in paragraph (3)(D);

(B) in the case of a violation of such provision in which it is established that the violation was due to reasonable cause and not to willful neglect, a penalty for each such violation of an amount that is at least the amount described in paragraph (3)(B) but not to exceed the amount described in paragraph (3)(D); and

(C) in the case of a violation of such provision in which it is established that the violation was due to willful neglect—

(i) if the violation is corrected as described in subsection (b)(3)(A),[1] a penalty in an amount that is at least the amount described in paragraph (3)(C) but not to exceed the amount described in paragraph (3)(D); and

(ii) if the violation is not corrected as described in such subsection, a penalty in an amount that is at least the amount described in paragraph (3)(D).

In determining the amount of a penalty under this section for a violation, the Secretary shall base such determination on the nature and extent of the violation and the nature and extent of the harm resulting from such violation.

(2) Procedures

The provisions of section 1320a–7a of this title (other than subsections (a) and (b) and the second sentence of subsection (f)) shall apply to the imposition of a civil money penalty under this subsection in the same manner as such provisions apply to the imposition of a penalty under such section 1320a–7a of this title.

(3) Tiers of penalties described

For purposes of paragraph (1), with respect to a violation by a person of a provision of this part—

(A) the amount described in this subparagraph is $100 for each such violation, except that the total amount imposed on the person for all such violations of an identical requirement or prohibition during a calendar year may not exceed $25,000;

(B) the amount described in this subparagraph is $1,000 for each such violation, except that the total amount imposed on the person for all such violations of an identical requirement or prohibition during a calendar year may not exceed $100,000;

(C) the amount described in this subparagraph is $10,000 for each such violation, except that the total amount imposed on the person for all such violations of an identical requirement or prohibition during a calendar year may not exceed $250,000; and

(D) the amount described in this subparagraph is $50,000 for each such violation, except that the total amount imposed on the person for all such violations of an identical requirement or prohibition during a calendar year may not exceed $1,500,000.

(b) Limitations

(1) Offenses otherwise punishable

No penalty may be imposed under subsection (a) and no damages obtained under subsection (d) with respect to an act if a penalty has been imposed under section 1320d–6 of this title with respect to such act.

(2) Failures due to reasonable cause

(A) In general

Except as provided in subparagraph (B) or subsection (a)(1)(C), no penalty may be imposed under subsection (a) and no damages obtained under subsection (d) if the failure to comply is corrected during the 30-day period beginning on the first date the person liable for the penalty or damages knew, or by exercising reasonable diligence would have known, that the failure to comply occurred.

(B) Extension of period

(i) No penalty

With respect to the imposition of a penalty by the Secretary under subsection (a), the period referred to in subparagraph (A) may be extended as determined appropriate by the Secretary based on the nature and extent of the failure to comply.

(ii) Assistance

If the Secretary determines that a person failed to comply because the person was unable to comply, the Secretary may provide technical assistance to the person during the period described in subparagraph (A). Such assistance shall be provided in any manner determined appropriate by the Secretary.

(3) Reduction

In the case of a failure to comply which is due to reasonable cause and not to willful neglect, any penalty under subsection (a) and any damages under subsection (d) that is [2] not entirely waived under paragraph (3) [3] may be waived to the extent that the payment of such penalty [4] would be excessive relative to the compliance failure involved.

(c) Noncompliance due to willful neglect

(1) In general

A violation of a provision of this part due to willful neglect is a violation for which the Secretary is required to impose a penalty under subsection (a)(1).

(2) Required investigation

For purposes of paragraph (1), the Secretary shall formally investigate any complaint of a violation of a provision of this part if a preliminary investigation of the facts of the complaint indicate such a possible violation due to willful neglect.

(d) Enforcement by State attorneys general

(1) Civil action

Except as provided in subsection (b), in any case in which the attorney general of a State has reason to believe that an interest of one or more of the residents of that State has been or is threatened or adversely affected by any person who violates a provision of this part, the attorney general of the State, as parens patriae, may bring a civil action on behalf of such residents of the State in a district court of the United States of appropriate jurisdiction—

(A) to enjoin further such violation by the defendant; or

(B) to obtain damages on behalf of such residents of the State, in an amount equal to the amount determined under paragraph (2).

(2) Statutory damages

(A) In general

For purposes of paragraph (1)(B), the amount determined under this paragraph is the amount calculated by multiplying the number of violations by up to $100. For purposes of the preceding sentence, in the case of a continuing violation, the number of violations shall be determined consistent with the HIPAA privacy regulations (as defined in section 1320d–9(b)(3) of this title) for violations of subsection (a).

(B) Limitation

The total amount of damages imposed on the person for all violations of an identical requirement or prohibition during a calendar year may not exceed $25,000.

(C) Reduction of damages

In assessing damages under subparagraph (A), the court may consider the factors the Secretary may consider in determining the amount of a civil money penalty under subsection (a) under the HIPAA privacy regulations.

(3) Attorney fees

In the case of any successful action under paragraph (1), the court, in its discretion, may award the costs of the action and reasonable attorney fees to the State.

(4) Notice to Secretary

The State shall serve prior written notice of any action under paragraph (1) upon the Secretary and provide the Secretary with a copy of its complaint, except in any case in which such prior notice is not feasible, in which case the State shall serve such notice immediately upon instituting such action. The Secretary shall have the right—

(A) to intervene in the action;

(B) upon so intervening, to be heard on all matters arising therein; and

(C) to file petitions for appeal.

(5) Construction

For purposes of bringing any civil action under paragraph (1), nothing in this section shall be construed to prevent an attorney general of a State from exercising the powers conferred on the attorney general by the laws of that State.

(6) Venue; service of process
(A) Venue

Any action brought under paragraph (1) may be brought in the district court of the United States that meets applicable requirements relating to venue under section 1391 of title 28.

(B) Service of process

In an action brought under paragraph (1), process may be served in any district in which the defendant—

(i) is an inhabitant; or

(ii) maintains a physical place of business.

(7) Limitation on State action while Federal action is pending

If the Secretary has instituted an action against a person under subsection (a) with respect to a specific violation of this part, no State attorney general may bring an action under this subsection against the person with respect to such violation during the pendency of that action.

(8) Application of CMP statute of limitation

A civil action may not be instituted with respect to a violation of this part unless an action to impose a civil money penalty may be instituted under subsection (a) with respect to such violation consistent with the second sentence of section 1320a–7a(c)(1) of this title.

(e) Allowing continued use of corrective action

Nothing in this section shall be construed as preventing the Office for Civil Rights of the Department of Health and Human Services from continuing, in its discretion, to use corrective action without a penalty in cases where the person did not know (and by exercising reasonable diligence would not have known) of the violation involved.

(Aug. 14, 1935, ch. 531, title XI, §1176, as added Pub. L. 104–191, title II, §262(a), Aug. 21, 1996, 110 Stat. 2028; amended Pub. L. 111–5, div. A, title XIII, §13410(a)(1), (d)(1)–(3), (e)(1), (2), (f), Feb. 17, 2009, 123 Stat. 271–276.)

§1320d–6. Wrongful disclosure of individually identifiable health information

(a) Offense

A person who knowingly and in violation of this part—

(1) uses or causes to be used a unique health identifier;

(2) obtains individually identifiable health information relating to an individual; or

(3) discloses individually identifiable health information to another person,

shall be punished as provided in subsection (b). For purposes of the previous sentence, a person (including an employee or other individual) shall be considered to have obtained or disclosed individually identifiable health information in violation of this part if the information is maintained by a covered entity (as defined in the HIPAA privacy regulation described in section 1320d–9(b)(3) of this title) and the individual obtained or disclosed such information without authorization.

(b) Penalties

A person described in subsection (a) shall—

(1) be fined not more than $50,000, imprisoned not more than 1 year, or both;

(2) if the offense is committed under false pretenses, be fined not more than $100,000, imprisoned not more than 5 years, or both; and

(3) if the offense is committed with intent to sell, transfer, or use individually identifiable health information for commercial advantage, personal gain, or malicious harm, be fined not more than $250,000, imprisoned not more than 10 years, or both.

(Aug. 14, 1935, ch. 531, title XI, §1177, as added Pub. L. 104–191, title II, §262(a), Aug. 21, 1996, 110 Stat. 2029; amended Pub. L. 111–5, div. A, title XIII, §13409, Feb. 17, 2009, 123 Stat. 271.)

§1320d–7. Effect on State law

(a) General effect

(1) General rule

Except as provided in paragraph (2), a provision or requirement under this part, or a standard or implementation specification adopted or established under sections 1320d–1 through 1320d–3 of this title, shall supersede any contrary provision of State law, including a provision of State law that requires medical or health plan records (including billing information) to be maintained or transmitted in written rather than electronic form.

(2) Exceptions

A provision or requirement under this part, or a standard or implementation specification adopted or established under sections 1320d–1 through 1320d–3 of this title, shall not supersede a contrary provision of State law, if the provision of State law—

(A) is a provision the Secretary determines—

(i) is necessary—

(I) to prevent fraud and abuse;

(II) to ensure appropriate State regulation of insurance and health plans;

(III) for State reporting on health care delivery or costs; or

(IV) for other purposes; or

(ii) addresses controlled substances; or

(B) subject to section 264(c)(2) of the Health Insurance Portability and Accountability Act of 1996, relates to the privacy of individually identifiable health information.

(b) Public health

Nothing in this part shall be construed to invalidate or limit the authority, power, or procedures established under any law providing for the reporting of disease or injury, child abuse, birth, or death, public health surveillance, or public health investigation or intervention.

(c) State regulatory reporting

Nothing in this part shall limit the ability of a State to require a health plan to report, or to provide access to, information for management audits, financial audits, program monitoring and evaluation, facility licensure or certification, or individual licensure or certification.

(Aug. 14, 1935, ch. 531, title XI, §1178, as added Pub. L. 104–191, title II, §262(a), Aug. 21, 1996, 110 Stat. 2029.)

§1320d–8. Processing payment transactions by financial institutions

To the extent that an entity is engaged in activities of a financial institution (as defined in section 3401 of title 12), or is engaged in authorizing, processing, clearing, settling, billing, transferring, reconciling, or collecting payments, for a financial institution, this part, and any standard adopted under this part, shall not apply to the entity with respect to such activities, including the following:

(1) The use or disclosure of information by the entity for authorizing, processing, clearing, settling, billing, transferring, reconciling or collecting, a payment for, or related to, health plan premiums or health care, where such payment is made by any means, including a credit, debit, or other payment card, an account, check, or electronic funds transfer.

(2) The request for, or the use or disclosure of, information by the entity with respect to a payment described in paragraph (1)—

(A) for transferring receivables;

(B) for auditing;

(C) in connection with—

(i) a customer dispute; or

(ii) an inquiry from, or to, a customer;

(D) in a communication to a customer of the entity regarding the customer's transactions, payment card, account, check, or electronic funds transfer;

(E) for reporting to consumer reporting agencies; or

(F) for complying with—

(i) a civil or criminal subpoena; or

(ii) a Federal or State law regulating the entity.

(Aug. 14, 1935, ch. 531, title XI, §1179, as added Pub. L. 104–191, title II, §262(a), Aug. 21, 1996, 110 Stat. 2030.)

§1320d–9. Application of HIPAA regulations to genetic information

(a) In general

The Secretary shall revise the HIPAA privacy regulation (as defined in subsection (b)) so it is consistent with the following:

(1) Genetic information shall be treated as health information described in section 1320d(4)(B) of this title.

(2) The use or disclosure by a covered entity that is a group health plan, health insurance issuer that issues health insurance coverage, or issuer of a medicare supplemental policy of protected health information that is genetic information about an individual for underwriting purposes under the group health plan, health insurance coverage, or medicare supplemental policy shall not be a permitted use or disclosure.

(b) Definitions

For purposes of this section:

(1) Genetic information; genetic test; family member

The terms "genetic information", "genetic test", and "family member" have the meanings given such terms in section 300gg–91 of this title, as amended by the Genetic Information Nondiscrimination Act of 2007.[1]

(2) Group health plan; health insurance coverage; medicare supplemental policy

The terms "group health plan" and "health insurance coverage" have the meanings given such terms under section 300gg–91 of this title, and the term "medicare supplemental policy" has the meaning given such term in section 1395ss(g) of this title.

(3) HIPAA privacy regulation

The term "HIPAA privacy regulation" means the regulations promulgated by the Secretary under this part and section 264 of the Health Insurance Portability and Accountability Act of 1996 (42 U.S.C. 1320d–2 note).

(4) Underwriting purposes

The term "underwriting purposes" means, with respect to a group health plan, health insurance coverage, or a medicare supplemental policy—

(A) rules for, or determination of, eligibility (including enrollment and continued eligibility) for, or determination of, benefits under the plan, coverage, or policy;

(B) the computation of premium or contribution amounts under the plan, coverage, or policy;

(C) the application of any pre-existing condition exclusion under the plan, coverage, or policy; and

(D) other activities related to the creation, renewal, or replacement of a contract of health insurance or health benefits.

(c) Procedure

The revisions under subsection (a) shall be made by notice in the Federal Register published not later than 60 days after May 21, 2008, and shall be effective upon publication, without opportunity for any prior public comment, but may be revised, consistent with this section, after opportunity for public comment.

(d) Enforcement

In addition to any other sanctions or remedies that may be available under law, a covered entity that is a group health plan, health insurance issuer, or issuer of a medicare supplemental policy and that violates the HIPAA privacy regulation (as revised under subsection (a) or otherwise) with respect to the use or disclosure of genetic information shall be subject to the penalties described in sections 1320d–5 and 1320d–6 of this title in the same manner and to the same extent that such penalties apply to violations of this part.

(Aug. 14, 1935, ch. 531, title XI, §1180, as added Pub. L. 110–233, title I, §105(a), May 21, 2008, 122 Stat. 903.)

HHS/OCR Guidance

What follows are selected elements of guidance published by OCR. This is by no means an exhaustive compilation of the OCR guidance materials and the guidance presented here does not cover the full scope of the law and regulations. You can find these materials in addition to many more on the OCR website. You can find these resources at https://www.hhs.gov/hipaa/for-professionals/index.html

Privacy Rule Guidance

- **The Privacy Rule does not require you to obtain a signed consent form before sharing information for treatment purposes.** Health care providers can freely share information for treatment purposes without a signed patient authorization.

- **The Privacy Rule does not require you to eliminate all incidental disclosures.** The Privacy Rule recognizes that it is not practicable to eliminate all risk of incidental disclosures. In August 2002, specific modifications to the Rule were adopted to clarify that incidental disclosures do not violate the Privacy Rule when you have policies which reasonably safeguard and appropriately limit how protected health information is used and disclosed.

- **The Privacy Rule does not cut off all communications between you and the families and friends of patients.** As long as the patient does not object, The Privacy Rule permits you to:
  - share needed information with family, friends, or anyone else a patient identifies as involved in his or her care;
  - disclose information when needed to notify a family member or anyone responsible for the patient's care about the patient's location or general condition;
  - share the appropriate information for these purposes even when the patient is incapacitated if doing so is in the best interest of the patient.

- **The Privacy Rule does not stop calls or visits to hospitals by family, friends, clergy or anyone else.** Unless the patient objects, basic information such as phone number, room number and general condition can:
  - be listed in the hospital directory;
  - be given to people who call or visit and ask for the patient;
  - be given to clergy along with religious affiliation--when provided by the patient--even if the patient is not asked for by name.

- **The Privacy Rule does not prevent child abuse reporting.** You may continue to report child abuse or neglect to appropriate government authorities.

- **The Privacy Rule is not anti-electronic.** You can communicate with patients, providers, and others by e-mail, telephone, or facsimile, with the implementation of appropriate safeguards to protect patient privacy.

- **The Privacy Rule protects all "individually identifiable health information" held or transmitted by a covered entity or its business associate, in any form or media,**

whether electronic, paper, or oral. The Privacy Rule calls this information "protected health information (PHI)."

- **"Individually identifiable health information"** is information, including demographic data, that relates to:
    - the individual's past, present or future physical or mental health or condition,
    - the provision of health care to the individual, or
    - the past, present, or future payment for the provision of health care to the individual,

and that identifies the individual or for which there is a reasonable basis to believe it can be used to identify the individual. Individually identifiable health information includes many common identifiers (e.g., name, address, birth date, Social Security Number).

- If the patient is present and has the capacity to make health care decisions, when does HIPAA allow a health care provider to discuss the patient's health information with the patient's family, friends, or others involved in the patient's care or payment for care?
    - If the patient is present and has the capacity to make health care decisions, a health care provider may discuss the patient's health information with a family member, friend, or other person if the patient agrees or, when given the opportunity, does not object. A health care provider also may share information with these persons if, using professional judgment, he or she decides that the patient does not object. In either case, the health care provider may share or discuss only the information that the person involved needs to know about the patient's care or payment for care.

- If the patient is not present or is incapacitated, may a health care provider still share the patient's health information with family, friends, or others involved in the patient's care or payment for care?
    - Yes. If the patient is not present or is incapacitated, a health care provider may share the patient's information with family, friends, or others as long as the health care provider determines, based on professional judgment, that it is in the best interest of the patient. When someone other than a friend or family member is involved, the health care provider must be reasonably sure that the patient asked the person to be involved in his or her care or payment for care. The health care provider may discuss only the information that the person involved needs to know about the patient's care or payment.

Security Rule Guidance

Who is Covered by the Security Rule

- The Security Rule applies to health plans, health care clearinghouses, and to any health care provider who transmits health information in electronic form in connection with a transaction for which the Secretary of HHS has adopted standards under HIPAA (the "covered entities") and to their business associates. For help in determining whether you are covered, use CMS's decision tool.

  Read more about covered entities in the Summary of the HIPAA Privacy Rule - PDF.

Business Associates

- The HITECH Act of 2009 expanded the responsibilities of business associates under the HIPAA Security Rule. HHS developed regulations to implement and clarify these changes.

  See additional guidance on business associates.

What Information is Protected

- **Electronic Protected Health Information.** The HIPAA Privacy Rule protects the privacy of individually identifiable health information, called protected health information (PHI), as explained in the Privacy Rule and here - PDF. The Security Rule protects a subset of information covered by the Privacy Rule, which is all individually identifiable health information a covered entity creates, receives, maintains or transmits in electronic form. The Security Rule calls this information "electronic protected health information" (e-PHI).[3] The Security Rule does not apply to PHI transmitted orally or in writing.

General Rules

- The Security Rule requires covered entities to maintain reasonable and appropriate administrative, technical, and physical safeguards for protecting e-PHI.

  Specifically, covered entities must:

  1. Ensure the confidentiality, integrity, and availability of all e-PHI they create, receive, maintain or transmit;
  2. Identify and protect against reasonably anticipated threats to the security or integrity of the information;
  3. Protect against reasonably anticipated, impermissible uses or disclosures; and
  4. Ensure compliance by their workforce.[4]

  The Security Rule defines "confidentiality" to mean that e-PHI is not available or disclosed to unauthorized persons. The Security Rule's confidentiality requirements support the Privacy Rule's prohibitions against improper uses and disclosures of PHI. The Security rule also promotes the two additional goals of maintaining the integrity and availability of e-PHI. Under the Security Rule, "integrity" means that e-PHI is not altered or destroyed in an unauthorized manner. "Availability" means that e-PHI is accessible and usable on demand by an authorized person.[5]

HHS recognizes that covered entities range from the smallest provider to the largest, multi-state health plan. Therefore the Security Rule is flexible and scalable to allow covered entities to analyze their own needs and implement solutions appropriate for their specific environments. What is appropriate for a particular covered entity will depend on the nature of the covered entity's business, as well as the covered entity's size and resources.

Therefore, when a covered entity is deciding which security measures to use, the Rule does not dictate those measures but requires the covered entity to consider:

- o Its size, complexity, and capabilities,
- o Its technical, hardware, and software infrastructure,
- o The costs of security measures, and
- o The likelihood and possible impact of potential risks to e-PHI.[6]

Covered entities must review and modify their security measures to continue protecting e-PHI in a changing environment.[7]

Risk Analysis and Management

- The Administrative Safeguards provisions in the Security Rule require covered entities to perform risk analysis as part of their security management processes. The risk analysis and management provisions of the Security Rule are addressed separately here because, by helping to determine which security measures are reasonable and appropriate for a particular covered entity, risk analysis affects the implementation of all of the safeguards contained in the Security Rule.
- A risk analysis process includes, but is not limited to, the following activities:
  - o Evaluate the likelihood and impact of potential risks to e-PHI;[8]
  - o Implement appropriate security measures to address the risks identified in the risk analysis;[9]
  - o Document the chosen security measures and, where required, the rationale for adopting those measures;[10] and
  - o Maintain continuous, reasonable, and appropriate security protections.[11]

Risk analysis should be an ongoing process, in which a covered entity regularly reviews its records to track access to e-PHI and detect security incidents,[12] periodically evaluates the effectiveness of security measures put in place,[13] and regularly reevaluates potential risks to e-PHI.[14]

Administrative Safeguards

- **Security Management Process**. As explained in the previous section, a covered entity must identify and analyze potential risks to e-PHI, and it must implement security measures that reduce risks and vulnerabilities to a reasonable and appropriate level.
- **Security Personnel.** A covered entity must designate a security official who is responsible for developing and implementing its security policies and procedures.[15]

- **Information Access Management.** Consistent with the Privacy Rule standard limiting uses and disclosures of PHI to the "minimum necessary," the Security Rule requires a covered entity to implement policies and procedures for authorizing access to e-PHI only when such access is appropriate based on the user or recipient's role (role-based access).[16]
- **Workforce Training and Management.** A covered entity must provide for appropriate authorization and supervision of workforce members who work with e-PHI. A covered entity must train all workforce members regarding its security policies and procedures, and must have and apply appropriate sanctions against workforce members who violate its policies and procedures.
- **Evaluation.** A covered entity must perform a periodic assessment of how well its security policies and procedures meet the requirements of the Security Rule.

Physical Safeguards

- **Facility Access and Control.** A covered entity must limit physical access to its facilities while ensuring that authorized access is allowed.
- **Workstation and Device Security.** A covered entity must implement policies and procedures to specify proper use of and access to workstations and electronic media. A covered entity also must have in place policies and procedures regarding the transfer, removal, disposal, and re-use of electronic media, to ensure appropriate protection of electronic protected health information (e-PHI).

Technical Safeguards

- **Access Control.** A covered entity must implement technical policies and procedures that allow only authorized persons to access electronic protected health information (e-PHI).
- **Audit Controls.** A covered entity must implement hardware, software, and/or procedural mechanisms to record and examine access and other activity in information systems that contain or use e-PHI.
- **Integrity Controls.** A covered entity must implement policies and procedures to ensure that e-PHI is not improperly altered or destroyed. Electronic measures must be put in place to confirm that e-PHI has not been improperly altered or destroyed.
- **Transmission Security.** A covered entity must implement technical security measures that guard against unauthorized access to e-PHI that is being transmitted over an electronic network.

Required and Addressable Implementation Specifications

- Covered entities are required to comply with every Security Rule "Standard." However, the Security Rule categorizes certain implementation specifications within those standards as "addressable," while others are "required." The "required" implementation specifications must be implemented. The "addressable" designation does not mean that an implementation specification is optional. However, it permits covered entities to determine whether the addressable implementation specification is reasonable and appropriate for that covered entity. If it is not, the Security Rule allows the covered entity to adopt an alternative measure that achieves the purpose of the standard, if the alternative measure is reasonable and appropriate.

Organizational Requirements

- **Covered Entity Responsibilities.** If a covered entity knows of an activity or practice of the business associate that constitutes a material breach or violation of the business associate's obligation, the covered entity must take reasonable steps to cure the breach or end the violation. Violations include the failure to implement safeguards that reasonably and appropriately protect e-PHI.
- **Business Associate Contracts.** HHS developed regulations relating to business associate obligations and business associate contracts under the HITECH Act of 2009.

Policies and Procedures and Documentation Requirements

- A covered entity must adopt reasonable and appropriate policies and procedures to comply with the provisions of the Security Rule. A covered entity must maintain, until six years after the later of the date of their creation or last effective date, written security policies and procedures and written records of required actions, activities or assessments.
- **Updates.** A covered entity must periodically review and update its documentation in response to environmental or organizational changes that affect the security of electronic protected health information (e-PHI).

Breach Notification Rule Guidance

The HIPAA Breach Notification Rule, 45 CFR §§ 164.400-414, requires HIPAA covered entities and their business associates to provide notification following a breach of unsecured protected health information.

A breach is, generally, an impermissible use or disclosure under the Privacy Rule that compromises the security or privacy of the protected health information. An impermissible use or disclosure of protected health information is presumed to be a breach unless the covered entity or business associate, as applicable, demonstrates that there is a low probability that the protected health information has been compromised based on a risk assessment of at least the following factors:

1. The nature and extent of the protected health information involved, including the types of identifiers and the likelihood of re-identification;
2. The unauthorized person who used the protected health information or to whom the disclosure was made;
3. Whether the protected health information was actually acquired or viewed; and
4. The extent to which the risk to the protected health information has been mitigated.

There are three exceptions to the definition of "breach."
1. The first exception applies to the unintentional acquisition, access, or use of protected health information by a workforce member or person acting under the authority of a covered entity or business associate, if such acquisition, access, or use was made in good faith and within the scope of authority.
2. The second exception applies to the inadvertent disclosure of protected health information by a person authorized to access protected health information at a covered entity or business associate to another person authorized to access protected health information at the covered entity or business associate, or organized health care arrangement in which the covered entity participates. In both cases, the information cannot be further used or disclosed in a manner not permitted by the Privacy Rule.
3. The final exception applies if the covered entity or business associate has a good faith belief that the unauthorized person to whom the impermissible disclosure was made, would not have been able to retain the information.

Breach Notification Requirements

Following a breach of unsecured protected health information, covered entities must provide notification of the breach to affected individuals, the Secretary, and, in certain circumstances, to the media. In addition, business associates must notify covered entities if a breach occurs at or by the business associate.

Individual Notice

Covered entities must notify affected individuals following the discovery of a breach of unsecured protected health information. Covered entities must provide this individual notice in written form by first-class mail, or alternatively, by e-mail if the affected individual has agreed to receive such notices electronically. If the covered entity has insufficient or out-of-date contact information for 10 or more individuals, the covered entity must provide substitute individual notice by either posting the notice on the home page of its web site for at least 90 days or by providing the notice in major print or broadcast media where the affected individuals likely reside. The covered entity must include a toll-free phone number that remains active for at least 90 days where individuals can learn if their information was involved in the breach. If the covered entity has insufficient or out-of-date contact information for fewer than 10 individuals, the covered entity may provide substitute notice by an alternative form of written notice, by telephone, or other means.

These individual notifications must be provided without unreasonable delay and in no case later than 60 days following the discovery of a breach and must include, to the extent possible, a brief description of the breach, a description of the types of information that were involved in the breach, the steps affected individuals should take to protect themselves from potential harm, a brief description of what the covered entity is doing to investigate the breach, mitigate the harm, and prevent further breaches, as well as contact information for the covered entity (or business associate, as applicable).

With respect to a breach at or by a business associate, while the covered entity is ultimately responsible for ensuring individuals are notified, the covered entity may delegate the responsibility of providing individual notices to the business associate. Covered entities and business associates should consider which entity is in the best position to provide notice to the individual, which may depend on various circumstances, such as the functions the business associate performs on behalf of the covered entity and which entity has the relationship with the individual.

Media Notice

Covered entities that experience a breach affecting more than 500 residents of a State or jurisdiction are, in addition to notifying the affected individuals, required to provide notice to prominent media outlets serving the State or jurisdiction. Covered entities will likely provide this notification in the form of a press release to appropriate media outlets serving the affected area. Like individual notice, this media notification must be provided without unreasonable delay and in no case later than 60 days following the discovery of a breach and must include the same information required for the individual notice.

Notice to the Secretary

In addition to notifying affected individuals and the media (where appropriate), covered entities must notify the Secretary of breaches of unsecured protected health information. Covered entities will notify the Secretary by visiting the HHS web site and filling out and electronically submitting a breach report form. If a breach affects 500 or more individuals, covered entities must notify the Secretary without unreasonable delay and in no case later than 60 days following a breach. If, however, a breach affects fewer than 500 individuals, the covered entity may notify the Secretary of such breaches on an annual basis. Reports of breaches affecting fewer than 500 individuals are due to the Secretary no later than 60 days after the end of the calendar year in which the breaches are discovered.

Notification by a Business Associate

If a breach of unsecured protected health information occurs at or by a business associate, the business associate must notify the covered entity following the discovery of the breach. A business associate must provide notice to the covered entity without unreasonable delay and no later than 60 days from the discovery of the breach. To the extent possible, the business associate should provide the covered entity with the identification of each individual affected by the breach as well as any other available information required to be provided by the covered entity in its notification to affected individuals.

Administrative Requirements and Burden of Proof

Covered entities and business associates, as applicable, have the burden of demonstrating that all required notifications have been provided or that a use or disclosure of unsecured protected health information did not constitute a breach. Thus, with respect to an impermissible use or disclosure, a covered entity (or business associate) should maintain documentation that all required notifications were made, or, alternatively, documentation to demonstrate that notification was not required: (1) its risk assessment demonstrating a low probability that the protected health information has been compromised by the impermissible use or disclosure; or (2) the application of any other exceptions to the definition of "breach."

Covered entities are also required to comply with certain administrative requirements with respect to breach notification. For example, covered entities must have in place written policies and procedures regarding breach notification, must train employees on these policies and procedures, and must develop and apply appropriate sanctions against workforce members who do not comply with these policies and procedures.

Sample Business Associate Agreement

A "business associate" is a person or entity, other than a member of the workforce of a covered entity, who performs functions or activities on behalf of, or provides certain services to, a covered entity that involve access by the business associate to protected health information. A "business associate" also is a subcontractor that creates, receives, maintains, or transmits protected health information on behalf of another business associate. The HIPAA Rules generally require that covered entities and business associates enter into contracts with their business associates to ensure that the business associates will appropriately safeguard protected health information. The business associate contract also serves to clarify and limit, as appropriate, the permissible uses and disclosures of protected health information by the business associate, based on the relationship between the parties and the activities or services being performed by the business associate. A business associate may use or disclose protected health information only as permitted or required by its business associate contract or as required by law. A business associate is directly liable under the HIPAA Rules and subject to civil and, in some cases, criminal penalties for making uses and disclosures of protected health information that are not authorized by its contract or required by law. A business associate also is directly liable and subject to civil penalties for failing to safeguard electronic protected health information in accordance with the HIPAA Security Rule.

A written contract between a covered entity and a business associate must: (1) establish the permitted and required uses and disclosures of protected health information by the business associate; (2) provide that the business associate will not use or further disclose the information other than as permitted or required by the contract or as required by law; (3) require the business associate to implement appropriate safeguards to prevent unauthorized use or disclosure of the information, including implementing requirements of the HIPAA Security Rule with regard to electronic protected health information; (4) require the business associate to report to the covered entity any use or disclosure of the information not provided for by its contract, including incidents that constitute breaches of unsecured protected health information; (5) require the business associate to disclose protected health information as specified in its contract to satisfy a covered entity's obligation with respect to individuals' requests for copies of their protected health information, as well as make available protected health information for amendments (and incorporate any amendments, if required) and accountings; (6) to the extent the business associate is to carry out a covered entity's obligation under the Privacy Rule, require the business associate to comply with the requirements applicable to the obligation; (7) require the business associate to make available to HHS its internal practices, books, and records relating to the use and disclosure of protected health information received from, or created or received by the business associate on behalf of, the covered entity for purposes of HHS determining the covered entity's compliance with the HIPAA Privacy Rule; (8) at termination of the contract, if feasible, require the business associate to return or destroy all protected health information received from, or created or received by the business associate on behalf of, the covered entity; (9) require the business associate to ensure that any subcontractors it may engage on its behalf that will have access to protected health information agree to the same restrictions and conditions that apply to the business associate with respect to such information; and (10) authorize termination of the contract by the covered entity if the business associate violates a material term of the contract. Contracts between business associates and business associates that are subcontractors are subject to these same requirements.

This document includes sample business associate agreement provisions to help covered entities and business associates more easily comply with the business associate contract requirements. While these sample provisions are written for the purposes of the contract between a covered entity and its business associate, the language may be adapted for purposes of the contract between a business associate and subcontractor.

This is only sample language and use of these sample provisions is not required for compliance with the HIPAA Rules. The language may be changed to more accurately reflect business arrangements between a covered entity and business associate or business associate and subcontractor. In addition, these or similar provisions may be incorporated into an agreement for the provision of services between a covered entity and business associate or business associate and subcontractor, or they may be incorporated into a separate business associate agreement. **These provisions address only concepts and requirements set forth in the HIPAA Privacy, Security, Breach Notification, and Enforcement Rules, and alone may not be sufficient to result in a binding contract under State law. They do not include many formalities and substantive provisions that may be required or typically included in a valid contract. Reliance on this sample may not be sufficient for compliance with State law, and does not replace consultation with a lawyer or negotiations between the parties to the contract.** *(note: emphasis added)*

Sample Business Associate Agreement Provisions

Words or phrases contained in brackets are intended as either optional language or as instructions to the users of these sample provisions.

Definitions

Catch-all definition:

The following terms used in this Agreement shall have the same meaning as those terms in the HIPAA Rules: Breach, Data Aggregation, Designated Record Set, Disclosure, Health Care Operations, Individual, Minimum Necessary, Notice of Privacy Practices, Protected Health Information, Required By Law, Secretary, Security Incident, Subcontractor, Unsecured Protected Health Information, and Use.

Specific definitions:

(a) Business Associate. "Business Associate" shall generally have the same meaning as the term "business associate" at 45 CFR 160.103, and in reference to the party to this agreement, shall mean [Insert Name of Business Associate].

(b) Covered Entity. "Covered Entity" shall generally have the same meaning as the term "covered entity" at 45 CFR 160.103, and in reference to the party to this agreement, shall mean [Insert Name of Covered Entity].

(c) HIPAA Rules. "HIPAA Rules" shall mean the Privacy, Security, Breach Notification, and Enforcement Rules at 45 CFR Part 160 and Part 164.

Obligations and Activities of Business Associate

Business Associate agrees to:

(a) Not use or disclose protected health information other than as permitted or required by the Agreement or as required by law;

(b) Use appropriate safeguards, and comply with Subpart C of 45 CFR Part 164 with respect to electronic protected health information, to prevent use or disclosure of protected health information other than as provided for by the Agreement;

(c) Report to covered entity any use or disclosure of protected health information not provided for by the Agreement of which it becomes aware, including breaches of unsecured protected health information as required at 45 CFR 164.410, and any security incident of which it becomes aware;

[The parties may wish to add additional specificity regarding the breach notification obligations of the business associate, such as a stricter timeframe for the business associate to report a potential breach to the covered entity and/or whether the business associate will handle breach notifications to individuals, the HHS Office for Civil Rights (OCR), and potentially the media, on behalf of the covered entity.]

(d) In accordance with 45 CFR 164.502(e)(1)(ii) and 164.308(b)(2), if applicable, ensure that any subcontractors that create, receive, maintain, or transmit protected health information on behalf of the business associate agree to the same restrictions, conditions, and requirements that apply to the business associate with respect to such information;

(e) Make available protected health information in a designated record set to the [Choose either "covered entity" or "individual or the individual's designee"] as necessary to satisfy covered entity's obligations under 45 CFR 164.524;

[The parties may wish to add additional specificity regarding how the business associate will respond to a request for access that the business associate receives directly from the individual (such as whether and in what time and manner a business associate is to provide the requested access or whether the business associate will forward the individual's request to the covered entity to fulfill) and the timeframe for the business associate to provide the information to the covered entity.]

(f) Make any amendment(s) to protected health information in a designated record set as directed or agreed to by the covered entity pursuant to 45 CFR 164.526, or take other measures as necessary to satisfy covered entity's obligations under 45 CFR 164.526;

[The parties may wish to add additional specificity regarding how the business associate will respond to a request for amendment that the business associate receives directly from the individual (such as whether and in what time and manner a business associate is to act on the request for amendment or whether the business associate will forward the individual's request to the covered entity) and the timeframe for the business associate to incorporate any amendments to the information in the designated record set.]

(g) Maintain and make available the information required to provide an accounting of disclosures to the [Choose either "covered entity" or "individual"] as necessary to satisfy covered entity's obligations under 45 CFR 164.528;

[The parties may wish to add additional specificity regarding how the business associate will respond to a request for an accounting of disclosures that the business associate receives directly from the individual (such as whether and in what time and manner the business associate is to provide the accounting of disclosures to the individual or whether the business associate will forward the request to the covered entity) and the timeframe for the business associate to provide information to the covered entity.]

(h) To the extent the business associate is to carry out one or more of covered entity's obligation(s) under Subpart E of 45 CFR Part 164, comply with the requirements of Subpart E that apply to the covered entity in the performance of such obligation(s); and

(i) Make its internal practices, books, and records available to the Secretary for purposes of determining compliance with the HIPAA Rules.

Permitted Uses and Disclosures by Business Associate

(a) Business associate may only use or disclose protected health information

[Option 1 – Provide a specific list of permissible purposes.]

[Option 2 – Reference an underlying service agreement, such as "as necessary to perform the services set forth in Service Agreement."]

[In addition to other permissible purposes, the parties should specify whether the business associate is authorized to use protected health information to de-identify the information in accordance with 45 CFR 164.514(a)-(c). The parties also may wish to specify the manner in which the business associate will de-identify the information and the permitted uses and disclosures by the business associate of the de-identified information.]

(b) Business associate may use or disclose protected health information as required by law.

(c) Business associate agrees to make uses and disclosures and requests for protected health information

[Option 1] consistent with covered entity's minimum necessary policies and procedures.

[Option 2] subject to the following minimum necessary requirements: [Include specific minimum necessary provisions that are consistent with the covered entity's minimum necessary policies and procedures.]

(d) Business associate may not use or disclose protected health information in a manner that would violate Subpart E of 45 CFR Part 164 if done by covered entity [if the Agreement permits the business associate to use or disclose protected health information for its own management and administration and legal responsibilities or for data aggregation services as set forth in optional provisions (e), (f), or (g) below, then add ", except for the specific uses and disclosures set forth below."]

(e) [Optional] Business associate may use protected health information for the proper management and administration of the business associate or to carry out the legal responsibilities of the business associate.

(f) [Optional] Business associate may disclose protected health information for the proper management and administration of business associate or to carry out the legal responsibilities of the business associate, provided the disclosures are required by law, or business associate obtains reasonable assurances from the person to whom the information is disclosed that the information will remain confidential and used or further disclosed only as required by law or for the purposes for which it was disclosed to the person, and the person notifies business associate of any instances of which it is aware in which the confidentiality of the information has been breached.

(g) [Optional] Business associate may provide data aggregation services relating to the health care operations of the covered entity.

Provisions for Covered Entity to Inform Business Associate of Privacy Practices and Restrictions

(a) [Optional] Covered entity shall notify business associate of any limitation(s) in the notice of privacy practices of covered entity under 45 CFR 164.520, to the extent that such limitation may affect business associate's use or disclosure of protected health information.

(b) [Optional] Covered entity shall notify business associate of any changes in, or revocation of, the permission by an individual to use or disclose his or her protected health information, to the extent that such changes may affect business associate's use or disclosure of protected health information.

(c) [Optional] Covered entity shall notify business associate of any restriction on the use or disclosure of protected health information that covered entity has agreed to or is required to abide by under 45 CFR 164.522, to the extent that such restriction may affect business associate's use or disclosure of protected health information.

Permissible Requests by Covered Entity

[Optional] Covered entity shall not request business associate to use or disclose protected health information in any manner that would not be permissible under Subpart E of 45 CFR Part 164 if done by covered entity. [Include an exception if the business associate will use or disclose protected health information for, and the agreement includes provisions for, data aggregation or management and administration and legal responsibilities of the business associate.]

Term and Termination

(a) <u>Term</u>. The Term of this Agreement shall be effective as of [Insert effective date], and shall terminate on [Insert termination date or event] or on the date covered entity terminates for cause as authorized in paragraph (b) of this Section, whichever is sooner.

(b) <u>Termination for Cause</u>. Business associate authorizes termination of this Agreement by covered entity, if covered entity determines business associate has violated a material term of the Agreement [and business associate has not cured the breach or ended the violation within the time specified by covered entity]. [Bracketed language may be added if the covered entity wishes to provide the business associate with an opportunity to cure a violation or breach of the contract before termination for cause.]

(c) <u>Obligations of Business Associate Upon Termination</u>.

[Option 1 – if the business associate is to return or destroy all protected health information upon termination of the agreement]

Upon termination of this Agreement for any reason, business associate shall return to covered entity [or, if agreed to by covered entity, destroy] all protected health information received from covered entity, or created, maintained, or received by business associate on behalf of covered entity, that the business associate still maintains in any form. Business associate shall retain no copies of the protected health information.

[Option 2—if the agreement authorizes the business associate to use or disclose protected health information for its own management and administration or to carry out its legal responsibilities and the business associate needs to retain protected health information for such purposes after termination of the agreement]

Upon termination of this Agreement for any reason, business associate, with respect to protected health information received from covered entity, or created, maintained, or received by business associate on behalf of covered entity, shall:

1.
   1. Retain only that protected health information which is necessary for business associate to continue its proper management and administration or to carry out its legal responsibilities;
   2. Return to covered entity [or, if agreed to by covered entity, destroy] the remaining protected health information that the business associate still maintains in any form;
   3. Continue to use appropriate safeguards and comply with Subpart C of 45 CFR Part 164 with respect to electronic protected health information to prevent use or disclosure of the protected health information, other than as provided for in this Section, for as long as business associate retains the protected health information;
   4. Not use or disclose the protected health information retained by business associate other than for the purposes for which such protected health information was retained and subject to the same conditions set out at [Insert section number related to paragraphs (e) and (f) above under "Permitted Uses and Disclosures By Business Associate"] which applied prior to termination; and
   5. Return to covered entity [or, if agreed to by covered entity, destroy] the protected health information retained by business associate when it is no longer needed by business associate for its proper management and administration or to carry out its legal responsibilities.

[The agreement also could provide that the business associate will transmit the protected health information to another business associate of the covered entity at termination, and/or could add terms regarding a business associate's obligations to obtain or ensure the destruction of protected health information created, received, or maintained by subcontractors.]

(d) <u>Survival</u>. The obligations of business associate under this Section shall survive the termination of this Agreement.

Miscellaneous [Optional]

(a) [Optional] <u>Regulatory References</u>. A reference in this Agreement to a section in the HIPAA Rules means the section as in effect or as amended.

(b) [Optional] <u>Amendment</u>. The Parties agree to take such action as is necessary to amend this Agreement from time to time as is necessary for compliance with the requirements of the HIPAA Rules and any other applicable law.

(c) [Optional] <u>Interpretation</u>. Any ambiguity in this Agreement shall be interpreted to permit compliance with the HIPAA Rules.

Sample Notice of Privacy Practices

OCR has published two variants of the Model Notice of Privacy Practices – one geared toward health plans and the other geared toward healthcare providers – each is available in English and in Spanish on the OCR website. What follows is the healthcare provider edition in English:

Your Information. Your Rights. Our Responsibilities.

This notice describes how medical information about you may be used and disclosed and how you can get access to this information. **Please review it carefully.**

Your Rights
You have the right to:
- Get a copy of your paper or electronic medical record
- Correct your paper or electronic medical record
- Request confidential communication
- Ask us to limit the information we share
- Get a list of those with whom we've shared your information
- Get a copy of this privacy notice
- Choose someone to act for you
- File a complaint if you believe your privacy rights have been violated

Your Choices
You have some choices in the way that we use and share information as we:
- Tell family and friends about your condition
- Provide disaster relief
- Include you in a hospital directory
- Provide mental health care
- Market our services and sell your information
- Raise funds

Our Uses and Disclosures
We may use and share your information as we:
- Treat you
- Run our organization
- Bill for your services
- Help with public health and safety issues
- Do research
- Comply with the law
- Respond to organ and tissue donation requests
- Work with a medical examiner or funeral director
- Address workers' compensation, law enforcement, and other government requests
- Respond to lawsuits and legal actions

Your Rights

When it comes to your health information, you have certain rights. This section explains your rights and some of our responsibilities to help you.

Get an electronic or paper copy of your medical record

- You can ask to see or get an electronic or paper copy of your medical record and other health information we have about you. Ask us how to do this.
- We will provide a copy or a summary of your health information, usually within 30 days of your request. We may charge a reasonable, cost-based fee.

Ask us to correct your medical record

- You can ask us to correct health information about you that you think is incorrect or incomplete. Ask us how to do this.
- We may say "no" to your request, but we'll tell you why in writing within 60 days.

Request confidential communications

- You can ask us to contact you in a specific way (for example, home or office phone) or to send mail to a different address.
- We will say "yes" to all reasonable requests.

Ask us to limit what we use or share

- You can ask us not to use or share certain health information for treatment, payment, or our operations. We are not required to agree to your request, and we may say "no" if it would affect your care.
- If you pay for a service or health care item out-of-pocket in full, you can ask us not to share that information for the purpose of payment or our operations with your health insurer. We will say "yes" unless a law requires us to share that information.

Get a list of those with whom we've shared information

- You can ask for a list (accounting) of the times we've shared your health information for six years prior to the date you ask, who we shared it with, and why.
- We will include all the disclosures except for those about treatment, payment, and health care operations, and certain other disclosures (such as any you asked us to make). We'll provide one accounting a year for free but will charge a reasonable, cost-based fee if you ask for another one within 12 months.

Get a copy of this privacy notice

You can ask for a paper copy of this notice at any time, even if you have agreed to receive the notice electronically. We will provide you with a paper copy promptly.

Choose someone to act for you

- If you have given someone medical power of attorney or if someone is your legal guardian, that person can exercise your rights and make choices about your health information.
- We will make sure the person has this authority and can act for you before we take any action.

File a complaint if you feel your rights are violated

- You can complain if you feel we have violated your rights by contacting us using the information on page 1.

- You can file a complaint with the U.S. Department of Health and Human Services Office for Civil Rights by sending a letter to 200 Independence Avenue, S.W., Washington, D.C. 20201, calling 1-877-696-6775, or visiting **www.hhs.gov/ocr/privacy/hipaa/complaints/**.
- We will not retaliate against you for filing a complaint.

Your Choices

For certain health information, you can tell us your choices about what we share. If you have a clear preference for how we share your information in the situations described below, talk to us. Tell us what you want us to do, and we will follow your instructions.

In these cases, you have both the right and choice to tell us to:

- Share information with your family, close friends, or others involved in your care
- Share information in a disaster relief situation
- Include your information in a hospital directory

If you are not able to tell us your preference, for example if you are unconscious, we may go ahead and share your information if we believe it is in your best interest. We may also share your information when needed to lessen a serious and imminent threat to health or safety.

In these cases we never share your information unless you give us written permission:

- Marketing purposes
- Sale of your information
- Most sharing of psychotherapy notes

In the case of fundraising:

- We may contact you for fundraising efforts, but you can tell us not to contact you again.

Our Uses and Disclosures

How do we typically use or share your health information?

We typically use or share your health information in the following ways.

Treat you

We can use your health information and share it with other professionals who are treating you.
Example: A doctor treating you for an injury asks another doctor about your overall health condition.

Run our organization

We can use and share your health information to run our practice, improve your care, and contact you when necessary.
Example: We use health information about you to manage your treatment and services.

Bill for your services

We can use and share your health information to bill and get payment from health plans or other entities.

Example: We give information about you to your health insurance plan so it will pay for your services.

How else can we use or share your health information?

We are allowed or required to share your information in other ways – usually in ways that contribute to the public good, such as public health and research. We have to meet many conditions in the law before we can share your information for these purposes. For more information see: www.hhs.gov/ocr/privacy/hipaa/understanding/consumers/index.html.

Help with public health and safety issues

We can share health information about you for certain situations such as:

- Preventing disease
- Helping with product recalls
- Reporting adverse reactions to medications
- Reporting suspected abuse, neglect, or domestic violence
- Preventing or reducing a serious threat to anyone's health or safety

Do research

We can use or share your information for health research.

Comply with the law

We will share information about you if state or federal laws require it, including with the Department of Health and Human Services if it wants to see that we're complying with federal privacy law.

Respond to organ and tissue donation requests

We can share health information about you with organ procurement organizations.

Work with a medical examiner or funeral director

We can share health information with a coroner, medical examiner, or funeral director when an individual dies.

Address workers' compensation, law enforcement, and other government requests

We can use or share health information about you:

- For workers' compensation claims
- For law enforcement purposes or with a law enforcement official
- With health oversight agencies for activities authorized by law
- For special government functions such as military, national security, and presidential protective services

Respond to lawsuits and legal actions

We can share health information about you in response to a court or administrative order, or in response to a subpoena.

Our Responsibilities

- We are required by law to maintain the privacy and security of your protected health information.
- We will let you know promptly if a breach occurs that may have compromised the privacy or security of your information.
- We must follow the duties and privacy practices described in this notice and give you a copy of it.
- We will not use or share your information other than as described here unless you tell us we can in writing. If you tell us we can, you may change your mind at any time. Let us know in writing if you change your mind.

For more information see:
www.hhs.gov/ocr/privacy/hipaa/understanding/consumers/noticepp.html.

Changes to the Terms of this Notice

We can change the terms of this notice, and the changes will apply to all information we have about you. The new notice will be available upon request, in our office, and on our web site.

Other Instructions for Notice

- Insert Effective Date of this Notice
- Insert name or title of the privacy official (or other privacy contact) and his/her email address and phone number.
- Insert any special notes that apply to your entity's practices such as "we never market or sell personal information."
- The Privacy Rule requires you to describe any state or other laws that require greater limits on disclosures. For example, "We will never share any substance abuse treatment records without your written permission." Insert this type of information here. If no laws with greater limits apply to your entity, no information needs to be added.
- If your entity provides patients with access to their health information via the Blue Button protocol, you may want to insert a reference to it here.
- If your entity is part of an OHCA (organized health care arrangement) that has agreed to a joint notice, use this space to inform your patients of how you share information within the OHCA (such as for treatment, payment, and operations related to the OHCA). Also, describe the other entities covered by this notice and their service locations. For example, "This notice applies to Grace Community Hospitals and Emergency Services Incorporated which operate the emergency services within all Grace hospitals in the greater Dayton area."

Intentionally Blank

Recognized Security Practicesa

The 2021 HITECH Amendment requires OCR to take into consideration whether a regulated entity has adequately demonstrated that recognized security practices were "in place" for the prior 12 months, in certain Security Rule enforcement and audit activities. OCR must take into consideration the RSPs implemented in the regulated entity's organization when OCR is making determinations regarding fines (called civil money penalties), audits, or other agreed upon remedies, such as resolution agreements OCR may reach with a regulated entity to resolve potential violations of the HIPAA Security Rule.

In short, if you had fully implemented one of the recognized security practice standards for the 12 months preceding a breach or audit, OCR may mitigate fines (civil monetary penalties), terminate an audit early and favorably, and/or reduce other actions taken against the entity for violations of the security rule.

> Visit **HIPAADeskReference.com** for an up-to-date link to the official OCR presentation on RSPs

Is RSP implementation mandatory?
No. Implementing RSPs is strictly voluntary, but may result in favorable, early termination of audits, reduction of fines (civil monetary penalties), and other favorable outcomes for the practice. There is no penalty for non-participation and it will not be used as an aggravating factor.

What are the standards included in the Recognized Security Practices?
- Section 2(c)(15) of the NIST Act (The **NIST Cyber Security Framework** – CSF)
- Section 405(d) of the Cybersecurity Act of 2015 (aka **Health Information Cybersecurity Practices** – HICP)
- "Other" programs that address cybersecurity and are recognized by statute or regulation.

What is the standard of implementation?
The RSP program requires that whichever RSP standard you choose is "fully implemented." That is, you cannot implement only part of the standard or implement the standard to only part of the organization. The only exception is elements of the standard that do not apply to the practice. For example, if the practice does not have medical devices, then controls applying to medical devices need not be implemented.

OCR will only take the RSP implementation into consideration once it has been fully implemented for a minimum of twelve months. Say, for example, you begin implementation on January 1 and are able to prove full implementation by May 1, OCR will consider the RSP implementation on May 1 of the following year (twelve months after the data of full implementation). It's worth noting that the standard must remain fully implemented to qualify. It is insufficient to only provide evidence of the initial adoption of the RSPs.

What evidence is required to prove implementation?

It is the responsibility of the practice to provide empirical evidence of the RSP implementation. Plans and policies to implement the RSP are not sufficient evidence by themselves. Practices should document and be prepared to present:

- Policies and procedures regarding the implementation and use of RSPs
- RSP implementation project plans and meeting minutes
- Diagrams and narrative detail of RSP implementation and use
- Application screenshots and reports showing RSP implementation and use
- Vendor contracts and statements of work regarding RSP implementation
- Include dates that support implementation and use of RSPs for previous 12 months

Other Available Resources

Visit **HIPAADeskReference.com** for additional resources, including:
- ✓ Discounts on HIPAA Courses
- ✓ Live HIPAA Training
- ✓ Live Remote Cybersecurity Awareness Training
- ✓ HIPAA News & Updates
- ✓ Free HIPAA Compliance Resources
- ✓ The HIPAA Quick Guide
- ✓ Discounts on Mock Audit Services
- ✓ …and more!

Courses Available at **HIPAADeskReference.com**:

HIPAA for Executive Leaders
A short course for executive leaders to learn how to oversee their practice's compliance program, what resources to allocate to it, what to expect from their compliance officer, and what questions and evidence to ask for to ensure compliance.

HIPAA Annual Training for Frontline Professionals
For frontline professionals who care for patients, this course covers how to handle patient data, what to do and not do, how to report incidents, and more. This is the ideal annual training for frontline staff members from the front desk to physicians.

HIPAA for Compliance Officers
This in-depth course dives into the text of the regulation, how to become, stay, and validate that the practice is compliant with HIPAA, and what to do when there's a problem.

HIPAA for IT Professionals
Geared for technology professionals, this course covers the security rule, HICP, and common technology controls to ensure the safety and security of ePHI across computers, servers, VOIP phones, networks, and cloud services.

Tools & Resources:
Weekly HIPAA Huddle Guides
The HIPAA Quick Reference Guide
HIPAA 5-Minute Audit
HIPAA Full Audit Tool

Services:
HIPAA Mock Audits
Live HIPAA Training Sessions
Live Cybersecurity Awareness Training w/ Hacking Threat Demonstration
Security Risk Assessment
HIPAA Consulting and Advisory Services

Books:
HIPAA for IT Professionals: A Reference Guide

www.ingramcontent.com/pod-product-compliance
Lightning Source LLC
Chambersburg PA
CBHW080043280326
41935CB00014B/1765